ROUTLEDGE LIBRARY EDITIONS: ENERGY

Volume 6

ENERGY STRATEGIES FOR THE UK

T0382737

ENERGY STRATEGIES FOR THE UK

S. C. LITTLECHILD AND K. G. VAIDYA

Routledge
Taylor & Francis Group

LONDON AND NEW YORK

First published in 1982 by Allen & Unwin

This edition first published in 2019
by Routledge
2 Park Square, Milton Park, Abingdon, Oxon OX14 4RN

and by Routledge
52 Vanderbilt Avenue, New York, NY 10017

Routledge is an imprint of the Taylor & Francis Group, an informa business

British Library Cataloguing in Publication Data
A catalogue record for this book is available from the British Library

ISBN: 978-0-367-21122-6 (Set)
ISBN: 978-0-429-26565-5 (Set) (ebk)
ISBN: 978-0-367-21115-8 (Volume 6) (hbk)
ISBN: 978-0-367-21135-6 (Volume 6) (pbk)
ISBN: 978-0-429-26560-0 (Volume 6) (ebk)

Publisher's Note
The publisher has gone to great lengths to ensure the quality of this reprint but points out that some imperfections in the original copies may be apparent.

Disclaimer
The publisher has made every effort to trace copyright holders and would welcome correspondence from those they have been unable to trace.

Energy Strategies for the UK

S. C. LITTLECHILD   K. G. VAIDYA

with

M. Carey   P. G. Soldatos   J. Rouse
I. H. Slicer   M. Anari   D. Basu

London
GEORGE ALLEN & UNWIN
Boston   Sydney

George Allen & Unwin (Publishers) Ltd,
40 Museum Street, London WC1A 1LU, UK

George Allen & Unwin (Publishers) Ltd,
Park Lane, Hemel Hempstead, Herts HP2 4TE, UK

Allen & Unwin Inc.,
9 Winchester Terrace, Winchester, Mass 01890, USA

George Allen & Unwin Australia Pty Ltd,
8 Napier Street, North Sydney, NSW 2060, Australia

First published in 1982

British Library Cataloguing in Publication Data

Littlechild, S. C.
  Energy strategies for the UK.
  1. Energy industries – Great Britain –
  Mathematical models   2. Power resources –
  Great Britain – Mathematical models
  I. Title   II. Vaidya, K. G.
  333.79'12'0724   HD9502.G72

ISBN 0-04-339029-3

Library of Congress Cataloging in Publication Data

Littlechild, S. C.
  Energy strategies for the UK.
  Includes bibliographical references and index.
  1. Energy policy – Great Britain. 2. Energy policy –
  Great Britain – Data processing. 3. Energy policy –
  Great Britain – Mathematical models. I. Vaidya, K. G.
  II. Title.
  HD9502.G72L57   333.79'0941   82-6761
  ISBN 0-04-339029-3   AACR2

Set in 10 on 11 point Times by Preface Ltd, Salisbury, Wilts.
and printed in Great Britain by Mackays of Chatham

Contents

List of Figures

List of Tables

Energy Units and Fuel Equivalents

Units in which energy consumption and production are expressed vary widely. The most common units and their equivalents are shown below. In the BEM, all energy is measured in petajoules (PJs). In the discussion of model results, however, petajoules are translated into the most usual units of measurement for the fuel being discussed (e.g. tonnes for coal). The fuel equivalents given in the table below are based on average calorific values of fossil fuels in the UK. They broadly correspond to conversion factors and fuel equivalents given in recent editions of the Digest of UK Energy Statistics, HMSO, although they may be somewhat different from fuel equivalents in other countries.

The following notes will help to clarify the table.

Energy   1 petajoule (PJ) = 1 million billion joules = 10^{15} J.

Other units commonly used include

1 megajoule (MJ) = 1 million joules = 10^6 J.
1 gigajoule (GJ) = 1 billion joules = 10^9 J.

Coal   The tonne as a measure of coal (and oil) is the metric measure where 1 tonne = 1000 kg = 0.9842 statute (long) ton = 2205 lb. mtce (million tonnes of coal equivalent) is a frequently used measure of energy and has been used occasionally in the book.

Oil   Oil statistics for the UK and Europe are generally expressed in tonnes but the USA and most oil companies continue to measure in barrels, where 1m. tonnes = 7.35m. barrels, or 1 barrel = 0.136m. tonnes. mtoe (million tonnes of oil equivalent), a frequently used measure of energy, has also been used in the book.

Natural gas   Natural gas is usually measured in therms. Strictly speaking, however, a therm is a measure of energy, and not a measure of volume of gas. Gas reserves, which are measured in terms of volume, are expressed in units of cubic feet or metres. The conversion factors are 1m. therms = 98m. cu. ft = 2.775m. cu. metres, or 1 trillion cu. ft (1 tcf) = 10,204m. therms. (A billion is a thousand million and a trillion is a million million throughout this book.)

Electricity   One gigawatt hour equals one million kilowatt hours (1 GWh = 10^6 KWh). Energy equivalents for electricity represent the amounts of primary fuel (coal, oil or gas) which have the same energy content as 1 GWh of electricity. Owing to conversion and transmission losses, however, the amount of energy actually required to produce 1 GWh of electricity will be several times greater than the energy equivalent.

One gigawatt (GW) of electricity generation capacity operating at maximum output throughout the year (i.e. 8,760 hours) produces 31.536 PJ/year (i.e. 0.0036 PJ × 8,760 hours). In the model, electricity generation capacity and capacities in the other energy industries are measured in PJ/year.

Energy units in Figures In the figures showing patterns of energy consumption and production, PJ (peta-joules) are used as a standard measure. For ease of comparison, the following measures are shown for individual fuels:

m. tce   million tonnes of coal equivalent
m. toe   million tonnes of oil equivalent
b. th.   billion therms
th. GWh   thousand gigawatt hours

Energy Units and Fuel Equivalents

Energy	Coal	Oil	Natural gas	Electricity
Energy				
1 petajoule (PJ)	0.0379 m. tonnes	0.0223m. tonnes	9.47813m. therms	277.778 GWh
Coal				
1m. tonnes	1m. tonnes	0.6m. tonnes	250m. therms	7500 GWh
Oil				
1m. tonnes	1.677m. tonnes	1m. tonnes	425m. therms	12500 GWh
Natural gas				
1m. therms	0.004m. tonnes	0.00235m. tonnes	1m. therms	29.307 GWh
Electricity				
1 gigawatt hour (GWh)	0.000136m. tonnes	0.00008m. tonnes	0.03413m. therms	1 GWh

Energy				
1 PJ				
26.377 PJ				
44.84 PJ				
0.105506 PJ				
0.0036 PJ				

Preface

The 'energy problem' has been at the forefront of public debate for at least a decade, and interest in it shows no sign of slackening. Whatever energy strategy is adopted will have far-reaching implications for our standards of living; for public safety, the environment and national security; for the livelihoods of coal miners and nuclear technologists; and not least for the welfare of many generations to come. It is important, therefore, that some method should be available for evaluating the strategies which are advocated by the various different interest groups, and if necessary for designing new strategies to achieve specified national objectives.

The Birmingham Energy Model has been designed with precisely this aim in mind. It is a large-scale computer-based model which is used to calculate and compare alternative strategies for the UK energy sector over the next fifty years, under a variety of different assumptions about costs, demands, technological constraints and policy objectives. This book explains how the model has been constructed and used to evaluate some of the strategies currently under active consideration. To our knowledge, it is the only single model available which (a) covers the whole of the UK energy sector over such a long-term period; (b) allows for interactions between the separate fuels on both supply and demand sides; (c) focuses on decision making and optimisation rather than on forecasting or simulation; and (d) is sufficiently flexible and convenient to be run repeatedly under a variety of different assumptions.

The research embodied in this book originated in a discussion between Stephen Littlechild and Malachey Carey in about 1973. Carey was then lecturer in economics at Newcastle Polytechnic, but had earlier (1970–2) been a statistician at the Department of Trade and Industry, where he had worked on the department's collection of energy models. At that time, and even today, these models each represented one particular aspect of the whole energy sector, and it was necessary to run them sequentially, 'iterating by hand', in order to obtain a comprehensive picture of the whole sector. It seemed to us that it would be both feasible and desirable to construct a single integrated model to do the work of the department's collection of sub-models.

The SSRC provided financial support for two successive research projects, entitled Integrated Models of the Energy Sector, Part I, from August 1974 to October 1977, and Part II from January 1978 to March 1981. The research was under the general direction of Littlechild throughout this period. Carey worked for three years as research fellow, and was mainly responsible for the survey of British energy research, the construction of the basic cost-minimisation model and the collection of the data. Kirit Vaidya, lecturer in economics at the University of Aston Management Centre, was also associated with the project from the very beginning, and played an increasingly important role in all aspects of the research, including taking responsibility for its direction during Littlechild's leave of absence in 1975 and 1979/80. Peter Soldatos, research associate from April 1976 to November 1979, carried out the computer programming and report writing (including graphs and tables), and extended the model to incorporate demand functions. Dipak Basu, research associate from May 1976 to August 1977, worked on the estimation of demand elasticities and on the oil and gas exploration and discovery functions. Mohammad Anari, research fellow from March 1979 to July 1980, extended the model to incorporate much more detail on the oil sector and estimated the price elasticities of demand for oil products. John Rouse and Ian Slicer, senior lecturer and principal lecturer, respectively, in the Department of Government and Economics at the City of Birmingham Polytechnic, assisted with the research project from 1978 to 1980; the former was mainly responsible for the analyses of 'soft energy' proposals and the latter for the security of supply considerations. Ian Slicer also prepared the index. In the early days of the project, assistance and advice were also received from Dr J. Tzoannos of Aston Management Centre (demand forecasting and the gas industry in particular) and Peter Hutchinson of the London Business School (computer programming and the matrix generator).

Several articles have been published by individual authors describing aspects of the work for which they were responsible, and Carey, Basu and Soldatos all received their Ph.D degrees for research related to this project. The material was assembled into book form, extensively and repeatedly rewritten, and in many cases extended, by Littlechild and Vaidya during 1979–81.

Because the research was carried out in Birmingham, and involved researchers from all three of the city's leading academic institutions, we have referred to it as the Birmingham Energy Model. But of course we have obligations to a great many people elsewhere in this country and abroad. Michael Posner encouraged us to pursue this research, and more thoroughly than we had originally envisaged. The SSRC provided a total of some £50,000 to finance research. Wendy Thompson has been especially helpful in the administration of the grant. Useful comments and advice have been received from many people, especially R. Ormerod (NCB), J. M. W. Rhys (Electricity Council), R. J. Hatfield (CEGB), T. Hendy and V. Janisz (British Gas), D. W. Pearce and R. J. Westoby (Aberdeen University), C. Robinson (University of Surrey) and A. S. Manne (Stanford University). Helpful appraisals of the entire first draft were received from D. A. Heald (University of Glasgow) and an anonymous reviewer. The University of Birmingham has provided extensive financial, secretarial and computational support, including the use of its word processing facilities. Roy Pearce (University of Birmingham Computer Centre) provided valuable assistance in running the model. We are indebted to Margaret Sheridan and Maria Jones for cheerfully and efficiently typing endless drafts of often illegible manuscripts, to Vivien Morris for initial preparation of the graphs, and to Tim Grogan in the Department of Geography drawing office for preparing camera-ready versions. Nick Brealey of George Allen and Unwin has been an indefatigable source of advice and encouragement.

Finally, we offer apologies to our wives – Kate Littlechild, Anne Vaidya, Linda Carey, Eve Soldatos and Catherine Slicer – who have had to suffer 'the energy book' far longer than they should have done.

BIRMINGHAM
August 1981

1

UK Energy Sector: Past, Present and Future

1.1 Introduction

It is widely believed that Britain has an 'energy problem'. Of course energy has become very expensive and is likely to become even more expensive in the future. But the real problem is what to do about it. For there is no shortage of proposed energy strategies, and the government is constantly under pressure, from all sides, to adopt one strategy rather than another.

The decision about strategy is not an easy one. The energy sector accounts for about one-tenth of the country's capital stock. Billions of pounds and hundreds of thousands of jobs are at stake. Considerations of safety, the environment, technological leadership and national security are all involved. Decisions made now will affect our children and grandchildren.

In designing an energy strategy, it would seem useful to have available some mechanism for evaluating the consequences of the various alternatives under consideration, calculating the 'trade-off' between the achievement of different goals, and identifying the particular strategies most likely to promote the national interest.

The Birmingham Energy Model is just such a mechanism. It is a large-scale linear programming model designed to calculate and compare optimal strategies for the UK energy sector over the next fifty years under a variety of different assumptions about costs, demands, technology, policy objectives and constraints. The purpose of this book is to explain how the Birmingham Energy Model is constructed and used, and to evaluate some current proposals for UK energy strategies in the light of the model's results.

This first chapter begins by setting the scene. It describes the changing pattern of energy consumption in the past, the present levels of resource availability, likely future developments in technology, the policy decisions to be taken, the kinds of forecasts that need to be made, the economic, social and political considerations likely to affect policy, and the various proposals put forward by the main protagonists. It should be emphasised that this review is at a very elementary level designed for those readers who are not familiar with the energy problem and techniques of energy modelling. An excellent and more comprehensive analysis of these topics is provided by Eden *et al.* (1981).

The last two sections of the chapter describe the scope of the Birmingham Energy Model and provide a chapter-by-chapter outline of the book.

1.2 Primary and Secondary Energy

In discussing energy, it is conventional to draw a distinction between primary and secondary energy or fuels. *Primary energy* refers to the form in which energy is recovered directly from nature. For Britain, the main sources of primary energy are coal, oil, natural gas and uranium. By convention, electricity generated by nuclear power plants, which use uranium as their fuel, is referred to as a primary fuel. Other sources of primary energy are more important in other countries and yet other sources may become more important in the future. They include water flowing over a dam (generating hydroelectricity), wind, waves and the sun.

Some primary fuels, notably coal and natural gas, may be used directly in final consumption. For the most part, however, primary energy is converted into *secondary energy*, which refers to the form in which energy is used. The main secondary fuels are electricity (produced from coal, oil or natural gas) and oil products (including petrol, kerosene, fuel oil and gas oil). Oil and gas may be produced synthetically from coal, in which case coal is the primary fuel with oil and gas the secondary fuels.

There are of course *conversion losses* in converting primary energy to secondary energy, and *conversion losses* in transporting energy from its place of production to the final consumer. Thus (quite apart from imports and exports of energy) the total final consumption of energy (measured in some common unit) is necessarily less than the total consumption of primary energy.

1.3 Changes in Production and Consumption

Since the Second World War, there have been dramatic changes in primary energy production and consumption patterns (Figure 1.1). Over the two centuries to 1955, annual coal consumption in Britain (including consumption in energy industries) increased steadily from less than 10m. tonnes to over 210m. tonnes. For almost all this period, consumption of other fuels was negligible. In contrast, over the next two decades coal consumption fell by half and petroleum (oil) consumption increased fivefold (from 30m. to over 150m. tonnes coal equivalent), thereby replacing coal as the major source of UK energy. By 1975, natural gas supplied half as much energy as coal, and nuclear energy had begun to make a substantial contribution.

The main difference between the production and consumption of primary energy was the export of coal, which increased steadily to a

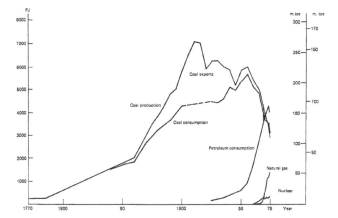

Figure 1.1   *Primary fuel consumption and coal production since 1770*

peak of 100m. tonnes in 1910, then continued to decline to a negligible level by 1940.

The pattern of primary energy consumption between 1948 and 1979 is shown cumulatively in Figure 1.2. (The graph is designed to be comparable to projections made from model solutions to be discussed in future chapters.) It shows the dominance of coal at the outset (71 per cent of total primary energy consumption), a decline in its relative importance as other fuels grew more rapidly up to the middle 1950s and a steady fall in the total amount of coal consumed thereafter. By the early 1970s oil had captured the largest share of primary energy consumption.

An important determinant of this change in the consumption pattern was the movement in relative prices. During the 1950s and 1960s the price of coal rose at about the same rate as the domestic price index, whereas the price of oil imports fell in absolute terms. Roughly speaking, the price of oil imports fell from about twice the price of coal in 1950 to three-quarters of it in 1970. However, because of the substantial fuel tax imposed in 1961, the movement of relative market prices has been less marked.

At the beginning of the 1960s, over 90 per cent of Britain's gas manufacturing capacity was based on coal (Figure 1.3). By the end of the 1960s over 80 per cent was based on oil. Within another decade, both coal and oil were completely displaced as sources of gas supply, and in 1975 natural gas provided almost 14,000m. therms of primary energy in 1979 (1468 PJ or 5.6 mtce). The consumption of natural gas continued to grow at a rapid rate until 1979, reflecting its price advantage over electricity and oil.

Coal has remained the dominant fuel in electricity production throughout the period (Figure 1.4). However, its share in total electricity

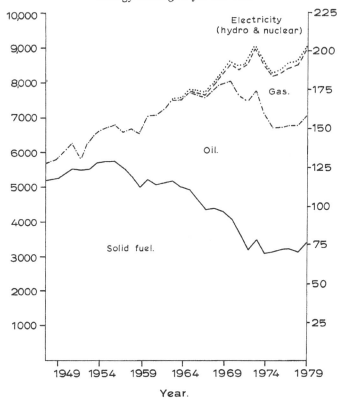

Figure 1.2 *Primary energy consumption, 1948–79*

production has fallen owing partly to the increase in electricity generated at oil-fired power stations in the late 1960s and early 1970s, and
partly to the expansion of nuclear electricity production (a sixteenfold
increase between 1960 and 1979). In 1979, the electricity industry was
the major consumer of coal taking almost 69 per cent (129m. tonnes) of
the total inland consumption.

The pattern of decline in the importance of coal and the increase in
the share of other fuels outlined above reflect changes in the final
demand for primary and secondary fuels. The final demand for coal in
the Domestic Sector started to fall in 1963, and by 1979 was one-third
the level in 1948 (Figure 1.5). The demand for oil rose to a peak in 1973
but has fallen back slightly since then owing to the rise in oil prices. Gas
has captured by far the largest share of the domestic sector energy
market reflecting its price advantage over its main rival, electricity. The
demand for electricity continued to grow steadily up to 1974 but has
been erratic since then, owing to higher prices. In the Iron and Steel
Sector (Figure 1.6), solid fuel remained the dominant fuel but its con-

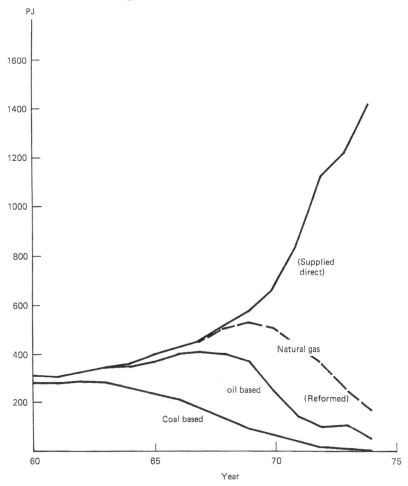

Figure 1.3 *Gas supply by source, 1960–74*

sumption had fallen to less than half the 1948 consumption by 1979. Oil consumption reached a peak in 1970 but since then has declined sharply to less than half the 1970 level. Final demands in the Other Industry Sector and Commercial and Other Sectors (Figures 1.7 and 1.8) show a familiar pattern, with declining consumption of coal and rising consumption of the three other fuels, but a fall in oil consumption after 1973 in response to higher oil prices. In the Transport Sector (Figure 1.9), coal was the most important fuel in 1948, but by 1979 over 99 per cent of total energy consumed was oil, with small amounts of electricity (mainly railways) and even less coal. It is worth noting that after the 1973 oil

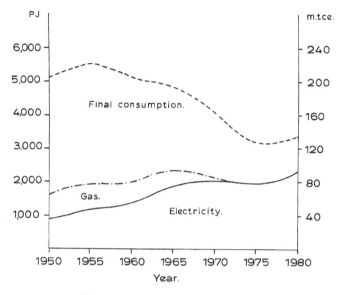

Figure 1.4   *Uses of Coal, 1948–79*

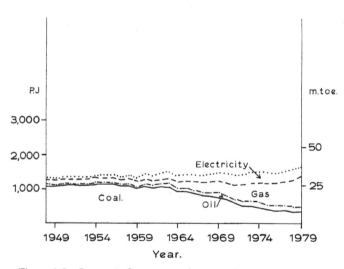

Figure 1.5   *Domestic Sector annual energy demand, 1948–79*

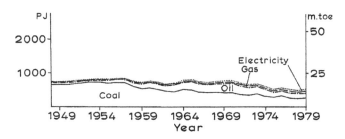

Figure 1.6   *Iron and Steel Sector annual energy demand, 1948–79*

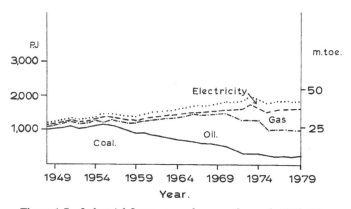

Figure 1.7   *Industrial Sector annual energy demand, 1948–79*

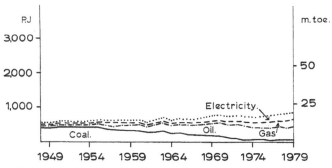

Figure 1.8   *Commercial Sector annual energy demand, 1948–79*

8

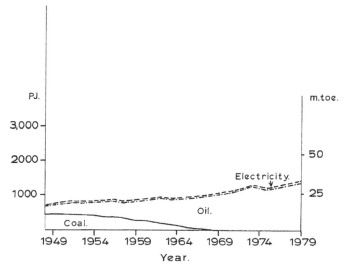

Figure 1.9   *Transport Sector energy demand, 1948–79*

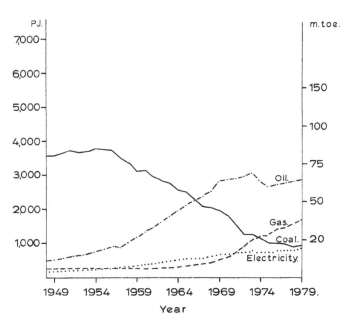

Figure 1.10a   *Annual total final energy demand, 1948–79*

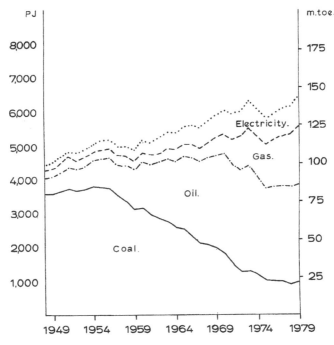

Figure 1.10b *Annual total final energy demand (cumulative), 1948–79*

price increase, there was a relatively modest fall in oil consumption which has since been restored.

Total final consumption of secondary fuels (aggregated over the five sectors) is shown in Figures 1.10a and b. It is evident that by 1979 the UK had completed a dramatic transition from a one-fuel economy to a four-fuel economy. Recent changes in relative prices of fuels and likely future changes in prices and conditions of demand and supply suggest that equally dramatic changes in the UK energy economy are to be expected during the next few decades.

1.4   Present and Future Reserves of Fuels

Britain presently has resources of all three major fossil fuels (Figure 1.11), but their precise extent is unknown. There is probably between 35 and 80 trillion cubic feet of natural gas which at the 1979 rate of consumption would last for between twenty and forty-five years. Total recoverable reserves of oil originally in place on the UK Continental Shelf are estimated to be within the range 2,400 and 4,400m. tonnes, which at the 1979 rate of annual oil consumption would last for between thirty and fifty years. Technically and economically recoverable reserves

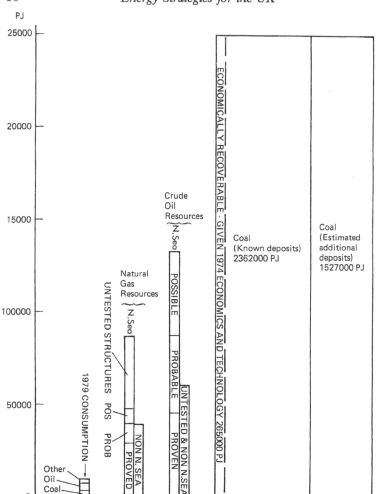

Figure 1.11 *Some estimates of UK fossil fuel resources, 1974*

of coal are estimated to stand at 45,000m. tonnes which would be adequate to meet UK demand at the 1979 consumption level for seventy years. Additional geological resources of coal in place are estimated to be 120,000m. tonnes. (Unless explicitly referenced, the sources for the estimates in this section are given in Chapter 4.)

In the world as a whole, world oil reserves were estimated in 1977 at about 75,000m. tonnes, sufficient for twenty-five years at 1977 consumption rates (World Energy Conference, 1978). Coal reserves (technically and economically recoverable, *not* geological reserves in place) were estimated at 430,000m. tonnes, sufficient for 174 years. The world proved reserves of natural gas were estimated to be adequate for approximately fifty years at the annual rate of consumption prevailing in the mid-1970s. Additional undiscovered recoverable resources were estimated to be more than three times the proved reserves. At the 1977 rate of annual world uranium consumption (33,000 tonnes) the 'reasonably assured' resources of economically recoverable uranium (2.2m. tonnes) are likely to be adequate for over 60 years. However, there are considerable uncertainties about future uranium consumption and nuclear technology. According to the World Energy Conference (1978), nuclear electricity programmes of many countries are expected to expand rapidly over the next few years, leading to uranium consumption rising to over 100,000 tonnes per year by 1990. The high consumption rate in 1990 and beyond would lead rapidly to a severe shortfall in supply unless new supplies and technical developments (such as the fast breeder) appear. An alternative view (see Foley, 1981) is that the increase in nuclear electricity production is likely to be slower and uranium reserves will be adequate even if there are no new technical developments.

It should be emphasised that estimates of the extent of available resources are necessarily uncertain and frequently need to be adjusted as new discoveries are made. For example, in late 1979, a large anthracite deposit was discovered in south-western China: its estimated size of 1500m. tonnes is of the order of one-third of total UK coal reserves. In the UK the National Coal Board has claimed that exploration in the UK (restarted in the mid-1970s after a decade of virtually no exploration) was revealing new deposits at the rate of 480m. tonnes per year, though this is likely to be a confirmation of reserves within the overall estimate of 45,000m. tonnes. Further, the quantities of economically recoverable reserves of all fuels in the UK and the world are responsive to the prices of fuels. A higher world price of oil is likely to make it worthwhile to extract higher cost oil. On the other hand, if world trade in coal expands and cheap imported coals are available, economically recoverable coal reserves in the UK may fall.

In general, the costs of extracting coal, oil and natural gas are likely to increase as the cheaper and more accessible reserves are exhausted. This tendency may, however, be partly offset by increased efficiency stemming from technological developments or from improved managerial effectiveness. In the case of electricity, it is widely believed that improvements in nuclear technology will reduce costs significantly. However, there are (as noted) considerable uncertainties about nuclear technology and a likelihood that uranium costs may rise sharply. Certain new technologies are likely to be adopted, notably synthetic oil and gas production from coal. While it is generally recognised that considerable technical advances will be made in renewable energy sources (e.g. wind, waves, solar) in the next few decades, their contribution to the UK energy sector is likely to remain small during the rest of this century.

1.5 The Nature of Energy Policy

For each fuel, decisions have to be made concerning the levels and nature of production, employment, investment and selling price. At some stage, a great deal of detail is involved, since decisions have to be made for each pit, oil field, generating station, etc. Some of the decisions are made on a day-by-day or week-by-week basis (e.g. levels of output), while others are much less frequent and longer term (e.g. whether or when to close particular exhausted or uneconomic collieries, oil fields or generating plant, and where or when to open new ones, etc.).

Within the UK today, these decisions are made by a variety of different organisations, notably the National Coal Board, the British Gas Corporation, the Electricity Council, the Electricity Area Boards, the CEGB, the British National Oil Corporation and numerous oil companies. All but the latter are public corporations or nationalised industries, ultimately responsible to the government via the Department of Energy. They are nominally responsible for day-to-day decisions, but require government approval for decisions affecting 'the public interest', such as major investments or plant closures. There are also extensive requirements for consultation with trade unions, consumer councils and some suppliers. The private oil companies (and other private companies operating on the fringes of the UK energy sector) are of course free to take their own decisions, with a view to the interests of their shareholders. They are, however, subject to a variety of government laws, regulations and pressures, as will be illustrated below.

Because of the strong interdependencies between the various fuel industries, it is most important that their decisions be co-ordinated in some way – by government, by the market, or by some combination of the two. An *energy policy* is a framework within which decisions are made as to how the energy sector evolves over time. At its most simple, it comprises three elements: (1) a set of *forecasts* of future conditions in the energy sector; (2) a set of *policy objectives* to be pursued; and (3) a set of *policy instruments* for achieving these objectives. The task of policy-makers is to make the forecasts, to decide upon the objectives, and finally to select the instruments most likely to achieve the chosen objectives under the conditions expected to hold.

We shall explore in turn the nature of the forecasts, objectives and instruments.

1.6 Forecasts

In order to take decisions about energy policy, it is necessary to make forecasts of future conditions, not just in the energy sector but also in the economy as a whole and, indeed, in the world economy. The following are some of the most important forecasts that need to be made.

(1) Estimates of the present and future relationships between the demand for each fuel and various 'explanatory variables' such as the price of the fuel, the prices of other (substitute) fuels, the prices of

and demand for complementary goods (e.g. motor cars, new houses), the level of national income, etc. Such relationships are often embodied in the concepts of 'elasticities of demand' with respect to price, income, etc.

(2) Forecasts of the rates of growth of these 'explanatory variables'.

(3) Forecasts of the rate of growth in the demand for each type of fuel, derived from (1) and (2).

(4) Forecasts of the amounts of coal, oil, natural gas and uranium resources likely to be available for extraction. Current forecasts of aggregate UK and world resources have been briefly described in Section 1.3 above, but for many planning purposes more detailed estimates are likely to be required by particular location.

(5) Judgements about the energy technologies likely to be available, as described briefly in Section 1.4.

(6) Estimates of the costs of extracting and processing the natural resources in order to convert them to useful energy. Important components of production and distribution costs include labour productivity, wage rates, technical efficiency of each process, the world market prices of fuels likely to be imported or exported (notably oil, gas and coal), etc.

It is perhaps unnecessary to emphasise that forecasts of these 'parameters' do not of themselves determine the optimal energy policy for the UK to follow. For example, a forecast relationship between the price of coal and the demand for it does not establish what price *ought* to be charged for coal, and hence does not determine the level of coal production. Even if the demand for coal is thought to be rather insensitive to its price, it remains to be decided whether that demand should be met by domestic or imported coal, or even left partially unfulfilled in order to conserve the limited coal supplies for consumption in the future.

1.7 Policy Objectives

Given the forecasts of demands, costs and resource availabilities, there is still considerable scope for choice in determining an energy policy. The following considerations will normally be relevant, although the importance attached to each will depend upon the circumstances of the time and the perceptions and preferences of the government (cf. Eden *et al.*, 1981, Ch. 17).

(1) The total cost of meeting the energy requirements of the country – what is sometimes called the total 'energy bill' – is obviously a most important consideration. Resources used to provide energy cannot be used to produce other goods and services. A lower energy bill thus allows a higher standard of living and a faster rate of growth.

(2) In calculating the total cost of a national energy policy, it is not only the costs measured by the energy industries themselves which are relevant. It may, for example, be cheaper for the gas or electricity industry to provide power on an 'interruptible' basis, but the

additional costs incurred by their customers (e.g. in providing back-up facilities or in lost production) need to be taken into account as well. To use economists' terms, it is important to look at total 'social' cost, and not merely at the 'private' costs of the major suppliers. Or, to put it another way, we need to look at the benefits provided by energy as well as at the costs of supplying it. Then, any benefits sacrificed by one energy policy may be included as one of the foregone 'opportunity costs' of that policy.

(3) This point can be taken still further. In some cases, it is not only the buyer and seller who incur costs. Third parties may be affected by their agreement. For example, opening up new coal mines (in the Vale of Belvoir, perhaps) will destroy some of the rural countryside. Adopting nuclear energy on a large scale will increase the chance of a nuclear accident, thereby increasing the safety risks of those living in the vicinity of (nuclear) power stations. At the same time, of course, it may reduce accidents in coal-mining. Thus, public policy must be concerned with so-called 'externalities', notably pertaining to the environment and health and safety.

(4) Whatever energy policy is pursued, there are likely to be changes in the size of each individual fuel industry, simply because of the dramatic changes which are likely to occur in technology and the world economy. These changes will have important repercussions on the level of employment in each industry. Those already employed will prefer to minimise the extent of disruption and/or improve their own employment prospects (e.g. with respect to wages, promotion and job security). Consumers and customer-firms, on the other hand, will tend to prefer lower energy costs, and place a lower value on employment considerations. Questions of equity and income (re)distribution are thus involved.

(5) National security considerations bulk quite large in the energy sector. It is considered desirable to avoid situations in which the UK is at the mercy of its suppliers if they can collude to exploit their monopoly power. The suppliers might be foreign (e.g. Arab oil sheikhs) or domestic (e.g. British coal miners). In such situations it is often felt desirable to maintain a balance between domestic and foreign suppliers so as to limit the political or economic power of any one group of suppliers. National security considerations would also be involved in deciding upon nuclear policy – for example, the threat of nuclear 'proliferation'.

(6) Finally, it may be thought desirable for the UK to maintain a leading position in certain technologies. This might favour a pro-nuclear policy in order to provide experience for the British nuclear power industry.

1.8 Policy Instruments

Instruments for the furtherance of energy policy might be roughly grouped into three classes. First there are taxes and subsidies designed to influence the choices made by producers and consumers. Examples include the tax on fuel oil, the subsidies for installing domestic insulation, the subsidies on domestic as opposed to imported coal, and the subsidies for converting oil-burning appliances to coal.

Second, there are the targets or directives that may be issued to the nationalised fuel industries. Examples include the requirements to break even financially, achieve specified financial targets or work within cash limits (which may be negative!), to maintain certain uneconomic pits in operation, to maximise the rate of introduction of North Sea oil and gas, to construct coal-fired instead of oil-fired generating plants, etc.

Finally, there are the legal restrictions on the private companies such as the licensing of North Sea oil and gas fields, the prohibitions on the sale of electricity and gas direct to consumers, and so on. The act of nationalisation (or denationalisation) might also be considered the exercise of a policy instrument.

The nature of the policy instruments adopted will vary according to the nature of the situation and the objectives sought. It will also reflect the political philosophy of the country and the prevailing government.

At one extreme, the fuel industries could be considered essentially as extensions of the government, with the latter deciding in detail on the prices and levels of output of each fuel, the technologies and inputs to be used, the size and location of facilities and workforce, etc. At the other extreme, policy might allow each industry complete freedom subject to certain minimal conditions (e.g. breaking even financially). The measures described in the last paragraph evidently lie between these two extremes of central planning and complete decentralisation.

1.9   The Development of Energy Policy in the UK

To illustrate how the various issues raised in the above discussion have influenced policy making, we briefly review the development of UK energy policy over the last quarter-century.

Until the mid-1950s the UK energy economy was overwhelmingly dependent on coal. Adequate domestic supplies were available, and alternative sources of fuel were limited. A national energy policy seemed unnecessary. The need for such a policy arose as the economy shifted first to a two-fuel basis with the growth in the importance of oil from the mid-1950s onwards, and subsequently to a four-fuel basis with the increased production of nuclear electricity and availability of natural gas in the 1960s.

The main concern during the 1960s, as set out in the White Paper on fuel policy (Ministry of Fuel and Power, 1965) was with the problems facing the coal industry. Availability of oil at a low price and technological advances in the gas and electricity industries (low-cost production of gas from oil and decreasing cost of nuclear electricity) meant that the demand for coal was falling and was expected to fall further in the future. The White Paper announced certain measures aimed at slowing down the decline in demand for coal.

In a subsequent White Paper on fuel policy (Ministry of Fuel and Power, 1967) a more comprehensive statement of energy policy was made. Security of supply, efficient use of resources and the balance of payments were among the most important considerations. In order to arrive at a set of long-term policy guidelines, forecasts were made of the future pattern of energy demand under different sets of assumptions. The costs of meeting energy demand under different assumptions were estimated. In addition to cost, changes in the coal industry, security of energy supply and implications for the balance of payments were assessed in arriving at a set of policy proposals.

The next major development in energy policy was the 1978 Green Paper (Department of Energy, 1978). It gave two alternative formulations of the objectives of energy policy:

2.1 The traditional objectives of energy policy have been given as: that there should be adequate and secure energy supplies, that they should be efficiently used and that the two foregoing objectives should be achieved at the lowest practicable cost to the nation . . .

2.2 An alternative formulation has been suggested by the Secretary of State for Energy in his note preceding the Energy Policy Review, namely that our objectives should be to ensure that:

(i) everyone can afford adequate heat and light at home;
(ii) industry's needs for energy are fulfilled at a price which reflects full resource cost and has regard to the long-term availability of the various fuels;
(iii) these objectives are met on a long-term basis, taking account of risks; the depletion of our reserves of oil and gas is regulated; research and development in energy supply and use is adequately funded; and investment in energy industries to meet these objectives is properly planned;
(iv) freedom of the consumer to choose between fuels provided at a minimum price which reflect economic cost should, where possible, be maintained and increased.

It is of course for the Government, subject to the approval of Parliament, to set out appropriate objectives for an integrated energy policy for the nation.

The Green Paper did not explore the differences between these objectives in great detail. However, in the light of uncertainty about future developments in the UK and world energy situations, an overriding concern was to keep the supply options open. Plans were proposed to expand the coal industry, increase the generation of electricity from nuclear power, and reduce the projected dependence on oil when supplies from North Sea ran down. The aim was not so much to choose a policy that would attempt to minimise the resource costs of meeting the forecast energy demands, as to retain a flexibility in energy policy.

There have been a number of important developments in energy policy since the 1978 Green Paper, notably the downward revision of energy demand projections, substantial increases in the price of gas, and the announcement of a firm nuclear electricity plant construction programme at a lower level than proposed in the Green Paper. Concern with security of supply is still important though in the short and medium terms the balance of payments presents less of a problem. However the overall approach to energy policy set out in the Green Paper still remains.

In recent years the UK has participated in several international energy policy-making exercises, notably within the European Economic Community (EEC) and the International Energy Agency (IEA). The EEC energy policy has set targets to reduce oil import dependency and to accelerate the programme of nuclear power station construction. Agreements have been reached at meetings under IEA auspices to share oil in the case of an international crisis, to set targets to reduce oil consumption and to take specific steps (e.g. reduction of oil used for electricity production) to make implementation of targets more effective.

A number of critics have made significant contributions to the debate on energy policy. We illustrate by mentioning just a few of the criticisms. The nuclear power programme remains a contentious issue. While the electricity industry and the current government emphasise the advantages of nuclear energy and therefore propose to expand it at the most rapid rate feasible, Cook and Surrey (1977) remain unconvinced and recommend that the nuclear programme should be continued at a 'tick-over rate' merely to keep the nuclear option open. Pearce and Jones (1979) further argue that difficulties of obtaining suitable sites and planning permission are likely to make rapid expansion of nuclear electricity capacity difficult if not impossible. Leach *et al.* (1979) question the energy demand projections made by the Department of Energy, produce very much lower demand projections on the assumption of effective conservation measures and claim that conservation is cheaper than expansion of energy production capacity.

Expansion of coal output projected in the Green Paper is more or less an endorsement of the coal industry's proposals and projections made in the *Plan for Coal* (National Coal Board, 1974) and *Coal for the Future* (National Coal Board, 1977) which envisaged an increase in annual coal production to 170m. tonnes by the year 2000. Subsequently, official coal consumption projections have been revised downwards (see Department of Energy, 1979). Robinson and Marshall (1981) are sceptical about plans to expand domestic coal production on the grounds that they are based on unrealistically high coal consumption projections and that deep-mined British (and Western European) coal is unlikely to be able to compete with strip-mined imported coal in the absence of substantial state subsidies and import restrictions.

Finally, there is debate about the appropriate extent of government intervention. Heald (1981) argues that 'available opportunities to establish a coherent policy towards the energy sector are now being missed', while Robinson (1981) suggests that 'the present system is so imperfect that a more market-oriented regime would be a significant improvement'. Eden. *et al.* (1981, p. 381) conclude that 'deliberate interference with [the price mechanism], in ways or for motives unconnected with market mechanisms, seems to have made things worse, not better'. Indeed, Enoch Powell, speaking at the 1976 National Energy Conference, denounced the whole concept of an energy policy.

1.10   Problems of Designing an Energy Policy

In Britain today, some of the more crucial energy policy decisions are as follows:

- whether each fuel industry should, broadly speaking, expand or contract over the next half-century;
- whether electricity should continue to be generated by a mixture of coal, oil and gas, or whether nuclear power should eventually become the main source of electricity;
- whether American-designed pressurised water reactors (PWRs) or British-designed advanced gas cooled reactors (AGRs) should be built to generate nuclear energy;
- whether the demand for energy should be reduced by conservation measures;
- whether conservation should be legally enforced or induced by appropriate pricing taxation and subsidy policies;
- whether British reserves of fossil fuels (especially gas and oil) should be rapidly exploited or conserved for future use (or, to put it another way, what volume of reserves should be bequeathed to future generations);
- whether such reserves as are extracted should be used in Britain or exported;
- whether synthetic fuels should be developed as a substitute for imports or domestic reserves;
- whether research into renewable energy sources (e.g. wind, waves and solar power) should be encouraged on a large scale, either now or in the future, and so on.

How should the government – or, more precisely, the Department of Energy or the Treasury – set about making such policy decisions? The task is a difficult one for many reasons: forecasts are notoriously unreliable, especially when looking twenty to fifty years into the future; the appropriate weight to attach to different objectives tends to vary over time depending upon political and economic conditions, and the set of instruments is constantly being revised as some of them become ineffective or unpopular and others are created.

There is, however, a further difficulty. Because of the scale and complexity of the energy problem, it is by no means obvious how the forecasts, objectives and instruments relate to one another. For example, if world coal prices and domestic coal extraction costs are both expected to remain constant in real terms, and the pattern of fuel production is chosen to minimise total costs of supply, what will be the consequences for output and employment in each region of the National Coal Board? How would the answer be different if coal prices and costs were expected to rise at the rate of 1 per cent per annum in real terms? Or, to choose another example, under specified assumptions about nuclear technology and costs, what sacrifice would be implied by a moratorium on further construction of nuclear plants? How would the answer be different if a policy of energy conservation were vigorously adopted?

1.11   The Birmingham Energy Model

These are the kinds of questions which the Birmingham Energy Model is designed to answer. It does not seek to make new forecasts, to argue for a particular set of objectives or to demonstrate that one set of instruments is superior to another. Rather, it attempts to clarify the relationships between the forecasts, objectives and instruments which are currently under discussion in Britain today. The purpose is not to espouse or criticise any one energy policy. Rather, the aim is to increase our understanding of the implications of different energy policies: to show what costs or sacrifices or 'trade-offs' are implied by choosing one policy rather than another.

More precisely, the Birmingham Energy Model is designed to answer the following question: what pattern of investment and production is required of each fuel over the next fifty years in order to achieve specified policy objectives under specified forecasts concerning energy costs, prices, technological performance and resource availability? The model does not consider which particular instruments are necessary or most appropriate to secure such a pattern of investment and production. Nor is it concerned with such wider questions as the desirability or effectiveness of central planning, private ownership versus public ownership, the role of competition, and so on. In short, the model does not purport to *make* policy, but it does purport to be a useful *aid* in making policy.

It is envisaged that the Birmingham Energy Model, perhaps in modified form, would be a useful complement to, and development of, the range of models currently available at the Department of Energy or the Treasury. It could also be used by private oil companies or nationalised industries to explore certain consequences for themselves of government policies – or, indeed, of their own policies. Finally, it could be used by independent organisations to appraise the models used by government and the energy policies adopted, much in the way that various business schools and consultancy groups have developed their own macroeconomic forecasting models.

1.12 Outline of the Book

The contents of the book are as follows:

Chapter 2 explores in some detail the purposes and characteristics of energy models, surveys the enormous variety of energy models which have been constructed in the past decade or so, and relates the Birmingham Energy Model to other models of similar structure. It includes a summary table and annotated bibliography of nearly one hundred published energy models.

Chapter 3 provides an intuitive non-mathematical description of the Birmingham Energy Model. Chapter 4 sets out the mathematical details of the model and describes the data and forecasts which are utilised in running it. Chapter 5 describes the nature of the 'Base Case' policy, involving the minimisation of the present value of total costs in the energy sector subject to meeting specified 'Base Case' demands and not exceeding specified 'Base Case' resource availabilities.

Chapter 6 describes a series of sensitivity analyses, to ascertain the effects of varying the base case assumptions concerning future prices, resource availabilities and discount rates. Chapter 7 examines the implications of introducing further policy considerations pertaining to self-sufficiency in oil, the energy balance of payments and coal imports.

The next two chapters examine the 'soft energy' proposals. Chapter 8 explores the effect of lower demands for fuel consequent upon a conservation programme, while Chapter 9 calculates the costs and consequences of a moratorium on nuclear energy.

The analysis so far has in all cases involved the minimisation of costs subject to meeting specified energy demands. In Chapter 10, energy demands are represented as functions of energy prices, and the model itself calculates what levels of energy demand it is most beneficial to meet. All the analyses of the preceding chapters are repeated in this new framework to ascertain how far the previous conclusions continue to hold.

Chapter 11 summarises the main results of each chapter and the general conclusions of the book. A Postscript describes the policy implied by an 'updated' version of the model using the latest forecasts and assumptions available at the time of going to press (August 1981), whereas the body of the book refers to conditions obtaining a couple of years earlier.

References are given at the end of the chapters in which they are mentioned, and collected in full at the end of the book.

References

Cook, R. L. and Surrey, A. J. (1977), *Energy Policy: Strategies for Uncertainty*, Martin Robertson, London.

Department of Energy (1978), *Energy Policy: A Consultative Document*, Cmnd 7101, HMSO, London.

Department of Energy (1979), *Energy Projections 1979*, Department of Energy, London.

Eden, R., Posner, M., Bending, R., Crouch, E. and Stanislaw, J. (1981), *Energy Economics*, Cambridge University Press, Cambridge, UK.

Foley, G. (1981), *The Energy Question* (2nd edn), Penguin, London.

Heald, D. (1981), 'U.K. energy policy: economic and financial control of the nationalised energy industries', *Energy Policy*, vol. 9, no. 2.

Leach, G., Lewis, C., Romig, F., van Buren, A. and Foley, G. (1979), *A Low Energy Strategy for the United Kingdon*, Science Reviews, London.

Ministry of Fuel and Power (1965), *Fuel Policy*, Cmnd 2798, HMSO, London.

Ministry of Fuel and Power (1967), *Fuel Policy*, Cmnd 3438, HMSO, London.

National Coal Board (1974), *Plan for Coal*, London.

National Coal Board (1977), *Coal for the Future*, London.

Pearce, D. W. and Jones, P. (1980), 'Nuclear power and UK energy policy', *International Journal of Environmental Studies*, vol. 15, no. 4.

Robinson, C. and Marshall, E. (1981), *What Future for British Coal?*, Hobart Paper No. 89, Institute of Economic Affairs, London.

Robinson, C. (1981), 'The errors of North Sea policy', *Lloyds Bank Review*, July, no. 141.

World Energy Conference (1978), *World Energy: Looking Ahead to 2020*, IPC Science and Technology Press, Guildford, UK.

2

A Survey of Energy Models

2.1 The Use of Mathematical Models

During the last decade an immense amount of time, money and effort has been devoted to the construction and operation of large-scale mathematical models of particular fuels or of the energy sector as a whole. It seems likely that, in Britain and the USA alone, nearly a hundred such models have been constructed, probably nearer a thousand if each modification and variant is included. There is a great deal of variety in these models, depending upon their purpose, focus, technique, time-horizon, country of origin, etc. In this chapter we shall attempt to indicate the range of models that has been developed, in order to place in context our own particular model.

Before doing so, it may be worthwhile to explain why mathematical models are useful at all. Let us first emphasise that a mathematical model can contribute very little to such fundamental political and social issues as whether the production of energy should be left to the market or be made subject to government planning, or what national goals should be aimed at. Nor can it say what consideration should be given to national self-sufficiency, international relations, unemployment and the quality of the environment. But appropriate models could contribute to making social, political and even moral choices by helping to clarify the consequences of such choices. Similarly, a mathematical model cannot directly evaluate the accuracy of the assumptions embodied in it concerning technologies and resource availabilities, demands and supplies, forecasts for the future, etc., but by tracing the implications of these assumptions it may well be able to highlight some of the questionable areas.

The claim for a mathematical model must be that it helps the user to clarify complex situations, that it helps to sort out the multitude of interrelationships which abound in his problem. This may simply take the form of providing some *qualitative* insights into the factors which are relevant in any particular decisions – for example, if investment in open face coal-mining takes place, then certain consequences will occur, some of which are expected to be favourable (such as reduction in operating costs and increased employment for miners) whereas others may not be (such as reduced investment in nuclear energy and consequent lack of nuclear experience). Of course, the *kinds* of consequences which are relevant have to be provided as an input to the model, but the second- and third-order consequences of any particular action may not have been immediately apparent. For example, reducing coal production costs may reduce the price of coal and cause a switch of domestic consumption away from oil, thereby saving foreign exchange but causing unemployment in the Scottish oil industry, etc.

However, the real forte of the mathematical model is in *quantitative* calculations. Ultimately, some way has to be found of weighing up and balancing the various qualitative considerations. If some criterion of cost or benefit can be specified, at least as a starting point, and if estimates can be made of the magnitudes involved, then the next task is to compute and compare the relative merits of various alternative policies. This is not a trivial task. If the model is at all complex, as it will be if a significant number of considerations have been incorporated, and if the model is sufficiently detailed to be practically useful and applicable, then an electronic computer is the only way of making the necessary computations and a mathematical model is the only way of organising these computations.

Within this framework, two main types of model can be distinguished: those which *optimise* and those which *simulate*. The simulation model traces through the implications of a specified policy: it does not of itself identify policies of particular interest nor does it modify or evaluate any proposed policy. An optimising model, by contrast, requires the specification of some criterion (albeit possibly a complex one) for judging alternative policies. Given such a criterion, it puts together, from the set of available actions and instruments, a bundle of decisions which constitute an optimal policy within the bounds of the various specified constraints. For example, a simulation model will trace the effects of investing £10m. in new electricity plant but will not of itself calculate whether greater benefits would be obtained from a higher investment; an optimisation model will calculate the most beneficial level of investment according to the specified criterion.

Optimisation thus provides a more valuable output at the cost of some simplification in the development of the model. Simulation is used chiefly where the notion of a 'good' policy is difficult to specify explicitly or where computation of a 'best' policy would be mathematically intractable.

Finally, it should be mentioned that both types of model allow *sensitivity analysis* to be carried out, to see how far the implications of a given policy, or the nature and benefits of an optimal policy, are affected by variations in the constraints imposed on the situation (e.g. resource availabilities) or by the introduction of new techniques (e.g. solar energy) or new constraints (e.g. on unemployment).

Further discussion of mathematical modelling can be found in most introductory texts on operational research (e.g. Rivett, 1968; Littlechild, 1977).

2.2   Classification of Energy Models

It will be convenient to classify energy models according to the following six criteria: affiliation of author(s), geographical focus, scope within the economy, activity examined, technique used and time horizon. It will soon become apparent that energy models are not randomly scattered in this six-dimensional space. For example, the affiliation of the author is roughly correlated with the scope of the model, and the technique used frequently depends upon the activity examined. But before discussing such phenomena, it will be useful to explain and illustrate each criterion in turn. Numbers in square brackets refer to the models listed in the appendix to this chapter.

(1)   Affiliation of author(s)
Energy industries and companies have long found it worthwhile to use mathematical models of varying degrees of size and sophistication, in order to help them with production planning and investment appraisal [8–24, 34, 42]. Somewhat later, *government departments and agencies* developed models to aid in the appraisal of particular industries and in making their own allocations of funds between industries [1–7, 30, 43, 44]. *Academics in university departments and research institutes* have always been interested in appraising the performance of both industry and government, and at the same time in developing new techniques of analysis [25–29, 35–41, 45–54]. Their models have typically been less oriented to operational considerations than to long-term strategy, and often concerned to push forward the frontiers of energy modelling as a partial end in itself. For further discussion and examples, particularly in electricity supply, see Turvey (1968, 1971), Anderson (1972) and Turvey and Anderson (1977).

(2)   Geographical focus
Industries and governments are predominantly concerned with energy problems within their own country. The earliest use of mathematical models was probably in the electricity industry of France (Nelson, 1964). The models of greatest relevance to the present book are those which refer to aspects of British energy policy [1–30] and to the USA, where the most sophisticated and closely related models have been developed [31–47]. Academics have recently developed models of wider geographic areas such as Western Europe, the North Sea, the Middle East, and the world as a whole; some examples are [48–54].

(3)   Scope within the economy
Here we may distinguish four main types of model. First, there are models pertaining to a *single fuel*, notably coal [14–20, 23], oil [24, 50–52], gas [5, 21] and electricity [8–13, 22, 23, 32, 34, 35]. (There are a few studies of less conventional fuels but these are typically not presented as formal models.) Second, there are models which examine the relationship between the major fuels in the whole *energy sector* [1–4, 6, 7, 14, 25–27, 29, 37, 39–44, 48]. Third, there are models which cover *all industries* in the economy, with particular emphasis on industries in the fuel sector [28, 30, 36, 38, 49, 53, 54]. Finally, there are models which focus on the *macro-economic interrelationships* between the energy sector and the rest of the economy, often in terms of aggregates such as employment, investment, the rate of growth, etc. [45–7].

(4) Activity examined

Many models attempt to estimate future *demands* for each fuel [8, 9, 13, 23], or for energy as a while [1, 14, 25–30]. Sometimes these are 'point estimates', in other cases demand is estimated as a function of prices, incomes, etc. Typically, these are statistical or econometric models. However there is a growing literature which is critical of such methods, and advocates instead a 'bottom-up' approach involving engineering estimates of fuel requirements for each energy-using process and sector [27–9]. Forecasting models of either kind are essentially outside the focus of our book, although for illustration a few examples are discussed in the Appendix. Of course, we need to embody particular forecasts in our own model, as discussed in Chapter 4.

Other models – perhaps almost all of the early mathematical models – take as given the levels of demand and focus instead on the problems of *supply*, notably production and investment planning [5, 6, 10–12, 15, 17–22, 33–4, 36–40, 43, 46–51, 53]. Yet other models look at the *interaction between supply and demand* activities, either to predict the prices and outputs that will occur, or to calculate in some sense the 'best' set of prices and outputs [3, 5, 7, 16, 24, 31–2, 41–2, 44–7, 48–9, 52–4]. This third type of model is becoming more common as computer capacity increases and experience is acquired with simpler models.

(5) Technique used

We have already referred to the use of statistical and econometric methods to estimate demand and supply functions. Such techniques are concerned to predict some aspect of the world, which is assumed to be quite independent of any decisions taken by the modeller. In this book we are more concerned with models used to aid in decision making. As indicated in the previous section, these latter models are basically of two types: *simulation* models which trace through the implications of a specified policy, and *optimisation* models which choose the best policy available according to a specified criterion.

Simulation is often used in a situation characterised by uncertainty; each 'run' of the model corresponds to a particular set of values of specified random variables. Here it will be convenient to use the term simulation in a more general sense, to include all non-optimising techniques used to cope with complexity. A simple example is the use of *scenario* models which trace the implications of certain crucial assumptions or decisions [19, 22, 32, 42, 51, 53]. *Input–output* models are used to calculate the net effects on other industries of a specified output in the fuel sector [30, 36, 38, 45–6]. Finally, an optimising technique may be used not to calculate a best policy but to predict the *equilibrium outcome* of specified market forces, for example, on the assumption that the market operates to maximise net value of output [36]. *Decision trees* have also been used to analyse the effects of uncertainty [43], and in some cases have been coupled with linear programming [35].

Optimising models use a variety of techniques. Because of its flexibility and cheapness, the most common technique is probably *linear programming*, for example, to minimise the cost of meeting a specified set of demands for energy [5, 6, 11, 17, 18, 21, 34, 36, 39, 40, 48, 50, 54].

Nowadays, a thousand variables and constraints can be handled without too much difficulty. Non-linearities may be handled either by making *linear approximations* or by using alternative *non-linear programming* techniques [10, 41, 47, 52]. Some of the very largest 'models' are in fact hitherto independent models *coupled together* and run iteratively, either by hand or by writing appropriate software for the purpose [7, 32, 36, 37–9, 44–7, 49]. For those unfamiliar with mathematical programming techniques, brief intuitive introductions can be found in elementary textbooks such as Rivett (1968) or Littlechild (1977). More advanced treatments are given by Charnes and Cooper (1961), Beale (1968) and Wagner (1969).

(6)   Time Horizon

Most of the models constructed by the fuel industries for operational purposes have a fairly *short-run* time horizon: depending upon the detail required, they may cover a matter of days, weeks or months up to, say, five years ahead [13, 17, 19, 20]. *Medium-run* models, covering five to thirty years ahead, usually take as given the basic technologies and focus on such questions as investment policy or the rate of depletion of oil and gas reserves [1–7, 10, 14–16, 21, 23, 24, 28, 30, 32, 35, 39a, 44–6, 51]. *Long-run* models, looking forward over thirty years, are necessarily more speculative; they are typically concerned with energy in a largely post-petroleum world, especially the choice between coal, nuclear and renewable energy as sources of electricity [22, 29, 34, 35, 39b, 41–3, 47, 48–9, 54].

2.3   A Crucial Gap in the UK Energy Models Available

In this book it is neither possible nor appropriate to attempt a systematic evaluation of the achievements and limitations of these hundred or so models. We must focus on one specific aspect: the availability and adequacy of models suitable for use by the Treasury or Department of Energy in formulating and evaluating UK energy policy.

There is evidently no shortage of mathematical models referring to aspects of the British energy sector: the Appendix describes over forty such models. Some are simply econometric forecasting models, but others are simulation or optimising models. Nevertheless, almost all the presently existing models have a crucial limitation: they limit themselves to one single fuel, and generally to either the supply side or the demand side (but not both) of that industry.

Many of the models have been constructed by the industries themselves for their own use in day-to-day management and short-term planning, and for these purposes the models are sufficient. However, the government has a responsibility to look at the interactions between the industries, to co-ordinate investment and production. It needs to take into account that coal, oil and gas may be converted into electricity, or coal and oil into gas; that the use of coal and oil reserves now will necessitate the development of other energy sources for the future, and so on. It must also examine the relationship between demand and supply: for many uses different fuels may be substituted, and ultimately the extent of all fuel usage depends upon the terms on which fuel is supplied (notably price) and the demand for products produced by energy (which in turn depends, *inter alia*, upon the price of those products). It is not sufficient simply to compare the efficiency of a coal-fired and an oil-fired boiler for producing electricity; at some stage one needs to ask whether that energy could be more efficiently supplied directly in the form of oil, gas or coal, and ultimately whether it is worth meeting that particular demand for energy at all. Finally, of course, the government has to take into account a whole range of economic, social and political considerations pertaining to employment, security, the environment, the state of the economy, and so on.

Of the models currently available in Britain, only one makes any attempt to cover the whole energy sector. This is the Department of Energy's model [7] which is, in fact, a data-processing model which integrates the results of sub-models [1–6] in order to balance the overall supply and demand for each fuel. Since these sub-models have not been formally integrated, they have to be run separately and linked by an *ad hoc* iterative procedure. This is most inconvenient for repeated usage, and it precludes extensive sensitivity analysis or exploration of the effects of uncertainty. It therefore seems an inadequate basis for policy making.

What seems to be required, then, is a single coherent and tractable model which (1) covers all major fuels in the whole energy sector, (2) incorporates both demand and supply sides, (3) takes into account the effects of price on demand and supply and the opportunities for substitution of fuels, (4) extends far enough into the future to cover the transition from the rapidly depleting fossil fuels (oil and gas) to coal, nuclear or renewable energy sources, (5) allows a variety of policy variables and constraints to be explored, and (6) is suitable for recurrent usage.

2.4   The Birmingham Energy Model

The purpose of the Birmingham Energy Model (henceforth often abbreviated to BEM) is to fill this crucial gap in the set of UK energy models. It is designed to satisfy the six criteria just specified.

The Birmingham Energy Model is an optimising model which chooses levels of investment and production for each fuel in each of ten five-year periods. In its simplest version (the 'cost model'), the levels of demand of each fuel are specified and the model calculates the energy policy which minimises the present value of the cost of meeting these demands. In the more sophisticated version (the 'demand model'), demands for each fuel are specified as functions of fuel prices and the model calculates the energy policy which maximises the net present value of the energy sector, that is, the benefits of energy consumption less the capital and operating costs of supplying the energy.

Although the objective function relates only to monetary costs or benefits, it is not suggested that these are the only relevant considerations for policy. Depending upon which aspect of the energy problem is being investigated, a variety of different policy constraints is imposed, pertaining to political, social and economic considerations such as the balance of payments, energy self-sufficiency, the extent of imports of oil and coal, unemployment, conservation, the use of nuclear energy, etc. The purpose of the simple benefit or cost function is to act as a 'driver', pushing the model in a generally desirable direction. The model ought not to be thought of as producing *the* optimal energy policy, but rather was a device for exploring the implications of various alternative policies, and as a means of generating policies worthy of further consideration.

A linear programming technique was chosen because of its power, flexibility and capacity. Efficient computer packages are available for solving very large programmes: a thousand variables and constraints present no difficulty. This is approximately the size of the BEM – such a size is necessary if one is to treat adequately the complex nature of the energy problem. Linearity is not an unrealistic or unduly severe restriction, since various non-linear elements are in fact included (notably the benefit of energy consumption) by means of piecewise linear approximations. These increase the number of variables and necessitate the development of special programming routines. None the less, it was possible for us to run any of our models and obtain results within twenty-four hours, and a government department with direct access to sophisticated equipment could probably do this in twenty-four minutes, possibly even in twenty-four seconds.

The wide scope of the model means that there is very little detail in certain areas. This is inevitable – indeed, in some respects, it is a merit of the model. It is not intended to choose between different coal faces or oil fields; the industries themselves have detailed models for such purposes. Rather, it allows one to concentrate on broad policy issues, comparing for example the magnitude of total investment in gas, coal and oil. However, the model can, if required, be developed to explore in more detail particular aspects of a given problem.

It might be argued that we know very little about next year's economic conditions, let alone about the next fifty years. In view of this uncertainty, is there any point in building such a long-term model? The reply must be that current policy-making already does make implicit judgements about the future, and the model simply makes these explicit. Moreover, the model provides a systematic and straightforward way of exploring the sensitivity of policy to uncertain forecasts (e.g. of world oil price or of domestic oil reserves). Finally, the techniques of linear programming under uncertainty (referred to above [35]) allow for the choice of optimal strategy this year in the light of various possible future developments – they calculate, in effect, a set of conditional plans depending upon how the future evolves. It would not be difficult to extend the model in this way.

2.5 Relation of BEM to Comparable US Models

Although the Birmingham Energy Model has no direct counterpart in Britain, a few comparable models exist elsewhere, mainly in the USA.

The Brookhaven Dynamic Energy System Optimising Model (DESOM) [39b] minimises the present value of the cost of meeting specified demands. Its base case covers a one-hundred-year horizon (six five-year periods, three ten-year periods and two twenty-year periods). It is thus similar in principle to our 'cost model', but in addition to the longer horizon it includes considerably more detail concerning fuel demands (disaggregated into twenty-two end uses rather than half a dozen sectors) and resource-production patterns (which are embodied in the associated Reference Energy System). We have not yet seen a report of the output or use of this model. There is obviously a trade-off between detail and manageability, and the BEM has on the whole opted more for the latter.

Manne's Energy Technology Assessment (ETA) Model [41] incorporates price-dependent demand functions and maximises consumer plus producer surplus, as our 'demand model' does. Both models are compact and self-contained: they do not need to link up with separate models of the economy. ETA covers a longer horizon (seventy-five years), and therefore includes certain future technologies omitted from our model (e.g. an 'advanced electric technology' and hydrogen via electrolysis). Such a long horizon has the advantage that the full consequences of exhausting fossil fuels (especially oil and gas) have to be faced and the benefits of developing completely new technologies can be better appraised, although the validity of the results for seventy-five years ahead is necessarily less certain.

ETA has been coupled with a macro-economic growth model to form ETA-MACRO [47]. This could, in principle, be done with BEM although at this stage it seems preferable to evaluate the energy model alone. It is also not clear whether the links between energy and the rest of the economy are sufficiently strong and complex to warrant a joint model, rather than, for example, adjusting the rate of growth of energy demand as part of sensitivity analysis. This point is discussed by Hogan and Manne (1977).

The Stanford PILOT [36] is a multi-period LP model coupled with an input–output model which maximises undiscounted consumption over forty years, designed to evaluate energy availabilities and conservation. It is evidently more comprehensive than BEM, but it is difficult to know how flexible it is, or how suited to evaluating energy policy.

The model developed by Nordhaus [1979] appears to be similar to BEM in several respects: it is a multi-fuel, multi-period linear programming model with the objective function couched in terms of cost of production and value of energy consumption, and a myriad of constraints pertaining to resource availabilities, capacities, import policy, etc. It is, however, a more ambitious piece of work, which utilises independent estimates of demand, discovery and cost functions, takes into account the stockpile problems of the nuclear fuel cycle, incorporates the rest of the world as well as the USA, extends over 120 years (in ten-year periods), incorporates market imperfections such as monopoly power and has been used to assess the trade-off between economic growth and environmental quality (with respect to carbon dioxide emissions). There is no doubt that it is an imaginative and skilfully designed model, but it is not clear how suitable it would be for 'everyday use'.

Finally, Hafele and Manne have developed a (relatively!) simple LP model [48] to appraise a model society over seventy-five years in order to analyse the transition from a fossil fuel to a mainly nuclear economy (as with ETA [41]). A variant of this model is apparently incorporated into a family of models designed to study the world energy situation [49]. The first application of those models is to a fifty-year period, within which fossil fuels are still the dominant source of supply. The sub-models as a whole are apparently linked by repeated manual iteration (as are the Department of Energy's sub-models [1–7]). Two levels of energy demand are explored under three different policy assumptions, but there is no optimising criterion: the emphasis is on 'internal consistency and global comprehensiveness' in order to generate plausible and surprise free scenarios. The demand for fuels is based upon purely physical considerations without use of own- or cross-price elasticities. It might be argued that the size of the problem (the whole world!), the lack of relevant information, and the interdisciplinary multi-national team approach necessitated such a decentralized family of models. Nevertheless the model as a whole seems significantly less sophisticated and convenient to use than the others described in this section, including the Birmingham Energy Model.

There are thus in existence today not more than half a dozen large-scale models which embody an optimising approach and incorporate the supply and demand of all major fuels over a long-term horizon. The Birmingham Energy Model is the only such British model, apart from the Department of Energy's collection of sub-models. From published descriptions, the BEM appears to stand comparison with any of these models. It is not the largest or most sophisticated, but it does appear to be a flexible and practicable tool for policy analysis, and is quite capable of extension to provide more detail or analyse other policy considerations deemed to be relevant.

Appendix: Abstracts of Leading Energy Models

In this Appendix we present brief abstracts and a summary table of the salient features of about sixty of the most important or relevant energy models. There now exist several very useful surveys and critiques of energy models which we have drawn upon. For the British models we have used Carey (1975), although this is now somewhat dated. For US models we have used Manne *et al.* (1979) and Kroch (1979). Other surveys include Brock and Nesbitt (1977), Charles River Associates (1978), Hoffman and Wood (1976). An earlier report by the Decision Sciences Corporation (1973) reviewed ninety-four US studies and models. There are also recent registers of energy research for the UK

Summary Table of Energy Models

GROUP I: UNITED KINGDOM

Model No.	Source/Author	Scope/Fuel	Activity	Technique	Horizon (years)/Reference Year
1	Dept. of Energy	Energy	Demand	Forecasting	30
2	Dept. of Energy	Energy	Conservation	Forecasting	30
3	Dept. of Energy	Energy	Fuel allocation	Econometric/Forecasting	30
4	Dept. of Energy	Energy	Transport	Econometric/Forecasting	30
5	Dept. of Energy	Gas	S and D	LP	30
6	Dept. of Energy	Electricity–Coal	Supply	LP	30
7	Dept. of Energy	Energy	S and D	Data Processing	30
8	Electricity Council	Electricity	Demand	Econometric	?
9	CEGB	Electricity	Demand	Econometric	6
10	CEGB	Electricity	Supply	Non-LP/iteration	30
11	CEGB	Electricity	Supply	LP	30
12	CEGB	Electricity	Supply	Calculus	<5
13	Electricity Area Boards	Electricity	Demand	Econometric	15
14	NCB	Energy	Demand	Economic/Econometric	15
15	NCB	Coal	Supply	Data Processing	15
16	NCB	Coal	S and D	Data Processing	5
17	NCB	Coal	Supply	LP	?
18	NCR	Coal	Area Supply	LP	5
19	NCR	Coal	Supply	LP/simulation	1
20	NCB	Coal	Supply Technology	Iteration	25
21	British Gas Corp.	Gas	Supply	LP	100, 200
22	UKAEA	Electricity	Supply	Simulation	30
23	UKAEA	Electricity	Demand	Econometric	30
24	Shell/BP	Oil	S and D	Economic	30

Summary Table of Energy Models

Model No.	Source/Author	Scope/Fuel	Activity	Technique	Horizon (years)/ Reference Year
25	Cambridge	Energy	Demand	Econometric/IO	1980, 85
26	NIESR	Energy	Demand	Econometric	1980
27	IIED	Energy	Demand	Technical Assessment/ Forecasting	50
28	Cheshire–Surrey, Thomas	Energy	Demand	Forecasting	25
29	Lovins	Energy	S and D	Technical Assessment/ Forecasting	
30	Systems Analysis Research Unit	Energy	Demand	IO/Econometric	30
GROUP II: USA					
31	MacAvoy–Pindyck	Gas	S and D	Econometric	1980
32	Baughman–Joskow	Regional Electricity	SD + Finance/ Regulatory	Econometric/Behavioural/ Simulation	1995
33	Zimmerman	Coal	Supply	Econometric	n.a.
34	Atomic Energy Commission	Electricity	Supply	LP	late C21
35	Manne	Breeder	Investment	Decision Tree/LP	2025
36	Stanford PILOT	Economy/Energy	Supply	Input–output/LP	40
37	Brookhaven RES	Energy	Supply	Network	1
38	Brookhaven–Illinois	Economy	Supply	Input–output	1
39a	Brookhaven BESOM	Energy	Supply	LP	1985, 2000
39b	Brookhaven DESOM	Energy	Supply	LP	100
40	Battelle	Energy	Supply	LP	1
41	Manne ETA	Energy	S and D	Non LP	75

42	SRI-Gulf	Energy	S and D	Behavioural	50
43	Synfuels	Energy	Supply	Decision Tree	2025
44	Project Independence PIES	Energy	S and D	Econometric/LP	1985, 90
45	Wharton	Energy/Macro	D and S	IO/Econometric	10
46	Hudson–Jorgenson	Energy/Macro	D and S	IO/Econometric	2000
47	Manne ETA-MACRO	Energy/Macro	D and S	Non LP/Econometric	75

GROUP III: WORLD

48	Häfele and Manne	World Energy	D and S	LP	75
49	IIASA	World Energy/Economy	D and S	Econometric/LP/Economic	2040
50	Deam/QMCERU	World Oil and Gas	Supply	LP	?
51	Odell–Rosing	North Sea Oil	Supply	Simulation	20
52	Kennedy	World Oil	D and S	Quadratic Programming	1980
53	WAES	World Energy	D and S	Economic/Technological	
54	Nordhaus	World Energy	D and S	LP	120

(Owens, 1980) the rest of Western Europe (Walton and Turner, 1981) and the world (Charpentier, 1974, 1975; Beaujean and Charpentier, 1976, 1978). Allen *et al.* (1981) compare global energy models while Taylor (1977) provides a useful survey of energy price and income elasticities; a more recent discussion, with a worldwide orientation, is given by Eden *et al.* (1981, Ch. 13). Westoby (1981) provides an incisive critique of long-run price elasticities in thirteen energy models (one of which is an earlier version of the BEM).

The studies summarised here are grouped by geographical focus: Group I, United Kingdom; Group II, USA; and Group III, world (or parts thereof). Within the UK group the order of presentation is by source of model: Department of Energy, fuel industries, other sources. Within the US group the order is by scope of model: individual fuels, energy sector, all industries, macro-economic relationships. The few studies in Group III are not arranged in any particular order. For ease of reference in the chapter, the models are numbered in order of presentation. However, the bibliographical references at the end of the chapter (as elsewhere in this book) are listed alphabetically by author.

Group I: United Kingdom

The Department of Energy
When the Energy Model Group was set up in 1967 within the Department of Energy, it was the intention to produce an integrated mathematical model that would illustrate the structure and development of the whole of the UK energy sector. As noted in Department of Energy (1978a), the latest published version of the Department of Energy forecasting methodology, it has been found preferable to develop a number of separate models describing parts of the UK energy sector with many of the interactions between the individual sub-models being handled by 'less mathematically formal means'. The main reasons for pursuing this course are given as data limitations and institutional constraints.

The descriptions and quotations in [1–7] below are from Department of Energy (1978). See also Hutber *et al.* (1974) for an earlier description.

1 Department of Energy Demand Model
The total energy demand is disaggregated into five main sectors (Domestic, Iron and Steel, Other Industry, Transport and Other Consumers). Statistical regression analysis is used to relate energy consumption (useful heat basis) to exogenous national economic variables in each sector, but there are variations in methods from one sector to another. In particular, forecasts for Iron and Steel and Transport are largely based on technological forecasts and advice from other departments.

2 Department of Energy Conservation Model
Since the Energy Demand Model described above is based on historical

relationships between energy consumption and economic variables it is thought that it does not adequately reflect the changed economic circumstances following the sudden rise in energy prices in 1973–74. The Conservation Model incorporates judgements about the technical efficacy of various conservation measures, the rate of adoption of conservation measures and how the latter is affected by energy prices and other conservation policies.

3 Department of Energy Fuel Allocation Model

Having estimated the total demand for energy in each sector (except Transport which is considered separately) and having adjusted the demand for conservation as noted above, the next stage is to calculate the likely market shares of each of the fuels in each sector. In general, for Domestic, Other Industry and Other Sectors, in applications in which substitution is feasible and limits to substitutability have not been reached, the model incorporates a movement away from fuels that are relatively expensive (at rates determined largely by normal rates of appliance replacement) towards the cheaper fuels. In these three sectors, the relative fuel shares are determined by the lagged effects of prices, other demand indicators and technical constraints limiting substitutability between fuels in certain uses. For an earlier description of treatment of demand, see Billington (1971).

Projections of fuel allocation in the Iron and Steel Sector are based on forecasts of technological developments in that sector. The Transport Sector is dealt with separately (see [4] below).

4 Department of Energy Transport Model

Projections of energy consumption in the Transport Sector are obtained by converting Department of Transport estimates of various forms of traffic growth (road, rail, air and water) into their energy requirements. The traffic growth projections are based on assumptions about macroeconomic variables. No substitution for oil products is permitted in road and air transport. The model incorporates judgements about the price trends of oil products, their short-term effects on fuel consumption as well as the long-term effects on oil consumption as a result of improvement in the fuel economy performance of vehicles.

5 Department of Energy Gas Supply Model

This is a linear programming model which covers the gas procurement, production and distribution activities of the British Gas Corporation in the UK. Activities such as procurement of gas from different sources (e.g. Southern Basin, UK Frigg and imported Norwegian gas, oil-associated gas) and transmission and storage of gas are included in the model. The objective function to be maximised, subject to several hundred constraints, is the present value of market surplus which is defined as consumer benefit less market surplus. More precisely, the market surplus is defined as the sum of the areas under the demand curves for the various market sectors less purchasing, processing, transmission, distribution and capital costs. Particular attention is paid to the problem of matching supply and demand load factors over the year. The time dimension in the model is represented by specifying the constraints and discounted market surplus for a number of 'snapshot' years. Levels of consumption, depletion, procurement, etc., for years between the snapshot years are obtained by extrapolation. One of the main concerns of this model is to assess the strategy for the depletion of natural gas. The market surplus approach endogenuously determines the optimum level of consumption and the price. Moreover, in producing consumption projections for all fuels, in the Fuel Allocation Model (see [3] above), the economically determined consumption projection is constrained by assumptions about the maximum rate at which consumers can change the mix of the stock of appliances in order to switch from one fuel to another.

6   Department of Energy Electricity and Coal Model

Electricity and coal sectors for England and Wales are incorporated into a single linear programming type model which has as its objective function the minimisation of the present value of combined costs of the CEGB and the NCB. The time dimension is represented by 'snapshot' years as in the gas supply model. Forecasts for Scotland and Northern Ireland are made independently and added to the final tabulations for the UK.

In the coal part of the model, coal tranches depicting differing levels of extraction costs ranging from low-cost open cast production to high-cost output from marginal pits are identified. The National Coal Board's production targets set out in the *Plan for Coal* and *Plan 2000* are assumed to be a constraining upper limit on the expansion of the industry. The demand uses for coal in final consumption and for making substitute natural gas are obtained from the Demand Model (see [1] above) and are an input in the Electricity and Coal Model. The levels of demand for coal in power stations, however, are obtained from the linear programming solution.

The electricity part of the model is represented by assembling all the power stations in England and Wales into groups according to the fuel they use, efficiency, location and age. Location is significant for coal-burning stations for which the model incorporates coal transportation costs from appropriate coal regions as well as differences in coal production costs in different regions.

Given the estimates of electricity demand obtained from the Demand Model, the Electricity and Coal Model takes account of the demand load duration on snapshot days and determines the utilisation and increase in capacity of different types of plant using different fuels in each of the snapshot years which minimise the present value of operating and capital costs.

Increases in capacity for electricity production by certain fuels are constrained in order to prevent large fluctuations in capacity installation from one period to the next, as well as to prevent capacity expansion which is thought to be impractical.

7 Department of Energy Data Processing Model

This model takes the output from the other six models described above and produces a consistent integrated picture of supply and demand for the UK energy sector. It performs tasks which were done by making *ad hoc* adjustments and iterations in the early stages of working with previous versions of the models described above.

(i) Run the four fuel supply models repeatedly, especially the gas and electricity LPs [2] and [4], assuming a different given pattern of demands each time. By noting the resultant marginal costs of supplies each time, a set of data linking fuel quantities supplied to marginal costs is obtained. These data represent a multi-dimensional space in quantities, marginal costs and time.

(ii) Using the data generated in (i), develop and estimate supply equations.

(iii) Solve the supply equations from (ii) simultaneously with the demand equations from [8], to obtain market prices and quantities for each fuel in each year (and in each market?).

(iv) In order to see the detailed implications of these market quantities, plug them back into the (mainly LP) supply models as fixed demands to be met and re-run the supply models.

8 Electricity Council Demand Models

Electricity consumption and maximum load forecasting are described in part in Edwards (1966) and Robson and Davis (1972, pp. 19–20). For consumption, two independent methods involving different levels of disaggregation are used and the results are then compared with each other, and with the results of the CEGB and Area Board forecasts [11] and [15].

Method 1.　Sales are divided into domestic, industrial and commercial and a separate single equation econometric model used for each. See also Boley (1973).

Method 2.　Domestic sales are broken down by cooking, water heating, etc., and appliances sales, consumption per appliance, and hence electricity usage is forecast for each. Industrial sales are forecast econometrically by standard industrial classification groups (about 16–20). Models and results set out in Baxter and Rees (1968) and Bell (1972). Market research for the commercial sector is less well developed.

　　Maximum half-hour demand (peak load) is forecast by applying a load factor, forecast from various econometric and market research methods, to the total consumption forecasts above.

9 CEGB Trend Projections

Until at least about 1970 the CEGB method of forecasting – they make an annual six-year forecast – was to extrapolate exponential trends fitted separately to the weather-corrected total electricity consumption and maximum half-hour demand over the previous ten years. These fitted very well, but since 1970 a linearly declining trend growth rate has given a much better fit. See Edwards and Clark (1962) and Jenkin (1973a).

10 CEGB 'Background' Supply Model (NLP) – CHOOSE
The objective function of this non-linear programming problem includes total capital and operating costs over a thirty-year period. The load duration curve in each year is represented by a non-linear function so that the operating cost part of the objective function is non-linear. Policy constraints are also included. Interaction between different years makes the problem difficult to solve. It is solved by setting up a series of related one-year problems and making these problems yield the same solution as the main problem by iteration. The model solves basically the same problem as the LP model [13] but is much less flexible. It was set up because computers at the time could not cope satisfactorily with the huge size of the corresponding LP. See Phillips *et al.* (1969).

11 CEGB 'Background' Supply Model (LP)
This is a sophisticated example of the conventional multi-period LP-type electricity model. Operating plus investment costs are to be minimised. The model allows the inclusion of variable fuel cost supply curves and the ability to convert plant from one fuel to another. See Jenkin (1973b, p. 4).

12 CEGB 'Background' Supply Model (CV)
In this electricity supply model the objective is to find the plant building programme that will minimise present valued capital and operating costs over thirty years. Plant installation, capital costs and operating costs for each plant type are all taken as functions of time. So also is peak demand. The problem is formulated as a calculus of variations model. It is solved directly, analytically; hence quite complex problems are handled without need for the programming procedures of [12] and [13] – which is especially useful when considering uncertainty (Jenkin, 1973b, Part II).

13 Electricity Area Board Demand Forecasts
The two Scottish Boards and the twelve Area Boards in England and Wales each make consumption and load forecasts for their own area, using both local knowledge and, where local data are available, econometric, trend and other techniques according to choice, similar to those of the Electricity Council and CEGB. The techniques used by the Area Boards are nowhere published in detail, but they are referred to in a few sentences in such papers as Edwards (1966, p. 4), Orson (1968, pp. 162–3) and Robson and Davis (1972, p. 20). Myers (1971) described consumption forecasting techniques of the South of Scotland Electricity Board. The forecasts of the twelve Area Boards in England and Wales are aggregated by the Electricity Council and compared with the various forecasts made by the CEGB and the Electricity Council itself.

14 NCB Energy Demand Model

An interactive conversational computer model. Energy demands are projected for market sectors (four at present). Total energy demand in each sector is calculated from the user's view of economic growth, government policy, price elasticities, technical trends, etc. The total is then divided up between fuels on the basis of rules which are partly logical, partly empirical and party assumed. These rules require that supplies and relative prices be provided exogeneously by the user. (The coal supply/cost model [17] can be used at this point, see [18].) Further assumptions about the electricity industry programme enable the derivation of demands for primary fuels. See Baker and Sadnicki (1975) and Ormerod (1979).

15 NCB Coal Supply/Cost Model

This is an interactive conversational computer model. It considers 'how capital and labour resources are allocated in the light of depletion of existing reserves and the development of new sources of capacity' and provides estimates of future trends in productivity and operating cost (Baker and Sadnicki, 1975, pp. 22, 30).

16 NCB Coal Supply–Demand Model

Baker and Sadnicki (1975, p. 30) state that supply–demand matching for coal is studied through linking models [14] and [15]. Typically a combination of several runs is made on varying assumptions. A primary aim is to identify the desirability or otherwise of investment schemes. The above authors say that the model would produce some picture of a possible financial out-turn for the industry.

17 NCB National LP Model

This is an LP model which minimises the production and transport costs of meeting a given level of demand. It represents the total production at each pit, divided into five coal types, and the transport of each from seventeen production areas to seven sales regions. The five coal types or market categories, for which demands are taken as given, are electricity, coke ovens, domestic bituminous, domestic naturally smokeless and other. See NBPI (1970, Appendix H, p. 85, para 12 and Appendix B, p. 46, para 2).

18 NCB Area Board Model

This LP cost-minimising model was developed as an aid to detailed area planning. The model considers in detail production, segregation, in-pit transport, coal preparation, marketing and manpower alternatives at each pit – each of these headings having several further subdivisions. Capacity of each part of the plant can be taken as given, or new capital investment can be considered. See NBPI (1970, Appendix H, p. 4, paras 9–11).

19   NCB Planning System
This is a three-stage modelling and planning exercise involving national, area and colliery models. It is recommended in NBPI (1970, Ch. 5 and Appendix B, p. 46, paras 1–5). It appears from communication with the NCB planning department that they now operate some such system. In the recommendation, the first stage is similar to [19], the second stage is similar to [20], but with less detail, and the third stage is a simulation-type colliery planning model. A consistent solution, or plan, is achieved by iteration between these classes of models.

20   NCB Coal Conversion Processes Model
An interactive conversational computer model which examines combining several known processes for the gasification and/or liquifaction of coal, to form 'coalplexes'. A network is specified by listing the sub-processes, together with the numbered input and output streams connecting them. The programme, by a convergent iterative process, calculates the flow rates and compositions of the output streams, and also the unit capital costs, from the flow rate and composition of the input stream. Total capital cost is calculated by summing the capital costs of the sub-processes. See Merrick (1975).

21   British Gas Corporation Depletion Model
Described in Lyness and Clark (1975), and is somewhat similar to the Department of Energy Gas Model [5] above. This twenty-five year LP model describes the supply of gas from various sources, and its transmission, storage and sales in various markets. Objectives considered include sales maximisation, cost minimisation, net revenue maximisation and market surplus maximisation.

22   UKAEA Digital Computer Code for Assessing the Economics of Nuclear Power (Discount G)
'Discount G is a computer code for simulating an electricity generating system consisting of both nuclear and conventional stations. It may be used to calculate the present worth of expenditure on the system, so that if the calculation is repeated with one type of station replaced by another, the economic benefit of this replacement can be determined as well as its effect on uranium and plutonium logistics. In this way, the code has been used as an aid in formulating development policy' (Iliffe, 1974). The latest version, G, is set out in full, including the computer code, in Iliffe (1973).

23   UKAEA 'TREND' Forecasting Model of the Electricity System
The model makes S-curve trend projections of electricity consumption and overall plant load factor, and forecasts the demand for plant by applying these to a fitted load duration curve. Using (trend) projections of the costs of different plant types, the benefits from the introduction of new plant types can be calculated. Other evaluations and comparisons of planning programmes can be made (Brookes, 1970).

24 Shell Scenario Models

Described in general terms in Lindsell (1972) of Shell-Mex and BP Ltd. Although this company is now split up again between the parent companies Shell and BP, the description is apparently still valid (see DuMoulin and Eyre, 1979, for a recent description). The model is, in method, a fairly simple affair of informed guesses and simple arithmetic with almost no use of a computer. The absence of formal or longer term forecasts for Britain is a reflection of (1) recent very large changes in the energy market, which mean that the parameters reflecting past consumer behaviour are often now no longer valid, and the new parameters may as yet be inestimable; (2) the relatively short investment lead time, and hence flexibility in changing production, transport and distribution capacity in the industry – a tanker or an oil refinery takes only about three years to build; and (3) the international nature of the industry – Britain is only a small part of the world oil market.

British Petroleum's model is not published but is thought to be similar to Shell's.

25 The Cambridge Growth Project

This demand model was built as a sub-model for the Cambridge Growth Project which is an input/output type model of the British economy. It is set out in Stone and Wigley (1968). The authors intended (see Ch. 1) to construct also a fuel supply model to interact with the demand model but nothing further has been reported on this. Fuel demands by intermediate industry are forecast for more than twenty industry sub-groups by projecting the (fuel input)/(industry output) coefficients. This is done by expressing these coefficients as functions mainly of time and relative fuel prices. Demand by households for a fuel is expressed as a function of relative fuel prices, consumer expenditure and temperature. Non-industrial demand for motor spirit and final demand by the government sector are treated separately. The model and forecasts have since been updated (see Cambridge Growth Project, 1978, and Peterson, 1979).

26 NIESR Energy Forecasts

The National Institute for Economic and Social Research occasionally publishes studies of the demand for energy in the UK, with forecasts for several years ahead (Ray and Blackaby, 1960; Ray 1967, 1972). The forecasts are disaggregated by several categories of intermediate and final demand. The main forecasting technique seems to be to link total energy demand by market to some measures of output or activity. This relationship is affected by changes in the pattern of output and in the efficiency of fuel consumption. The share of energy demand going to each fuel is projected by studying trends in the rate of substitution between fuels, the pattern of output, fuel efficiencies, etc., in each market.

27 IIED Low Energy Strategy

Argues against econometric 'top-down' extrapolation of past trends, and in favour of disaggregated 'bottom-up' approach. Identifies 400 end-uses, projects future activity levels, calculates energy intensity of these activities, then aggregates. Considers Low and High economic growth projections over fifty years. Calculations embodied in report by Leach *et al.* (1979); methodology summarised by Lewis (1979). Inspired by French case study by Chateau and Lapillonne (1978).

28   *Cheshire–Surrey and Thomas Sectoral Approaches*
Cheshire and Surrey (1978) estimate UK energy demand for the year 2000 using a disaggregated sectoral approach (cf. [27]) rather than trend extrapolation. Thomas (1980) examines sensitivity and assumptions of this model. Develops computer version, with three demand sectors (domestic, transport, production) and twenty-one subsectors, which produces annual energy balance sheet. Alternative policies and data can be analysed. Model allows fuel substitution according to relative prices subject to capital stock constraints. Distinguishes several types of demand (e.g. competitive, premium, non-substitutable).

29   *Lovins Soft Energy Path*
Lovins (1979) contrasts the 'conventional' scenario (how to expand existing energy sources to meet projected homogeneous demands) with the 'soft' scenario (how to meet heterogeneous demands with minimum of energy supplied in most effective way for each use). More extensive exposition in Lovins (1976).

30   *Systems Analysis Research Unit Energy Demand Model*
Input–output model with twenty-four sectors (of which four are fuels and one government expenditure). Relation between GDP and energy use influenced by fuel mix (determined by price and income elasticities with constraints on speed of change), basket of final goods (calculated using price and income elasticities), and changes in efficiency of energy use (reflecting price-independent learning and price-dependent capital–energy substitution). Calibrated on 1958–75 data; projections to 2005. Model suggests fuel prices have strong effect. Can be used to explore usual scenarios, for example, non-nuclear. See Roberts (1980).

Group II: USA

31   *MacAvoy–Pindyck Gas Model*
Covers exploration of gas reserves, production, pricing, transportation costs and wholesale demand, by detailed regions of USA. Econometric approach, designed to analyse effects of wholesale price regulation on current and future demand and supply. See MacAvoy and Pindyck (1973, 1975). Gas Reserves discovery submodel draws on work of Fisher (1974).

32   *Baughman–Joskow Regionalized Electricity Model (REM)*
Constructed to analyse policy issues affecting electricity producers, consumers, regulators and equipment manufacturers. Consists of three

sub-models – demand, supply and financial/regulatory. Econometric demand model forecasts demands by region and sector as functions of prices of electricity, coal, oil and gas. Supply model based on behavioural decision rules to calculate least cost expansion pattern seen from single period (rather than explicit multi-period minimisation). Financial/regulatory submodel simulates industry processes of raising capital and setting prices in accordance with state and federal regulations. Used to assess future of US nuclear industry. See Baughman and Joskow (1976) and Baughman *et al.* (1979).

33   Zimmerman Coal Model
Small-scale highly specialised supply-oriented model of US coal industry, long-run marginal costs related to cumulative output by fitting log normal distribution of production costs to geological characteristics of coal seams. Used to examine policies related to strip-mining regulation, air pollution legislation and energy independence. See Zimmerman (1977).

34   Atomic Energy Commission (ALPS)
An LP system developed by US Atomic Energy Commission to assess benefits of alternative courses of electricity development. Electricity demands specified exogenously. Production and investment plans chosen to minimise present value of costs with emphasis on choice of nuclear technology. Very large scale (4,000 rows × 9,000 columns) due to nuclear detail and number of time periods (annual through 2020 and on to late twenty-first century). Used in cost–benefit appraisal of the fast breeder reactor. See Hardie *et al.* (1972).

35   Manne: Breeder Decision Analyses
'Sequential probabilistic linear programming is employed to calculate optimal electricity plant-mix decisions during the decade of the 1980s – given the uncertainty on the date of availability of the breeder. The model allows for the possibility that future uranium resource scarcities will lead to an increase in electricity prices and hence a reduction in the projected demands. Somewhat surprisingly, the near future decisions are insensitive to the distant future uncertainties. There seems to be a low value of information on the date of availability of the resource saving breeder technology' (Manne, 1974). More sophisticated analyses using ETA-MACRO [57] are described by Manne (1976), Manne and Richels (1978, 1980) and Richels and Plummer (1977).

36   Stanford PILOT
An input–output model of the economy linked to an inter-temporal linear programming model. Contains five energy sectors and eighteen non-energy sectors; the latter may be aggregated to seven. Capital formation endogenous. Available reserves are a function of endogenous drilling effort. No substitution on energy demand side. Maximand is undiscounted sum of gross national consumption over forty years subject to certain balance constraints. LP with piecewise linear approxima-

tions. Used to evaluate six scenarios related to energy availability and conservation. The model can also be used in a 'welfare equilibrium mode' by introducing utility and production functions in order to calculate market equilibrating prices over the dual programme. See Parikh (1976, 1977), Dantzig (1977) and Connolly et al. (1977).

37 Brookhaven Reference Energy System (RES)

'A network representation of all of the technical activities required to supply various forms of energy to end-use activities' (Tessmer et al. 1975). Quantified for a given year with specified energy demands and required energy supplies. Used to evaluate effects of new technologies on resource consumption, cost and the environment, by comparing Perturbed Energy System with RES. Used in conjunction with Brookhaven–Illinois input–output model [48] and optimising models [49].

38 Brookhaven–Illinois Input–Output Model

Specialised input–output model of the national economy, with output of energy sectors measured in physical units (BTUs) rather than dollars. Based on Bureau of Economic Analysis input–output table with seventy-eight regular producing sectors, plus additional sectors for new energy technologies (110 sectors in total?). Has fixed coefficients, implying no substitution between inputs as relative prices change. Used in conjunction with Reference Energy System, [5] and optimising model [48]. See Tessmer et al. (1975) and Behling et al. (1975).

39 Brookhaven Energy System Optimising Model (BESOM)

Single period optimising model using same input parameters as Reference Energy System [37], encompassing entire energy system and allowing full inter-fuel substitutability. Calculates minimum cost allocation of energy supplies to meet specified energy demands for a single planning year (typically 1985 or 2000). LP model of transportation type with additional capacity and balance constraints. See Cherniavsky (1974). Multi-period extension (DESOM) calculates minimum present value of costs. See Marcuse et al. (1976), Cherniavsky et al. (1977). Both optimising models used in conjunction with input–output model [6] to analyse interactions with rest of economy, for example, strategic planning of electrification and oil stockpiling. See Tessmer et al. (1975).

40 Battelle Model

Single period cost-minimising LP model, similar to Brookhaven BESOM model [49] but with substantial regional disaggregation (238 demand regions and 125 supply regions, plus transportation costs). See Chilton and Kimeson (1976).

41 Manne Energy Technology Assessment Model (ETA)

'Designed to overcome the objections to long term demand projections that are independent of supply conditions and prices' (Manne, 1979a). Partial equilibrium model covering US energy sector. Energy demands aggregated into electric and non-electric, with demand functions incorporating own- and cross-price elasticities. Supply side handled via conventional LP process analysis (electric energy from coal-fired power plants, light water reactors, fast breeders and more advanced electric technology, non-electric energy from oil, gas, synthetic fuels or hydrogen via electrolysis). Non-linear optimisation (maximand present value of consumer plus producer surplus over seventy-five-year horizon) used to approximate inter temporal market equilibrium for energy sector. See Manne (1976) and, for an application to R & D expenditure, Auer *et al.* (1976). Model used in nuclear power debate (Keeny *et al.*, 1977; Modeling Resource Group, 1978).

42 SRI–Gulf
Highly detailed regional model (eight demand and twenty supply regions) of US energy sector over fifty years horizon. Behavioural supply and demand functions with algorithm to generate market clearing prices. Originally developed to analyse synthetic fuels strategy for Gulf Oil. See Cazalet *et al.* (1975, 1977). Used in [53] below.

43 Synfuels
Decision tree used to design possible development strategy for synthetic fuels in USA, taking advantage of sequential nature of decisions and information flows. Based on SRI–Gulf model [52] of energy network. 'The analysis is credited with persuading the Administration to cut back from President Fund's original goal of one million barrels (of synthetic fuel) down to 350,000 barrels a day by 1985' (Manne *et al.*, 1979). See Synfuels Interagency Task Force (1975).

44 Project Independence Evaluation System (PIES)
Consists of an econometric demand model, a series of special-purpose regional supply models and an integrating model with LP structure which combines outputs from other components and solves for market clearing prices, supplies and demands in a typical future year – 1985 or 1990. Demand functions incorporate own- and cross-price elasticities, but because latter are non-symmetric they do not integrate into a social welfare function, hence an iterative equilibrating procedure has to be employed instead of an optimising one. Model used to assess US dependence on oil imports and impact of domestic price controls. See Federal Energy Administration (1974, 1976), Hogan (1975, 1977), and for a critique Hausman (1975).

45 Wharton Annual Energy Model
A demand-oriented macro-economic model integrated with a detailed input–output sub-model of the energy sector. Annual with five- to ten-year horizon. The sub-model contains fifty-nine intermediate industries and 126 sectors, and has variable coefficients based upon a single elasticity of substitution for a broad class of substitutes. See Preston (1975) and Klein and Finan (1976).

46   Hudson–Jorgenson Model
Macro-economic model coupled with Long-Term Inter-industry Trans-actions Model (LTITM). The former is a two-sector neo-classical growth model with five behavioural equations relating to supply of goods and labour, demand for factors of production and aggregate consumption function; there are eight price and quantity variables; the production function mainly determines the growth of capital stock. See Hudson and Jorgenson (1975). The LTITM is a ten-sector input–output model with variable coefficients. See Behling *et al.* (1976).

47   Manne ETA–MACRO
'Merger between ETA [51] and a macroeconomic growth model provid-ing for substitution between capital, labour and energy inputs' (Manne *et al.*, 1979). Extent of trade-off summarised by single elasticity of sub-stitution parameters. Model designed to explore effects of higher energy costs (e.g. due to non-nuclear policy) on (reduced) growth of GNP and capital stock. See Hitch (1977, pp. 1–45) and Manne (1979a, b, c). The last reference is an application to the international energy situation.

Group III: The World

48   Häfele and Manne (1975)
LP model of about 400 constraints, not counting simple upper bounds, designed to describe the energy dynamics of a hypothetical 'model so-ciety' of the scale and level of technology of the US, Western Europe, Japan or the USSR, over twenty-five three-year sub-periods, from the present dependence on fossil fuels, through the inevitable transition to a mainly nuclear fuel economy. See Häfele and Manne (1975).

49   IIASA Global Models
A set of energy models developed by the Energy Systems Program at the International Institute for Applied Systems Analysis (IIASA) in Austria is designed to study global and regional aspects of the long-term transition to sustainable energy systems. Family of models includes a macro-economic model (MACRO) of potential GNP; two energy demand models (MUSE and MEDEE) which use outputs of MACRO to calculate final energy demands; an energy demand model for develop-ing regions (SIMA); an energy supply and conversion model (MES-SAGE) using LP to calculate minimum present value of costs over mul-tiple periods (presently till 2040); and an economic impact model (IMPACT) to determine whether the economy can sustain investment programme (capital, materials, equipment, manpower) required by MESSAGE. The models have been used to investigate two scenarios (High and Low energy demand) under three different policy assump-tions (nuclear moratorium, all-out nuclear effort, energy conservation program) for a seven-region model of the world over fifty years. See Anderer *et al.* (1981) and Häfele (1981) and, for earlier outlines, Häfele and Basile (1978). MESSAGE is a significant extension of [63] which focused on strategies for a transition from fossil to nuclear fuels.

50 QMCERU World Model
Research conducted by a team under Professor R. J. Deam at the Queen Mary College Energy Research Unit: 'A large linear programming computer model has been constructed which currently covers the world's oil and gas industry and will eventually embrace all other significant forms of energy. QMCERU (1974, Part I) describes and discusses some of the concepts on which the model was based, the technical and accounting aspects of its construction, the computer support systems required and the significance and implication of results obtained.' See also QMCERU (1973) and QMCERU (1974, Part II).

51 Odell and Rosing North Sea Oil Simulation Model
On certain assumptions about numbers of exploration wells drilled and probabilities of success of each, a mean value for discoveries of new reserves in each of four different size classes is determined for each of the next twenty years. To these eighty means are then added or subtracted various random elements to give 'actual' discoveries. These discoveries are revised upwards by random amounts at random intervals over about twenty years – doubling on average. To each discovery is applied a depletion pattern, selected at random from a predefined set. The above programme is repeated many times to simulate many possible paths for total annual production and these are compared with potential demand. See Odell and Rosing (1976) and critical review by Kemp (1977).

52 Kennedy World Oil Model
Deals with production, consumption, trade patterns and pricing in world oil market. Assumes OPEC will set Gulf crude oil price to maximise OPEC revenues. Includes linear crude oil supply functions for other sources and linear demand functions for four refined products in six world regions in 1980 (with zero cross-elasticities). Quadratic programming used to maximise net economic benefits in order to calculate market equilibrium. See Kennedy (1974).

53 WAES Global Energy Prospects
Workshop on Alternative Energy Strategies is an international project, involving seventy-five experts in fifteen countries. Uses scenarios to span wide range of future energy supply and demand patterns at world level. Takes 'soft' approach (cf. [37]). See Wilson (1976) and WAES (1977).

54 Nordhaus World Energy Model
LP model of world energy system over 120 years in ten-year periods. Minimises cost of energy minus marginal utilities of each activity, where latter derived from estimated demand functions based on 1955–72 data for seven countries. Constraints pertain to resources, conversion, delivery, US imports and energy consumption, growth of production, nuclear stockpile for nuclear fuel cycle, etc. Also run for two or three major regions (USA, OPEC, Rest of World). Market imperfections can be incorporated (e.g. monopoly in oil and gas). Attempt to assess trade-off

between economic growth and environmental quality (diffusion of carbon dioxide). See Nordhaus (1979).

References

Allen, E. L., Edmonds, J. A. and Kuenne, R. E. (1981), 'A comparative analysis of global energy models', *Energy Economics*, vol. 3, no. 1.

Anderer, J., with McDonald, A. and Nakicenovic, N. (1981), *Energy in a Finite World: Paths to a Sustainable Future* (Vol. 1), Report by the Energy Systems Program Group of the International Institute for Applied Systems Analysis, Wolf Häfele, Program Leader, Ballinger Publishing Co., Cambridge, Mass.

Anderson, D. (1972), 'Models for determining least-cost investments in electricity supply', *Bell Journal of Economics and Management Science*, vol. 3, Spring.

Auer, P. L., Manne, A. S. and Yu, O. S. (1976), *Nuclear Power, Coal, and Energy Conservation – With a Note on the Costs of a Nuclear Moratorium*, EPRI SR-34, Special Report, Electric Power Research Institute, Palo Alto, California.

Baker, A. and Sadnicki, M. J. (1975), 'The use of interactive computer models of demand and supply', in *Understanding Energy Systems*, Proceedings of a Joint Conference of the Institute of Fuel and the Operational Research Society, London, April.

Baughman, M. L. and Joskow, P. L. (1976), 'The future of the U.S. nuclear energy industry', *Bell Journal of Economics*, Spring.

Baughman, M. L., Joskow, P. J. and Kamat, D. P. (1979), *Electric Power in the U.S.: Models and Policy Analyses*, MIT Press, Cambridge, Mass.

Baxter, R. E. and Rees, R. (1968), 'Analysis of the industrial demand for electricity', *Economic Journal*, vol. 78, June.

Beale, E. M. L. (1968), *Linear Programming in Practice*, Pitman, London.

Beaujean, J. and Charpentier, J. (eds) (1976), *A Review of Energy Models*, No. 3, December, RR-76-18, International Institute for Applied Systems Analysis, Laxenburg, Austria.

Beaujean, J. and Charpentier, J. (eds) (1978), *A Review of Energy Models*, No. 4, July, RR-78-12, International Institute for Applied Systems Analysis, Laxenburg, Austria.

Behling, D. J., Marcuse, W., Swift, M. and Tessmer, R. G. Jr. (1975), 'A two level iterative model for estimating inter-fuel substitution effects', *Summer Computer Simulation Conference*, San Francisco, 21–23 July.

Behling, D. J. Jr., Dullian, R. and Hudson, E. (1976), *The Relationship of Energy Growth to Economic Growth under Alternative Energy Policies*, Brookhaven National Laboratories.

Bell, A. R. (1972), 'Industrial electricity – an example of an intermediate good', *Journal of Industrial Economics*, pp. 95–109.

Billington, B. J. (1971), 'Formulating and estimating a model for estimating the demand for fuels', Paper presented at the *Colloquium on Statistical Model Building, Prediction and Control*, Institute of Electrical Engineers, London, 30th April.

Boley, T. A. (1973), 'Electricity demand: econometric models and changing coefficients', *UN Economic Commission for Europe, Symposium on Mathematical Models of Sectors of the Energy Economy*, Alma Ata, USSR, August.

Brock, M. and Nesbitt, D. (1977), *Large-scale Energy Planning Models: A Methodological Analysis*, Standard Research Institute, Menlo Park, California.

Brookes, L. G. (1970), 'A Forecasting model of the electricity system', *Atom*, No. 165, July.

Cambridge Growth Project (1978), *Input–output and Energy Demand Models for the UK*, Final Report to the Commission of the European Communities. Department of Applied Economics, Cambridge.

Carey, M. (1975), 'A survey of quantitative models and studies of the UK energy sector', *Discussion Paper*, Series B No. 33, Faculty of Commerce and Social Science, University of Birmingham, England.

Cazalet, E. *et al.*, (1975), *A Western Energy Development Study*, Stanford Research Institute for Gulf Oil Corporation, SRI Project 4000.

Cazalet, E. G. (1977), *Generalised Equilibrium Modelling: The Methodology of the SRI–Gulf Energy Model*, Decision Focus Incorporated, Palo Alto, California.

Charles River Associates (1978) 'Review and Evaluation of selected large-scale energy models', CRA Report No. 231, Cambridge, Mass., 1978.

Charnes, A. and Cooper, W. W. (1961), *Management Models and Industrial Applications of Linear Programming*, Vols 1 and 2, Wiley, New York.

Charpentier, J. (1974), *A Review of Energy Models*, No. 1, May, RR-74-10, International Institute of Applied Systems Analysis, Laxenburg, Austria.

Charpentier, J. (1975), *A Review of Energy Models*, No. 2, July, RR-75-35, International Institute of Applied Systems Analysis, Laxenburg, Austria.

Chateau, B. and Lapillonne, B. (1978), 'Long term energy demand forecasting: A new approach', *Energy Policy*, vol. 6, no. 2.

Cherniavsky, E. A. (1974), 'Brookhaven energy system optimization model', *Brookhaven National Laboratory Topical Rep*. BNL 19569.

Cherniavsky, E. A., *et al.* (1977) 'Dynamic energy system optimisation model', Brookhaven National Laboratory, Upton, N.Y.

Cheshire, J. H. and Surrey, A. J. (1978), 'Estimating UK energy demand for year 2000', *SPRU Occasional Paper*, Series No. 5, SPRU, University of Sussex.

Chilton, C. H. and Kimeson, R. M. (1976), *A National Energy Model*, Battelle Pacific-Northwest, Richland, Washington.

Connolly, T. J., Dantzig, G. B. and Parikh, S. C. (1977), 'The Stanford Pilot Energy/Economic Model', Systems Optimization Laboratory, Department of Operations Research, Stanford University, *Technical Report SOL 77-19*.

Dantzig, G. B. (1977), 'Large-scale systems optimizations with application to energy', Systems Optimization Laboratory, Department of Operations Research, Stanford University, *Technical Report SOL 77-3*.

Decision Sciences Corporation Report DSc 114 (1973), 'Quantitative energy studies and models: a state-of-the-art review', prepared for the Council on Environmental Quality, Executive Office of the President.

Department of Energy (1978a), *Energy Forecasting Methodology*, Energy Paper No. 29, HMSO, London.

Department of Energy (1978b), *Energy Forecasts*, Energy Commission Paper No. 5, HMSO, London.

DuMoulin, M. and Eyre, J. (1979), 'Energy scenarios: a learning process', *Energy Economics*, vol. 1, no. 2.

Eden, R., Posner, M., Bending, R., Crouch, E. and Stanislaw, J. (1981), *Energy Economics: Growth Resources and Politics*, Cambridge University Press, Cambridge, UK.

Edwards, R. S. and Clark, D. (1962), 'Planning for expansion in electricity supply', *British Electrical Power Convention*, Paper 3, Brighton.

Edwards, Sir R. (1966), 'Economic planning and electricity forecasting', *World Power Conference*, Tokyo Meeting, October. (Also an Electricity Council booklet.)

Federal Energy Administration (1974), *Project Independence Report*, US Government Printing Office, Washington, D.C.

Federal Energy Administration (1976), *National Energy Outlook*, US Government Printing Office, Washington, D.C.

Fisher, F. M. (1974), *Supply and Costs in the US Petroleum Industry: Two Econometric Studies*, Johns Hopkins Press, Baltimore.

Griffin, J. M. (1979), *Energy Conservation in OECD, 1980–2000*, Ballinger, Cambridge, Mass.

Häfele, W. and Manne, A. D. (1975), 'Strategies for a transition from fossil to nuclear fuels', *Energy Policy*, vol. 3, no. 1.

Häfele, W. and Basile, P. 'Modelling of long-range energy strategies with a global perspective', paper presented at the *8th International Conference on Operational Research*, Toronto, June.

Häfele, W. (1981), *Energy in a Finite World: A Global Systems Analysis*, Report by the Energy Systems Program Group of the International Institute for Applied Systems Analysis, Wolf Häfele, Program Leader, Ballinger, Cambridge, Mass.

Hardie, R. W., Black, W. E. and Little, W. W. (1972), 'ALPS, A Linear Programming System for Forecasting Optimum Power Growth Patterns', Hanford Engineering Development Laboratory, Richland, Washington.

Hausman, J. A. (1975), 'Project independence report: an appraisal of the U.S. energy needs up to 1985', *Bell Journal of Economics and Management Science*, Autumn.

Hitch, C. J. (ed.) (1977), *Modeling Energy-Economy Interactions: Five Approaches*, Resources for the Future, Washington, D.C.

Hoffmann, K. and Wood, D. O. (1976), 'Energy system modelling and forecasting', in *Annual Review of Energy*, Vol. 1, J. M. Hollander (ed.), Annual Reviews, Inc., Palo Alto, California.

Hogan, W. W. (1975), 'Energy Policy models for project independence', *Computers and Operations Research*, vol. 2, pp. 251–71.

Hogan, W. W. (1977), 'Project independence evaluation system: structure and algorithms', *Proceedings of American Mathematical Society Symposia in Applied Mathematics*, San Antonio, Texas, Vol. 21.

Hogan, W. W. and Manne, A. (1977), 'Energy-Economy Interations: the Fable of the Elephant and the Rabbit', Energy Modelling Forum, *Working Paper, EMF 1–3*, Stanford University.

Hudson, E. A. and Jorgenson, D. W. (1975), 'U.S. energy policy and economic growth', *Bell Journal of Economics and Management Science*, vol. 5, no. 2.

Hutber, F. W., Billington, B., Butchart, R., Endie, B., Kendall, P. and Parker, E. (1974), 'The Department of Energy's national energy models', Proceedings of Joint Conference of the Institute of Mathematics and the OR Society, Grosvenor House Hotel, London.

Iliffe, C. E. (1973), 'DISCOUNT G: a digital computer code for assessing the economics of nuclear power', *TRG Report 2285(R)*, UKAEA, London.

Iliffe, C. E. (1974), 'The system approach in economic assessment of nuclear power', in *Energy Modelling*, a special publication of the journal *Energy Policy*, IPC Science and Technology Press, Guildford, UK.

Jenkin, F. P. (1973a), 'Energy forecasting – the problem of choice of forecast', UN Economic Commission for Europe, *Symposium on Mathematical Models of Sectors of the Energy Economy*, Alma Ata, USSR.

Jenkin, F. P. (1973b), 'CEGB electricity supply models', UN Economic Commission for Europe, *Symposium on Mathematical Models of Sectors of the Energy Economy*, Alma Ata, USSR.

Keeney, S. M. *et al.* (1977), *Nuclear Power Issues and Choices*, Report of the Nuclear Energy Policy Study Group (NEPS), Ballinger, Cambridge, Mass.

Kemp, A. G. (1977), Review of *Optimal Development of the North Sea's Oil Fields*, by P. R. Odell and K. E. Rosing, *Energy Policy*, vol. 5, no. 2.

Kennedy, M. (1974), 'An economic model of the world oil market', *Bell Journal of Economics and Management Science*, Autumn.

Klein, L. R. and Finan, W. F. (1976), 'The structure of the Wharton annual energy model', presented at the *EPRI Energy Modeling Forum*, October.

Kroch, E. (1979), 'A brief review of energy modeling efforts', *Research Working Paper No. 240A*, Graduate School of Business, Columbia University.

Leach, G., Lewis, C., Romig, F., van Buren, A. and Foley, G. (1979), *A Low Energy Strategy for the United Kingdom*, Science Reviews, London.

Lewis, C. (1979), 'A low energy option for the UK', *Energy Policy*, vol. 2, no. 2.

Littlechild, S. C. (ed.) (1977), *Operational Research for Managers*, Philip Allan, Deddington, UK.

Lindsell, D. A. (1972), 'Forecasting oil demand', in *Energy Forecasting in the UK*, Proceedings of the Institute of Petroleum and the Institute of Fuel Joint Conference, April.

Lovins, A. B. (1976), 'Energy strategy: the road not taken', in *Future Strategies for Energy Development, A Question of Scale*, Oak Ridge Associated Universities, Oak Ridge, Tennessee.

Lovins, A. B. (1979), 'Re-examining the nature of the ECE Energy Problem', *Energy Policy*, vol. 7, no. 3.

Lyness, F. K. and Clark, D. J. (1975), 'Modelling the exploitation of natural gas reserves', in *Understanding Energy Systems* Proceedings of Joint Conference of the Institute of Fuel and OR Society, London.

MacAvoy, P. W. and Pindyck, R. S. (1973), 'Alternative regulatory policies for dealing with the natural gas shortage', *Bell Journal of Economics and Management Science*, Autumn.

MacAvoy, P. W. and Pindyck, R. S. (1975), *The Economics of the Natural Gas Shortage (1960–1980)*, North Holland, Amsterdam.

Manne, A. S. (1974), 'Waiting for the breeder', *The Review of Economic Studies Symposium*.

Manne, A. S. (1976), 'ETA: a model for energy technology assessment', *Bell Journal of Economics*, Autumn.

Manne, A. S. and Richals, R. G. (1978), 'A decision-analysis of the US breeder reactor program', *Energy*, vol. 3, no. 6.

Manne, A. S. (1979a), 'ETA–MACRO: a model of energy–economy interactions', *Advances in the Economics of Energy and Resources*, vol. 2.

Manne, A. S. (1979b), 'Long-term energy projections for the USA', International Energy Program, *Discussion Paper*, Stanford University, September.

Manne, A. S. (1979c), 'International energy supplies and demands: a long-term perspective', International Energy Program Discussion Paper, Stanford University, November.

Manne, A. S. and Richels, R. G. (1980), 'Evaluating nuclear fuel cycles', *Energy Policy*, vol. 8, no. 1.

Manne, A. S., Richels, R. G. and Weyant, J. P. (1979), 'Energy policy modeling: a survey', *Operations Research*, vol. 27, no. 1.

Marcuse, W., Bodin, L., Cherniavsky, E. and Sanborn, Y. (1976), 'A dynamic time dependent model for the analysis of alternative energy policies', in K. B. Haley (ed.), *Operational Research '75*, North Holland, Amsterdam.

Merrick, D. (1975), 'Optimisation of coal conversion processes', in *Understanding Energy Systems*, Proceedings of a Joint Conference of the Institute of Fuel and the Operational Research Society, London.

Modeling Resource Group (MRG) (1978), 'Energy modeling for an uncertain future', Committee on Nuclear and Alternative Energy Systems (CONAES), National Research Council, National Academy of Sciences, Washington D.C.

Myers, C. L. (1971), 'Forecasting electricity sales', *The Statistician*, vol. 20, no. 3.

NBPI (1970), National Board for Prices and Incomes, *Coal Prices, Second Report*, Report No. 152, Cmnd 4455, HMSO, London.

Nelson, J. R. (ed.) (1964), *Marginal Cost Pricing in Practice*, Prentice-Hall, Englewood Cliffs, N.J.

Nordhaus, W. D. (1979), *The Efficient Use of Energy Resources*, Yale University Press, New Haven.

Odell, P. R. and Rosing, K. E. (1976), *Optimal Development of the North Sea's Oil Fields*, Kogan Page, London.

Ormerod, R. J. (1979), 'Regional energy models for decision making', *Euro III Conference*, April.

Orson, R. W. (1968), 'Forecasting in the electricity supply industry', in M. Young (ed.), *Forecasting and the Social Sciences*, Social Science Research Council, Heinemann, London.

Owens, S. (1980), *Energy – A Register of Research, Development and Demonstration in the United Kingdom*, Part 2, Social Sciences, Social Science Research Council, London.

Parikh, S. C. (1976), 'Analysing U.S. energy options using the pilot energy model', Systems Optimization Laboratory, Department of Operation Research, Stanford University, *Technical Report SOL 76-27*.

Parikh, S. C. (1977), 'Progress report on the pilot energy modeling project', Systems Optimization Laboratory, Department of Operations Research, Stanford University, *Technical Report SOL 77-11*.

Phillips, D., Jenkin, F. P., Pritchard, J. A. T. and Rybicki, K. (1969), 'A mathematical model for determining generating plant mix', *Proceedings of the Third Power Systems Computation Conference*, Rome, Vol. 2.

Peterson, W. (1979), 'Fuel use in the UK: a study of substitution responses', in A. Strub (ed.), *Energy Models for the European Community*, a special publication of the journal *Energy Policy*.

Pindyck, R. S. (1979), *The Structure of World Energy Demand*, MIT, Cambridge, Mass.

Preston, R. (1975), 'The Wharton long-term model: input–output within the context of a macro forecasting model', *International Economic Review*.

Queen Mary College Energy Research Unit (1973), 'World energy modelling: the development of Western European oil prices', *Energy Policy*, vol. 1, no. 1.

Queen Mary College Energy Research Unit (1974), 'World energy modelling: Part I, concepts and methods; Part II, preliminary results from the petroleum/natural gas model', in *Energy Modelling*, a special publication of the journal *Energy Policy*.

Ray, G. F. and Blackaby, F. T. (1960), 'Energy and expansion', *National Institute Economic Review*, no. 11.

Ray, G. F. (1967), 'Long-term forecasts of the demand for cars, selected consumer durables and energy: Section III: The demand for energy', *National Institute Economic Review*, no. 40.

Ray, G. F. (1972), 'Medium-term forecasts reassessed: Part III: Energy', *National Institute Economic Review*, no. 62.

Richels, R. G. and Plummer, J. L. (1977), 'Optimal timing of the US Breeder', *Energy Policy*, vol. 5, no. 2.

Rivett, P. (1968), *Concepts of Operational Research*, C. A. Watts, London.

Roberts, P. C. (1980), 'Systems analysis research unit model, co-ordination group from Depts. of Energy, Transport and Environment', reported in *Management Science and Government*, vol. 35, no. 2.

Robson, L. F. and Davis, D. A. (1972), 'Electricity forecasting', in *Energy Forecasting in the UK*, Proceedings Joint Conference of the Institute of Petroleum and the Institute of Fuel.

Stone, R. and Wigley, K. (1968), *The Demand for Fuel 1948–1975: A Sub-model of the British Fuel Economy*, No. 8 in A Programme for Growth, Chapman and Hall for the Department of Applied Economics, University of Cambridge.

Synfuels Interagency Task Force (1975), *Recommendations for a Synthetic Fuels Commercialisation Program*, U.S. Government Printing Office, Washington D.C.

Taylor, L. D. (1977), 'The demand for energy: a survey of price and income elasticities', in W. D. Nordhaus (ed.), *International Studies of the Demand for Energy*, Ch. 1, North Holland, Amsterdam.

Tessmer, R. G., Hoffman, K. C., Marcuse, W. and Behling, D. J. (1975), 'Coupled energy system – economic models and strategic planning', *Computers and Operations Research*, vol. 2, 213–24.

Thomas, S. D. (1980), 'Modelling UK energy demand to 2000', *Energy Policy*, vol. 8, no. 1.

Turvey, R. (1968), *Optimal Pricing and Investment in Electricity Supply*, Allen and Unwin, London.

Turvey, R. (1971), *Economic Analysis and Public Enterprises*, Allen and Unwin, London.

Turvey, R. and Anderson, D. (1977), *Electricity Economics, Essays and Case Studies*, World Bank Research Publication.

WAES (Workshop on Alternative Energy Strategies) (1977), *Energy: Global Prospects 1985–2000*, McGraw Hill, New York.

Wagner, H. M. (1969), *Principles of Operations Research*, Prentice-Hall, Englewood Cliffs, N.J.

Wilson, C. L. (1976), 'Energy demand studies: major consuming countries', in P. S. Baxle (ed.), *First Technical Report of the WAES* (Workshop on Alternative Energy Strategies), MIT Press, Cambridge, Mass.

Walton, A. and Turner, L. (1981), *Energy Policy Research Register 1980–81, for Austria, Denmark, France, Fed. Republic of Germany, Italy, Netherlands, Norway, Sweden and Switzerland*, Royal Institute of Internal Affairs, London.

Westoby, R. (1981), 'Long-run price elasticities for energy: an overview of existing energy models', *Discussion Paper 81-05*, University of Aberdeen, Department of Political Economy.

Zimmerman, M. B. (1977), 'Modeling depletion in a mineral industry: the case of coal', *Bell Journal of Economics*, Spring.

3

The Birmingham Energy Model: General Description

3.1 Introduction

The Birmingham Energy Model (henceforth abbreviated to BEM) is designed as an integrated long-term mathematical programming model of the UK energy sector explicitly including all the conventional and some unconventional fuels. The aim is to use the model to examine, compare and evaluate various ways in which the UK energy sector might develop over the next fifty years. There are two versions of the model. In the first version, which will be referred to as the 'cost model', or 'fixed demand model', the objective function is to minimise the net present value of the operating and capacity costs incurred in meeting specified levels of energy demand over the next forty years. This version of the model enables us to assess the implications of alternative energy demand projections for the total energy bill and the detailed pattern of energy supply.

The second version, referred to as the 'demand model' or 'variable demand model', differs from the cost model only in the treatment of demand. Instead of demand *levels*, demand *functions* are specified, in which the demand for each fuel is linearly dependent on the prices of one or more fuels. The objective is to maximise the present value of consumers' benefits from consumption of all fuels (the levels of which are endogenously determined by the model), less the capital and operating costs of meeting the total energy demand. The demand model is thus a more fully integrated model of the UK energy sector than the cost model, since patterns of supply as well as demand are determined endogenously within it. On the other hand, the cost-minimisation version is simpler.

In order to prevent confusion between the two models, and for ease of exposition, the cost model and the assessment of policy implications within it have been developed separately from the demand model. The bulk of this book (Chapters 3–9) refers solely to the cost model. The nature of the demand model, and the results obtained from using it, are described in Chapter 10.

Subsequent sections of this chapter describe the UK energy sector (Section 3.2) and the overall structure of the model (Section 3.3). These sections are presented verbally in order to explain the reasoning underlying the mathematical formulation. The mathematical formulation and data assumptions are presented in the next chapter.

3.2 Representation of the UK Energy Sector

The model with a basic set of assumptions described in this and the next chapter is referred to as the Base Case. Variations on the Base Case are considered in later chapters.

The fuel products distinguished in the model, their sources and methods of production (where appropriate) are set out in Table 3.1. There are four basic fuels, namely, coal, oil, gas and electricity.

Table 3.1 *Fuel Products, Their Sources and Methods of Production*

Fuel products	Sources and methods of production
Coal	Domestic extraction (imports permitted in one scenario)
Crude oil	Domestic extraction, imports and synthetic production from coal. Exports permitted
Gas	Domestic extraction, imports and synthetic production from coal. Exports permitted
Electricity	Coal-fired, oil/gas-fired, nuclear and gas turbine power stations
Petrol	Refined from crude oil (joint product), reformed from Naphtha, cracked from fuel oil (joint product)
Naphtha (for non-energy use in industry)	Refined from crude oil (joint product), cracked from fuel oil (joint product)
Kerosene	Refined from crude oil (joint product)
Gas/diesel oil	Refined from crude oil (joint product), cracked from fuel oil (joint product)
Fuel oil	Refined from crude oil (joint product)

In the BEM Base Case model, coal extraction from indigenous resources is the only source of coal. This is consistent with most recent studies of the UK energy sector, which implicitly assume that, owing to the large UK reserves of coal, imports of coal in any significant amount will not be permitted by the UK government. The implications of permitting coal imports are investigated in Chapter 7, along with other related policy issues.

Crude oil and gas may be extracted from indigenous resources, manufactured from coal or imported. Crude oil and gas may also be exported. However, oil is rarely used as a fuel in its crude form. The crude oil refining process produces five main products (petrol, naphtha, kerosene, gas oil and fuel oil) which are used in different markets for different purposes. Naphtha is used as a feedstock in the petrochemicals industry while the remaining oil products are used as fuels for final

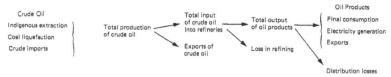

Figure 3.1 *Simplified schema of the oil industry in BEM*

consumption, electricity generation or export. Total output of oil products is slightly less than crude oil import because of losses in refining and distribution (see Figure 3.1).

Electricity can be produced by coal-fired, oil-fired, gas-fired or nuclear power stations.

An overall view of the UK energy sector as it is represented in BEM is shown in Figure 3.2. Primary energy (coal, oil, natural gas and nuclear energy) may be either consumed directly or used to produce secondary energy (electricity, oil products, synthetic gas and synthetic oil manufactured from coal). Hydroelectricity is omitted from the model since it is a relatively unimportant primary energy source in Britain. Assumptions about the availability of, and costs of obtaining or producing, the nine fuel products are set out and discussed in the next chapter.

The supply of oil products perhaps needs further explanation. Oil refining is a process which converts crude oil, a complex mixture of hydrocarbons, into a range of marketable oil products. The refining process consists of three sub-processes: (1) physical separation of crude oil through distillation, (2) conversion, and (3) purification or treatment of refined products.

The physical separation of crude oil into oil products is done by the process of distillation which makes use of the differences in boiling points of the oil products in order to make the separation. The oil products obtained after distillation are known as straight line products (e.g. straight line gasoline) and are generally classified into light, middle and heavy distillates. The output of various oil products obtained by distillation may not give the refiner the products in the proportions in which he wishes to market them, bearing in mind the differing market conditions faced by the different products. Therefore a wide range of conversion processes has been developed. The two most important processes included in the model are reforming and cracking. Reforming is used to convert naphtha (which would otherwise be used as a feedstock in the manufacture of chemicals) into petrol. Cracking is a process whereby naphtha, fuel oil or reduced crude can be converted into petrol and other by-products. It is no coincidence that both the processes described above convert other oil products into petrol. Since the advent of the motor car, one of the most important requirements has been to increase the quantity of motor spirit (petrol) from petroleum, since motor spirit is a premium fuel commanding a high price.

The next stage in the energy industries shown in the diagram is the distribution and transmission of fuels to the various markets. For oil products, transport and distribution costs include the costs of purifying,

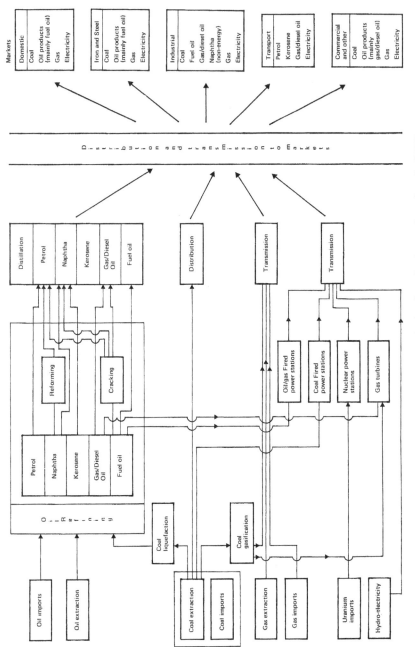

Figure 3.2 *Fuels, their sources, methods of production and markets in BEM*

treating and blending the oil products. Capital and operating costs for distribution and transmission are included for each fuel in the model.

The total energy market is disaggregated into five sub-markets: (1) Domestic; (2) Iron and Steel; (3) Industrial (excluding Iron and Steel); (4) Transport; and (5) Commercial and Other. Such disaggregation seems desirable since the nature of demand and the possibilities of substitution will vary from one market to another. In the Domestic Sector the most important energy requirements are for space and water heating, cooking and operating various household appliances. In the Industrial Sector, energy for manufacturing processes is the most important requirement. The nature of the requirement naturally influences the choice of fuel. In the Domestic Sector, gas and electricity will usually be preferred to coal since they are cleaner and more convenient fuels, even when coal has a substantial cost advantage. In many industrial uses, by contrast, the choice will often be made almost entirely on the fuel cost advantage.

The Iron and Steel Sector is considered separately, partly because it is the most energy-intensive industry, and partly because for technical reasons the scope for substitution between fuels is rather limited. The Transport Sector is considered separately owing to the predominance of oil products as energy sources and the limited possibility of substitution for oil in road transport in the short and medium terms.

The cost of distributing energy to large consumers in the Industrial Sector is different from the cost of distribution to small consumers in the domestic sector. Such cost differences can be better handled by separating overall energy demand into demand for energy in different sectors.

3.3 Intuitive Structure of the BEM

This section (and the next chapter) describe the mathematical programming formulation of the BEM. The model covers a total time span of fifty years (1977–2026), divided up into ten periods of five years each (viz. 1977–81, 1982–86, 1987–91 and so on up to 2022–2026). Levels of average annual production, consumption and trade for various fuels in each five-year period are determined by the model solution. It is often convenient to refer to each period by a representative year (viz. 1980, 1985, 1990, . . . , 2025).

An intuitive overall view of the mathematical programming structure is provided by Figure 3.3. Broadly the objective is to choose the pattern of production and investment so as to minimise the cost of meeting specified demands for energy over the entire fifty-year programme period. The constraints ensure that production and distribution capacities are not exceeded and that total consumption of each fuel does not exceed availability (i.e. amount produced or extracted). The objective function and each block of the constraints are described in greater detail below. Sources of data are given in the next chapter: as far as possible we have relied on published sources, with occasional guidance from industry personnel.

Choose values for variables:

so as to minimise present value of

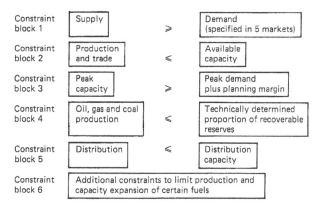

subject to constraints for each fuel and each period:

Figure 3.3   *The mathematical programming formulation of BEM*

The Objective Function

The objective function is the present value of the sum of (1) operating and capacity costs of each fuel-production process, *plus* (2) operating and capital costs of distributing the fuels, *plus* (3) costs of importing fuels, *less* (4) any revenue from exporting fuels, and *less* (5) the value of production and distribution capacity remaining at the end of the programme period.

This formulation of the objective function enables us to compare the total cost of meeting different levels of energy demand. Furthermore, additional policy constraints (e.g. limiting oil imports) can be imposed upon the model, and the value of the objective function with the additional constraint indicates the extra cost of the policy constraint. This approach will be used in assessing certain policy issues in later chapters (especially Chapter 7).

Constraint Block 1: Supply ⩾ Demand

This set of constraints requires that the average annual availability of a fuel in each five-year time period (1977–81, 1982–86, and so on) should meet the average annual consumption for the fuel during that time period. As we have shown in Table 3.1 and Figures 3.1 and 3.2, each fuel may be produced by a number of processes, including importation. For example, oil may be extracted from indigenous resources, manufactured from coal or imported. The total availability of a fuel is obtained by adding all the fuel available from different sources. The demand for the fuel consists of the final consumption in the various markets plus consumption of the fuel in producing another fuel. Account is also taken of losses in distribution. In the cost model, the final consumption of each fuel in each market is exogenously specified. The model can therefore be used to explore the implications for energy supply of alternative demand projections.

The model does not permit accumulation of stocks or meeting demand from stocks. This is not a serious matter since, as noted above, output in our model is specified as average annual output over a five-year period. It can reasonably be assumed that stock changes will even out over a five-year period and average demand can therefore be constrained to be met from current supply without undue distortion.

Constraint Block 2: Output and Trade ≤ Available Capacity
This set of constraints requires that the output of a fuel by a given process during each time period does not exceed the production capacity of that process during that period. Initial capacities available for production of each fuel by each process at the beginning of the first period are specified. These consist of capacities available in 1977 as well as additional capacities then under construction and becoming available in later years. For each type of capacity the time lag between the decision to construct the capacity and the capacity being available for production is specified, together with the maximum operating life of the plant.

In purely mathematical programming terms, the time lag is significant only at the beginning of the first period when capacities cannot be adjusted immediately. After the initial constraining effects of the time lags, the model is free to choose the amount of capacity to install, subject to certain smoothing and capacity expansion constraints discussed below. However, in making energy policy decisions the lead times are important throughout the programme period. For example, if nuclear electricity capacity should be higher in ten years' time and there is a lead time of ten years, the decision to install must obviously be made now.

The capacity available for production during any time period is not equal to the total physical capacity, since a part of the latter may be unavailable for production at a given time owing to breakdowns and overhead requirements. Provision for this has been made in the model.

In order to import and export gas, special pipeline and storage facilities are required. Sets of constraints limiting maximum imports and exports of gas to the available capacities are also included in this constraint block.

Constraint Block 3: Production Capacity ≥ Peak Demand + Planning Margin

For electricity and gas, a set of constraints requires that production capacity should be sufficient to meet peak demand plus specified planning margin requirements. While the constraints specified for these two fuels are similar, a number of important dissimilarities must be noted. Electricity cannot be stored in any significant quantities and therefore production and distribution must respond immediately to different levels of demand at different times of the day and the year. The proportions of the year during which the demand for electricity is at low, medium and high levels are specified in the model. The varying loads that the electricity industry has to meet is likely to be an important consideration in the mix of plant chosen for electricity production (i.e. coal, oil, gas or nuclear).

There are less complex considerations in meeting peak demand for gas. Since domestic consumers do not store gas, and gas suppliers have only limited storage capacity, the distribution capacity needs to be sufficient to meet peak demand (see constraint block 5 below), as does gas extraction and import capacity.

Constraint Block 4: Extraction ≤ Available Resources

The extraction of a fuel must not exceed available resources. However, in BEM the sets of constraints which limit extraction of fuels in any time period incorporate a number of additional technical considerations. Constraints for oil and gas are considered separately from those for coal.

Owing to the reduction in the oil pressure underground, the productivity of an oil well usually declines exponentially with the cumulative amount extracted. The rate of extraction is roughly proportional to the volume of remaining reserves. In BEM, maximum oil extraction in any one year is constrained to be a constant fraction of existing resources available for extraction. Since the size and location of all resources are not fully known at the beginning of the programme period, constraint block 4 is couched in terms of the proven resources at the beginning of the programme period and makes an assumption about the rate at which new resources become available for extraction. The constraints on extraction of gas are identical in mathematical form to those for oil extraction.

Coal extraction is dealt with in a different manner. As noted earlier, the UK has much larger reserves of coal than of oil and gas. There are likely to be considerable variations in costs of coal extraction between different localities owing to depth and thickness of seam and other technical considerations. The total coal resources are divided into five 'tranches', where the pits in each tranche are characterised by the same extraction cost. The set of constraints then requires that total extraction from each tranche must not exceed the total reserves in that tranche.

For all three fuels, total extraction in any time period is also constrained by the existing extraction capacity (see constraint block 2). For coal, extraction capacity is specified for each tranche.

Constraint Block 5: Distribution Capacity ≥ Peak Demand
For electricity and gas, a set of constraints requires that distribution capacity should be sufficient to meet peak demand. These constraints are similar to those imposed on production capacity in constraint block 3, and the reasons for imposing them are evident from the discussion there.

Constraint Block 6: Other Constraints on Production Capacities
There are limitations on the rates at which production capacities for certain activities may be expanded owing to resource limitations not represented in the constraints set out above. For example, expansion of nuclear electricity production is likely to be constrained by the ability of the heavy electrical goods industry to supply capital equipment.

Constraints are imposed on the maximum nuclear electricity production capacity and maximum coal extraction capacity available up to the year 2000. It is assumed that beyond the year 2000, any desired level of capacity can be attained with appropriate forward planning. Capacity expansion smoothing constraints are imposed for a number of activities (including nuclear electricity and coal) in order to reduce fluctuations in capacity-construction activity from one time period to the next. The smoothing constraints are imposed throughout the programme period and therefore extend to the year 2026.

Finally, a technical capacity constraint on the minimum gas turbine capacity required for starting up conventional power stations is also included in this constraint block.

4

The Birmingham Energy Model: Mathematical Formulation and Data

4.1 Introduction

This chapter presents a detailed description of the mathematical formulation of BEM and of the Base Case assumptions made about costs, energy consumption, resource availability and technology. While the model and the Base Case data are presented together, the model is organised so as to facilitate its repeated running with alternative assumptions about data. This flexibility is particularly useful for two reasons. Since the model extends far into the future, it is important to assess the implications of alternative assumptions about crucial parameters such as energy reserves and international energy prices; such sensitivity analysis is described in Chapter 6. Second, the main value of the model lies not in recommending an unequivocably optimal energy strategy, but in providing a vehicle for assessing the implications of different energy policies; such analyses are described in Chapters 7–9.

For ease of cross-reference between Chapters 3 and 4, the constraint block numbers in the present chapter correspond to those used in the previous chapter. The notation used in the mathematical formulation is defined as it is introduced. A complete list of the notation used and the corresponding notation in the computer programme is set out in the appendix to this chapter.

4.2 Production Processes, Fuels and Markets

The following production processes, fuels and markets correspond to the general description of the UK energy sector in Section 3.2 of the previous chapter. The model permits seventeen production technologies which are listed in Table 4.1, together with the numbers assigned to the production technologies in the mathematical formulation and computer programme (subscripts $j = 1, \ldots, 17$). In Tables 4.2 and 4.3 respectively are listed the fuels and market sectors with the indices and numbers assigned to them.

Table 4.1 *Production Processes in BEM*

Production processes	Assigned number (subscript j)
Coal extraction: tranche I	1
Oil extraction	2
Gas extraction	3
Synthetic oil from coal	4
Synthetic gas from coal	5
Electricity from coal	6
Electricity from oil	7
Electricity from gas	8
Nuclear electricity	9
Electricity from gas turbines	10
Coal extraction: tranche II	11
Coal extraction: tranche III	12
Coal extraction: tranche IV	13
Coal extraction: tranche V	14
Oil Refinery output	15
Reforming (petrol from naphtha)	16
Cracking (petrol, naphtha and gas/diesel oil from fuel oil)	17

Table 4.2 *Fuels in BEM*

Fuels	Assigned number (subscript i)
Coal	1
Crude oil	2
Gas	3
Electricity	4
Petrol	5
Naphtha (non-energy product)	6
Kerosene	7
Gas oil	8
Fuel oil	9

Table 4.3 *Market Sectors in BEM*

Market sector	Assigned number (subscript or superscript m)
Domestic	1
Iron and Steel industry	2
Industry (excluding Iron and Steel)	3
Transport	4
Commercial and Other	5

4.3   The BEM Constraints

The mathematical formulation and data are set out below, corresponding to the previous verbal description of the BEM constraints. In general, Roman capital letters represent variables (to be determined within
the model) while small letters and Greek letters represent coefficients
and constants (specified before running the model).

Sources of data are given in the appropriate tables. There are of
course several differences of opinion about what the levels of future
costs and performances are likely to be. This is only natural given the
uncertainty about the course of events over the next fifty years. However, there is also disagreement concerning costs and performance in the
recent past. As far as possible, we have used official published data
sources, mainly from government and industry. We have not made a
systematic critical assessment of these estimates, although we have
taken into account informal advice from within the industries about the
views currently held there. For as yet unestablished technologies such as
synthetic oil and gas, these estimates are necessarily very tentative.
Later chapters test the sensitivity of the results to changes in certain
crucial assumptions (e.g. oil and gas reserves, world prices, nuclear capital costs); it would be a simple matter to explore the effects of changing
the other assumptions if it seemed worthwhile.

Constraint Block 1: Supply ⩾ *Demand*
The requirement that average annual supply must be sufficient to meet
average annual demand for each fuel in each five-year time period is
represented by constraints (1) and (2). Essentially, constraint (1) says
that for each fuel (other than gas and electricity) and for each (five-year)
time period, total output from all relevant processes, plus imports but
less exports, should be sufficient to meet total final demand for that fuel
(after allowing for distribution losses) plus the amount of that fuel
required as an input in the production of other fuels. Constraint (1)
refers to all fuels other than electricity; the latter requires the slightly
modified constraint (2) owing to the need to meet peak demand for the
fuel.

$$\sum_j a_{ij} X_{jbt} + M_{it} - S_{it} \geq \xi_i \sum_m y_{imt} + \sum_j b_{ijt} X_{jt} \tag{1}$$

$t = 1, \ldots, 10$
$i = 1, 2, 3, 5, 6, 7, 8, 9$ (i.e. for all fuels except electricity)

In the above inequality, the notation used is as follows:

X_{jbt} = average annual output from process j in time period t (variable).
         Subscript b indicates the load duration curve block, and is always
         equal to unity for all fuels except electricity
M_{it} = average annual level of imports of fuel i during period t (variable)
S_{it} = average annual level of exports of fuel i during period t (variable).

No trade in electricity is permitted in the model, that is, the variables M_{it} and S_{it} are set at zero for electricity ($i = 4$)

y_{imt} = average annual demand for fuel i, in market m, during period t (constant)

a_{ij} = output coefficient indicating whether fuel i is produced by process j. Here $a_{ij} = 0$ if fuel i is *not* produced by process j, $a_{ij} = 1$ if fuel i is the *sole* product of process j, and $0 < a_{ij} < 1$, with $\sum_i a_{ij} = 1$, if several fuels are joint products of process j. Joint products occur only in oil refinery operations

b_{ijt} = input coefficient indicating amount of input of fuel i required for the production of one unit of output of process j in period t

$\xi_i = (1 - e_i)^{-1}$ where e_i is the proportion of fuel i lost during distribution (constant)

The values of coefficients a_{ij} and b_{ijt} are shown in Table 4.4. Coefficients a_{ij} for coal show that it can be produced (extracted) by processes 1, 11, 12, 13 and 14. In this case, each process represents a coal tranche, where each tranche is distinguished by the cost of coal extraction from the tranche. Tranche I is the cheapest and tranche V the most expensive. The oil refinery process (15) produces five joint products in the proportions indicated by the fractions in the table. As stated above, each b_{ijt} coefficient in the table represents the amount of fuel i required to produce one unit of output of process j. For example, in order to produce synthetic oil which would produce 1 GJ of energy, an amount of coal which would produce 1.43 GJ (i.e. $(0.7)^{-1}$ GJ) of energy would be required. The low coefficients for electricity show the heavy losses involved in converting coal, oil and gas into electricity. The higher coefficients for the oil products show the more moderate loss of energy involved in the refinery processes. The average loss in distribution of all fuels except coal is assumed to be 9 per cent (i.e. $e_i = 0.09$ and $\xi_i = (1 - e_i)^{-1} = 1.1$ for $i = 2, 3, \ldots, 9$). No distribution loss is assumed for coal ($e_1 = 0$ and $\xi_1 = 1$).

For electricity, the requirement that supply must be sufficient to meet demand is expressed in inequality (2). This differs from (1) only in that it must hold separately for base load, medium load and peak load conditions. Owing to the difficulty of storing the fuel, it is necessary that supply should be sufficient to meet the levels of demand when they arise. A similar difficulty in meeting fluctuating gas demand also arises. The simpler device of requiring that there be sufficient capacity to meet peak demand has been used for gas (see constraint blocks 3 and 5).

$$\sum_j a_{ij}X_{jbt} \geq \xi_i \frac{w_{ib}h_{ib}}{\zeta_i \varphi_i} \sum_m y_{imt} + \sum_j b_{ijt}X_{jbt} \tag{2}$$

where $t = 1, \ldots, 10$, $b = 1, 2, 3$ and $i = 4$ (electricity). The new notation introduced is as follows:

X_{jbt} = average annual output from process j at demand level b in time

Table 4.4 Values of input and output coefficients a_{ij} and b_{ijt}

Production process j / Fuels i	Value of input coefficient a_{ij}									Value of output coefficient b_{ijt}								
	Coal	Oil	Gas	Electricity	Petrol	Naphtha (non-energy)	Kerosene	Gas oil	Fuel oil	Coal	Oil	Gas	Electricity	Petrol	Naphtha (non-energy)	Kerosene	Gas oil	Fuel oil
1 Coal extraction: tranche I	1																	
2 Oil extraction		1																
3 Gas extraction			1															
4 Synthetic oil from coal		1								$(0.7)^{-1}$								
5 Synthetic gas from coal			1							$(0.7)^{-1}$								
6 Electricity from coal				1						$(0.35)^{-1}$								
7 Electricity from oil				1														$(0.35)^{-1}$
8 Electricity from gas				1								$(0.35)^{-1}$						
9 Nuclear electricity				1														
10 Electricity from gas turbines				1													$(0.25)^{-1}$	
11 Coal extraction: tranche II	1																	
12 Coal extraction: tranche III	1																	
13 Coal extraction: tranche IV	1																	
14 Coal extraction: tranche V	1																	
15 Oil refinery output					0.11	0.13	0.16	0.27	0.33		$(0.9)^{-1}$							
16 Petrol from naphtha					0.52	0.32	0.16											
17 Reforming output					1										$(0.95)^{-1}$			$(0.95)^{-1}$

Note: Blank spaces represent zero coefficients.

period t. There are three levels of demand denoted by subscript b: base load ($b = 1$), medium load ($b = 2$) and peak load ($b = 3$)

w_{ib} = level of demand in load block b as a fraction of peak demand level

h_{ib} = fraction of the year during which demand for fuel i is at level b

φ_i = demand load factor for fuel i

The annual load duration curve for electricity is shown in Figure 4.1. The actual smooth curve is represented in the model by three blocks. Peak load demand ($w_1 = 1.0$) occurs for 10 per cent of the year ($h_1 = 0.10$); medium load demand is at 65 per cent of peak load ($w_2 = 0.65$) and occurs for 40 per cent of the year ($h_2 = 0.40$); and base load demand is at 45 per cent of peak load ($w_3 = 0.45$) and occurs for the remaining 50 per cent of the year ($h_3 = 0.50$). The load factor φ_i represents total annual electricity production as a proportion of the production that would occur if peak load demand were sustained throughout the year. It is defined by

$$\varphi_i = \sum_{b=1}^{3} w_{ib} h_{ib}$$

For electricity ($i = 4$) we have $\varphi_4 = 0.585$, that is, electricity has a 58.5 per cent load factor. The proportion of total annual demand which occurs in load block b is given by

$$\frac{w_{ib} h_{ib}}{\sum_b w_{ib} h_{ib}} = \frac{w_{ib} h_{ib}}{\varphi_i}$$

This is the fraction which appears in equation (2). For electricity, these proportions are 17 per cent for peak load, 44 per cent for medium load and 38 per cent for base load demand.

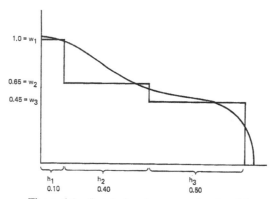

Figure 4.1   *Load–duration curve for electricity*

The levels of demand for each fuel in each market are based on projections made by the Department of Energy (1978a, b). The models used for making the Department of Energy projections are described in Department of Energy (1978c) and briefly summarised in the appendix to Chapter 2. The first step (performed in the Energy Demand Model) is to produce projections of total energy consumption in each market sector based on historical relationships between macro-economic variables and energy consumption. Since historical relationships are unlikely to reflect adequately the likely effects of recent increases in energy prices, judgements about price and efficiency effects on energy consumption are made in the Conservation Model. The energy consumption projections for each market are then adjusted for conservation effects. The disaggregation of total energy consumption in each sector, paying particular attention to premium and non-premium rises of different fuels, is carried out by the Fuel Allocation Model. For completing the allocation of gas and electricity, the Fuel Allocation Model interacts with the Gas Supply Model.

Energy consumption projections for each market sector and total energy consumption are shown in Figures 4.2 to 4.7(a) and set out in tables at the end of this chapter. In the Domestic Sector (see Figure 4.2) coal and oil consumption are projected to decline, the former mainly owing to the inconvenience of handling while the latter owing to high price. Gas is expected to retain a large share of the domestic market which has been identified as a premium market for this fuel. Electricity consumption is expected to remain stable and retain its market share up to 1995 but to grow faster thereafter and increase its market share. This is presumably explained by the depletion of cheap North Sea gas reserves and increasing reliance on more expensive sources of gas.

In the Iron and Steel Sector (see Figure 4.3) the underlying assumption is that the proportions in which the various fuels are demanded are

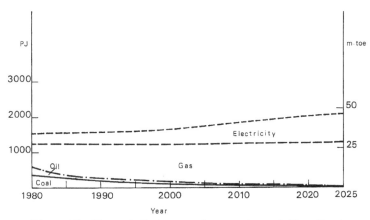

Figure 4.2   *Domestic Sector annual energy demand (Base Case)*

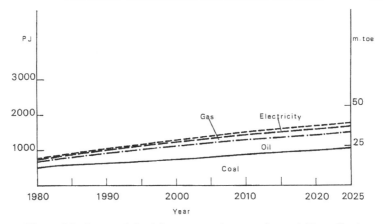

Figure 4.3   *Iron and Steel Sector annual energy demand (Base Case)*

technically determined. The projections show a more or less steady upward trend in the consumption of all fuels. More recent projections (see Department of Energy, 1979) make adjustments in these projections based on the recent fall in output in the sector and technical developments leading to substitution of electricity for coal. These later adjustments are incorporated in a later run of the model (see section 11.2).

The Industrial Sector consumption projections (see Figure 4.4) imply a dramatic revival in coal consumption. The consumption of oil products is expected to reduce but is not completely eliminated. There are certain

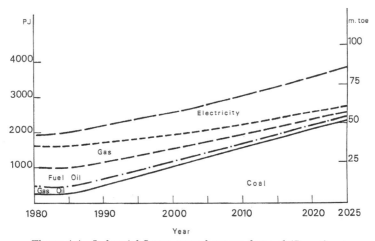

Figure 4.4   *Industrial Sector annual energy demand (Base Case)*

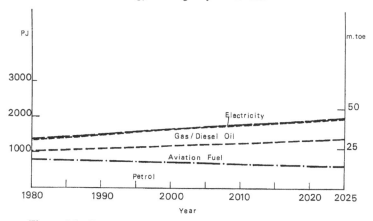

Figure 4.5   *Transport Sector annual energy demand (Base Case)*

premium rises for gas oil, where it is expected that substitution will not be possible. With the exception of certain premium uses of gas, it is expected that in the long run gas will not be able to compete with coal as cheaper gas runs out nor with electricity. Consumption of electricity is therefore also expected to rise.

As shown by Figure 4.5, the Transport Sector is heavily dominated by oil products. The projections incorporate the assumption that there will be substantial conservation effects on petrol consumption which will decline. There may also be conservation effects in gas/diesel oil consumption but the overall level of consumption will still increase because

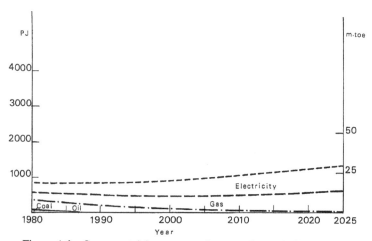

Figure 4.6   *Commercial Sector annual energy demand (Base Case)*

it will be related to overall economic activity which is expected to grow. Aviation fuel consumption is expected to grow rapidly. Electricity consumption (mainly in railways) is expected to remain at a low level, assuming no significant electrification over this period.

The overall pattern of energy consumption in the Commercial Sector (see Figure 4.6) is expected to be similar to that for the Domestic Sector. Consumption of coal and oil is projected to decline, gas retains a substantial market share, but after 1995 electricity consumption grows much faster.

The total final energy demand projections which are aggregated from the sectoral demand projections (see Figure 4.7a) indicate a growing importance for coal and electricity. Total final coal consumption grows from about 46m. tonnes in 1980 to 71m. tonnes in 2000 (i.e. at an annual growth rate of 2.2 per cent) and 129m. tonnes in 2025 (i.e. an annual growth rate of 2.4 per cent between 2000 and 2025). Electricity consumption almost doubles by the year 2000 (an annual growth rate just below 3.3 per cent) and then rises in 2025 to 70 per cent above the level in the year 2000 (an annual growth rate of 2.1 per cent between 2000 and 2025). Oil consumption is projected to remain stable at about 68m. tonnes throughout the programme period. Final gas consumption rises from 15000m. therms in 1980 to 17800m. therms in 2000 (annual growth rate about 0.9 per cent) and 20400m. therms in 2025 (annual growth rate about 0.5 per cent between 2000 and 2025). Total final energy consumption in 1980 is about 150 mtoe. By the year 2000 it rises to 187 mtoe (a growth rate of 1.1 per cent per year) and by the year 2025 it rises to 253 mtoe (a growth rate of 1.2 per cent per year between 2000 and 2025) (see Figure 4.7b).

Constraint Block 2: Production and Trade $\geq$ Available Production and Trade Capacities
This constraint block represented by inequality (3) below states that the output of any energy producing process cannot exceed the production capacity available (after allowing for maintenance, repair and breakdowns).

$$g_j \left[\sum_{v=1}^{t} h_{jvt} Z_{jv} + z_{jt}^0 \right] \geq X_{jbt}/h_{ib} \tag{3}$$

$$t = 1, \ldots, 10$$
$$j = 1, \ldots, 17$$
$$b = 1, \ldots, 3$$

where recall X_{jbt} denotes output from process j at demand level b in period t, and

Z_{jv} = amount of capacity for process j installed in period v (variable)

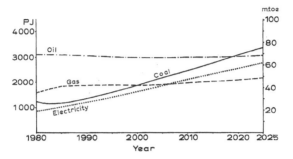

Figure 4.7a *Annual total final energy demand (Base Case)*

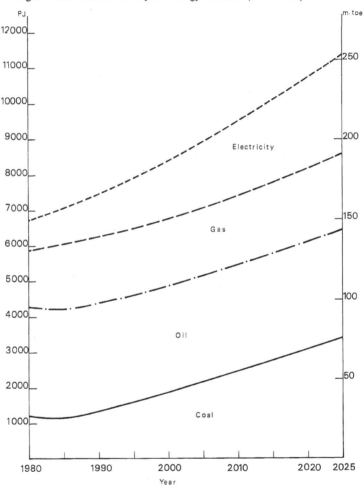

Figure 4.7b *Annual total final energy demand: cumulative (Base Case)*

h_{jvt} = proportion of capacity for process j, installed in period v, which is still effective in period t (constant)

z_{jt}^0 = amount of capacity for process j which was in existence or contracted for at the beginning of the programme period, and which is still effective in period t (constant)

g_j = average availability of plant for process j (constant)

X_{jbt} and h_{ib} have been described in constraint block 1. Note that h_{ib} and subscript b both take the value 1 for all fuels except electricity, for which it is required that capacity should be sufficient to meet peak demand.

The total installed capacity for any process is unlikely to be available for production at all times owing to planned maintenance and repair requirements as well as unplanned breakdowns. The coefficient g_j represents average availability as a proportion of installed capacity. In Table 4.5, the average plant availabilities for each process assumed in BEM are shown. Other considerations in determining whether capacity installed in one time period will be available for production in another time period are (1) the construction lead time for a plant and (2) the length of life of a plant. Assumptions on these are also set out in Table 4.5. The coefficient h_{jvt} is zero if plant installed in period v is not available in period t, either because of the construction lead time or because period t is beyond the life of plant installed in period v; otherwise h_{jvt} takes the value 1. In principle, it would be possible to assign values

Table 4.5 *Plant Construction Lead Times, Plant Life and Average Plant Availabilities for Energy Production Processes*

Production Process	Plant construction lead time (years)	Plant life (years)	Average plant availability (proportion of total capacity)
1 Coal extraction: tranche I	8	30	1.00
2 Oil extraction	4	20	0.85
3 Gas extraction	4	20	0.85
4 Synthetic oil from coal	5	20	0.90
5 Synthetic gas from coal	5	20	0.90
6 Electricity from coal	6	30	0.70
7 Electricity from oil	6	30	0.70
8 Electricity from gas	6	30	0.70
9 Nuclear electricity	8	25	0.65
10 Electricity from gas turbines	2	20	0.90
11 Coal extraction: tranche II	8	30	0.90
12 Coal extraction: tranche III	8	30	0.90
13 Coal extraction: tranche IV	8	30	0.90
14 Coal extraction: tranche V	8	30	0.90
15 Oil refinery output	4	30	0.90
16 Petrol from naphtha	4	30	0.90
17 Reforming output	4	30	0.90

between zero and unity to h_{jvt} in order to reflect higher plant outages as the plant gets older, but for simplicity a single average outage figure is assumed for each process. While our construction lead time assumptions are obtained from official sources, the actual lead times may in some cases be considerably longer owing to unanticipated technical difficulties or delays due to public enquiries and in obtaining planning permission. The main effect of (anticipated) longer lead times would be to delay the availability of new capacity during the early part of the programme period.

Existing and/or contracted capacity at the beginning of the programme period, denoted by z_{it}^0 in constraint (3), is shown in Table 4.6.

In addition to the set of production capacity constraints, constraint block (2) also includes the following two trade capacity constraints, which require that imports and exports of each fuel should not exceed the capacities available for engaging in such trade. In principle the constraints are applicable to any and all fuels, but in the present version of BEM the constraints are applied to gas only. (For other fuels, capacity costs are included in import and export prices.)

$$\sum_{v=1}^{t} h_{ivt}^m ZM_{iv} + zm_{it}^0 \geqslant M_{it} \tag{4}$$

$$\sum_{v=1}^{t} h_{ivt}^s ZS_{iv} + zs_{it}^0 \geqslant S_{it} \tag{5}$$

$$t = 1, \ldots, 10$$

at present for $i = 3$ (gas) only, where

M_{it}, S_{it} = average annual level of imports and exports, respectively, during period t (variables)

ZM_{iv}, ZS_{iv} = import and export capacities, respectively, for fuel i installed in period v (variables)

h_{ivt}^m, h_{ivt}^s = fractions of import and export capacity imports and exports, respectively, for fuel i, installed in period v, which are still effective in period t (constant)

zm_{it}^0, zs_{it}^0 = existing and/or contracted import and export capacity, respectively, for fuel i at the beginning of the planning period which is still effective in period t (constants)

The coefficients h_{ivt}^m and h_{ivt}^s have similar functions to coefficient h_{jvt} in inequality (3). Each takes the value of unity if the capacity is available in time period t and zero if it is not. The construction lead time and lifetime for import and export capacities are assumed to be four and thirty years, respectively. The initial import and export capacities (zm_{it}^0 and zs_{it}^0) for gas are assumed to be zero, indicating the negligible amount of trade currently taking place and acknowledging that substantial investment would be required before trade can be increased.

Table 4.6   Existing and Contracted Capacities for Energy Production Processes (PJ/year)

Production Process	1977	1978	1979	1980	1981	1982	1983	1984	1985	1986	1987	1988	1989	1990
1 Coal extraction: tranche I	1200	1200	1200	1200	1200	1500	1500	1500	1500	1500	(a)			
2 Oil extraction	2000	3000	4000	5000	5000	(a)								
3 Gas extraction	1812	1850	1850	1900	1900	(a)								
6 Electricity from coal	1500	1500	1500	1500	1500	1500	1500	1500	1500	1500	(a)			
7 Electricity from oil	350	350	350	480	550	(a)								
9 Nuclear electricity	160	238	234	238	272	340	340	340	340	340	(a)			
10 Electricity from gas turbines	100	106	112	118	124	130	(a)							
11 Coal extraction: tranche II	1000	1000	1000	1000	1000	1200	1200	1200	1200	1200	(a)			
12 Coal extraction: tranche III	900	900	900	900	900	900	900	900	900	900	(a)			
13 Coal extraction: tranche IV	400	400	400	400	400	400	400	400	400	400	(a)			
14 Coal extraction: tranche V	0													
15 Oil refinery output	6570	(a)												
16 Petrol from naphtha	1260	(a)												
17 Reforming output	675	(a)												

Sources: Digest of UK Energy Statistics (various years); CEGB Statistical Yearbook (various years); Nuclear Power Company Ltd. (1978); Parameters for nuclear power stations designed and constructed by the Nuclear Power Co., Ltd, Leicester, U.K. Department of Energy, Fact Sheet No. 5.

(a) Indicates end of contracted capacity expansion. Starting from year marked with this symbol straight-line depreciation of existing and contracted capacity over a period equal to plant lifetime is assumed.

Constraint Block 3: Capacity ⩾ Peak Demand + Planning Margin
This constraint block requires that available production capacity for gas and electricity should be sufficient to meet peak demand and, in addition, sufficient spare capacity should be available for contingencies such as repair and maintenance.

$$\sum_j a_{ij}\left[\sum_{v=1}^{t} h_{jvt}Z_{jv} + z_{jt}^0\right] + \sum_{v=1}^{t} h_{ivt}ZM_{iv} \geq \frac{\xi_i}{\varphi_i}P_i\sum_m y_{imt} \tag{7}$$

$$t = 1, \ldots, 10$$
$$i = 3, 4 \text{ (gas, electricity)}$$

With the exception of P_i, all the notation in inequality (3) has been introduced before. The left-hand side of inequality (7) represents available production and import capacities (the latter for gas only). On the right-hand side, $\xi_i/\varphi_i \ \Sigma_m y_{imt}$ represents peak demand. P_i represents the planning margin for fuel i. For gas, the planning margin assumed is 15 per cent while for electricity it is 28 per cent. Hence, the corresponding values of P_i in inequality (7) are $P_3 = 1.15$ for gas and $P_4 = 1.28$ for electricity. While these are the actual planning margins used by the gas and electricity industries, it has been argued by some that the 28 per cent planning margin set by the CEGB Corporate Plan (1977) is too high.

Constraint Block 4: Extraction ⩽ Available Resources
This constraint block sets limits on the extraction of oil, gas and coal from UK reserves. For oil and gas, the amount extracted in any period must not exceed a specified fraction of the proven reserves in that period, which are in turn equal to initially proven reserves plus new discoveries to date, less extraction to date. Formally we have

$$X_{j1t} \leq \frac{1}{\beta_i}\left[R_j^0 + \sum_{t=1}^{t-1} n_\tau(\Delta R_{j\tau} - x_{j1\tau})\right]$$

which is represented in BEM by the equivalent expression

$$\beta_j X_{j1t} + \sum_{\tau=1}^{t-1} n_\tau X_{j1\tau} \leq R_j^0 + \sum_{\tau=1}^{t-1} n_\tau \Delta R_j \tag{8}$$

$$t = 1, \ldots, 10$$
$$j = 2, 3 \text{ (oil extraction, gas extraction)}$$

where recall X_{j1t} is (base load) output and

$\beta_j =$ oil and gas extraction depletion factor, where $1/\beta_j$ represents the maximum fraction of remaining reserves which may (for technological reasons) be extracted in any period (constant)

n_t = length in years of period t (in all runs of BEM reported in this book, n_t = 5 for all periods)

R^0_j = reserves of fuel to be extracted by process j which are proven at the beginning of the programme period (constant)

ΔR_{jt} = average annual discoveries, during period t, of fuel to be extracted by process j (constant)

Constraint (8) incorporates the assumption that the productivity of oil and gas wells declines with the cumulative amount extracted. A decline curve commonly used to extrapolate the production rate is the exponential function $x(t) = x_0 e^{-t/\beta}$, where x_0 is the output rate at time $t = 0$ and $\beta > 0$ is a constant which varies from well to well. The amount $R(t)$ remaining in the reserves at time t is then

$$R(t) = \int_t^\infty x(t')\, dt' = \beta x_0 e^{-t/\beta} = \beta x(t)$$

The ratio of remaining reserves to current production is thus a constant, β, which varies from well to well. The value $\beta_j = 14$, assumed in the model, is a reasonable approximation for UK reserves. It implies that production in any period is approximately 7 per cent (one-fourteenth) of existing proven reserves. Note, however, that the extraction depletion factor represents the maximum amount that can be extracted: it is always possible to extract less than the maximum. (For further discussion, see Eden *et al.*, 1981, pp. 89–93.)

It is assumed that proven reserves at the beginning of the programme period are available for extraction immediately. Since development and construction lead times are about five years, new reserves proven during any time period are not available for extraction until the following period.

Data concerning the oil and gas reserves assumed in the model are shown in Table 4.7. The model assumes that the total amount of reserves available is at the approximate mid-point of the range of total (proven, probable and possible) reserves as estimated by the Department of Energy. Probable and possible reserves of oil and gas are

Table 4.7 *UK Oil and Gas Reserves in BEM Base Case*

	Brown Book estimates (thousand PJ)		BEM Base Case total reserves
	Proven	*Range of total estimates*	*(thousand PJ)*
Oil reserves	54	99–197	150
Gas reserves	29	32–92	57.6

Source: Tables 1 and 2 in *Development of the Oil and Gas Reserves of the UK 1980* (Brown Book) Department of Energy, 1980. Range of estimates is for ultimately recoverable reserves (proven, probable and possible) on the UK Continental Shelf. In the case of gas, the range of estimates is for remaining reserves at the beginning of the programme period.

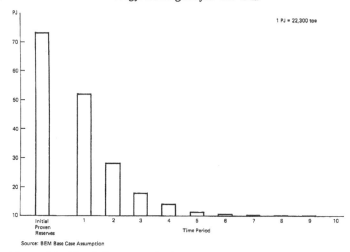

Figure 4.8   *Total discovery of oil reserves in each programme period*

assumed to be discovered and exploited at a declining rate as shown by Figures 4.8 and 4.9. While mathematical functions are used to describe smooth discovery rates for both fuels, the model and computer routines are devised to accept any specified discovery rate assumptions. The implications of alternative assumptions about reserves are assessed in Chapter 6.

British coal reserves from the dozen or so mining regions are divided into five 'tranches' according to the average cost of coal extraction. The

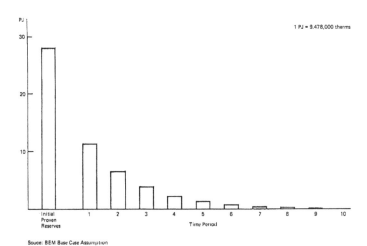

Figure 4.9   *Total discovery of gas reserves in each programme period*

Table 4.8   *Recoverable Reserves of Coal by Regions and Tranches*

Tranche	Region	Reserves (m. tonnes)
I	North Derbyshire, South Notts., South Midlands, North Notts., North Yorks.	3,630
II	Doncaster, Scottish, Barnsley, South Yorks.	2,785
III	North East, Western	2,520
IV	South Wales, Kent	1,065
V	Estimated additional reserves not known by region	35,000
Total		45,000

Source: NCB Estimates.

regions comprising each tranche and the total recoverable reserves assumed to be available are shown in Table 4.8.

The set of inequalities (9) limits total coal extraction from each tranche over the whole fifty-year programme period to not more than the total reserves in each tranche.

$$\sum_{t=1}^{10} n_t X_{j1t} \leq R_j^0 \tag{9}$$

$j = 1, 11\text{--}14$ (coal tranches $1, \ldots, 5$)

where recall X_{j1t} is average annual output in period t and n_t is the duration of period t.

Constraint Block 5: Distribution Capacity $\geq$ Peak Demand
Whereas constraint blocks 2 and 3 require that annual and peak demand cannot exceed available *production* capacity, constraint block 5 requires that *distribution* capacity for gas and electricity is sufficient to meet peak demand.

$$\sum_{v=1}^{t} h_{ivt}^w W_{imv} + w_{imt}^0 \geq \frac{\xi_i}{\varphi_i} \bar{y}_{imt} \tag{10}$$

$$t = 1, \ldots, T$$
$$m = 1, \ldots, M$$
$$i = 3, 4 \text{ (gas, electricity)}$$

The following new variables and coefficients are introduced in constraint (10).

W_{imv} = distribution capacity for fuel i in market sector m, installed in period v (variable)

h_{ivt}^w = proportion of distribution capacity for fuel i, installed in period v, which is still effective in period t (constant)

w_{imt}^0 = distribution capacity for fuel i in market sector m, which was existing and/or contracted at the beginning of the programme period and which is still effective in period t (constant)

Recall that ξ_i/ϕ_i is the ratio of peak demand to annual demand $\bar{y}_{imt}$.

Peak distribution capacity constraints are imposed on gas and electricity and not on the remaining fuels for the reasons stated in setting peak production capacity constraints in constraint block 3.

The initial distribution capacity is assumed to be sufficient to meet peak demand during the first time period. The model chooses whether to install new capacity to meet higher peak demand or to replace retiring capacity. Capacity lifetimes and construction lead times are assumed to be thirty years and four years, respectively.

Constraint Block 6: Other Constraints on Production Capacities
Two further constraints are included in the BEM which reflect assumptions made in the 1978 Green Paper. First, the new construction of nuclear capacity between 1979 and 2000 (periods 1–5) is limited to 35 GW.

$$\sum_{t=1}^{5} Z_{jt} \leq 35 \text{ GW} \tag{11}$$

$j = 9$ (nuclear electricity)

where recall Z_{jt} denotes the construction of new capacity in period t.

It should be noted here that Pearce and Jones (1980) have challenged the feasibility of so large a construction programme. Assuming a six-year construction time and an average size of 1.3 GW, this implies the construction of about twenty-seven stations between 1982 and 1994, or about two stations per year.

> Such a construction rate appears well beyond the physical capacity of the relevant construction industries and, more important, would be unlikely to achieve social acceptability in terms of the speed with which the necessary development applications could be processed by the local planning system. (p. 271)

Pearce, Edwards and Beuret (1979) have also pointed out the difficulties of acquiring suitable sites. In fact, the government has subsequently announced a rather more modest programme of nuclear construction, involving the planned construction of at least one nuclear power station per year for ten years from 1982, in order to meet an estimated need for 20 GW of new generating capacity by the year 2000 (*The Times*, 24 July 1981). We take up these points later.

Second, the total capacity for extracting coal in the years up to 2000 (periods 1–5) is limited to a maximum of 170m. tonnes per annum.

$$\sum_{\substack{\text{all coal} \\ \text{extraction} \\ \text{activities}}} \left[\sum_{\tau=1}^{t} Z_{j\tau} + z_{jt}^{0} \right] \leq 170 - 12.5 \, (5 - t) \, \text{m. tonnes} \qquad (12)$$

$$t = 3, 4, 5$$

Once again, doubts have been expressed as to the feasibility of this target (e.g. Robinson and Marshall, 1981).

More general construction smoothing constraints (13) are set for a number of activities to ensure that unrealistically large fluctuations in capacity levels do not take place from one time period to the next.

$$|Z_{jt} - Z_{j,t-1}| \leq n_t D_j \qquad (13)$$

$$t = 2, \ldots, 10$$
$$j = 1, \ldots, 14$$

where D_j is the maximum absolute difference in annual construction activity for process j from one period to the next.

A final capacity constraint within this constraint block is of a technical nature requiring that a minimum of 5 per cent of the total electricity production capacity should be gas turbines, which are required to start up conventional power stations. This constraint is written as:

$$Z_{kt} \geq 0.05 \sum_{j=6}^{10} Z_{jt} \qquad (6)$$

$$t = 1, \ldots, 10$$
$$k = 10 \, (\text{gas turbine})$$

4.4 The BEM Objective Function

The objective function is set out in full below and its components are explained. Briefly, it comprises the production and distribution costs of all fuels, the capital costs of new production distribution and import capacity, and the costs of importing fuels less the revenue from exporting fuels.

$$\min PV(TC) = \sum_{t} n_t d_t \sum_{j} C_{jt}^{x} \sum_{b} X_{jbt} \quad \text{(operating cost)}$$

$$+ \sum_{t} d_t \sum_{j} C_{jt}^{z} Z_{jt} \quad \text{(capital cost)}$$

$$+ \sum_{t} m_t d_t \sum_{i} \sum_{m} C_{imt}^{y} \bar{y}_{imt} \quad \text{(operating cost of distribution)}$$

$$+ \sum_t d_t \sum_i \sum_m C^w_{imt} W_{imt} \quad \text{(capital cost of distribution)}$$

$$+ \sum_t d_t n_t \sum_i [(P^m_{it} + C^m_{it}) M_{it} - (P^m_{it} - C^{xs}_{it}) S_{it}]$$
(net cost of trade)

$$+ \sum_t d_t \sum_i [C^{zm}_{it} ZM_{it} + C^{zs}_{it} ZS_{it}] \quad \text{(capital cost of trade)}$$

The values of the coefficients in the objective function and the sources from which information on these coefficients has been obtained are shown after explaining the notation introduced for the first time in the objective function.

All the terms in the objective function are weighted by the discount factor d_t in order to obtain present values (or, more precisely, 1976 values) of costs (or export revenue) incurred over the programme period. The calculation of the discount factor is as follows. First, it is assumed that cash inflows and outflows can be regarded as occurring in the middle of each year, so that, at discount rate r, £1 spent in any year is equivalent to $1/(1 + r)^{1/2}$ at the beginning of that year. It is further assumed that money spent in any five-year period is equally likely to be spent in any year of that period, so its expected value at the beginning of the period is

$$(1/5) \sum_{i=1}^{5} [1/(1 + r)]^{i-1/2}$$

Finally, the value of expenditure in period t is related back to the beginning of the ten-period programme (1976) by the factor $[1/(1 + r)]^{5(t-1)}$. The formula for the discount factor is thus

$$d_t = (1/5) \sum_{i=1}^{5} [1/(1 + r)]^{i-1/2} [1/(1 + r)]^{5(t-1)}$$

$$t = 1, \ldots, 10$$

In the Base Case, the discount rate is 5 per cent. This corresponds to the current required rate of return for appraising investments in the UK Public Sector. Consequences of lower and higher discount rates are assessed as a part of the sensitivity analysis in Chapter 6.

Although we have assumed a fifty-year programme period which is separated into ten five-year time periods, the constraints and the objective function are stated generally for t time periods each consisting of n_t years. The model can easily be run for different lengths of programme periods and different numbers and lengths of time periods within it.

The first term in the objective function represents the operating cost of extracting and producing energy by all the energy production processes. Since X_{jbt} is the annual output of process j in time period t, $\sum_j C^x_{jt} \sum_b X_{jbt}$ is the average annual operating cost. Weighting the above with the discount factor gives the 1976 value of operating costs for one year. To obtain the 1976 value of total operating costs in the time period consisting of n_t years, the term is multiplied by n_t. The second term represents the 1976 value of the capital cost of extracting and producing energy. The capital and operating costs per unit are shown in Table 4.9.

The next two terms in the objective function represent the 1976 values of operating and capital costs of distribution. The costs per unit assumed in the model are shown in Table 4.10. The last two terms represent import cost less export revenue and the cost of installing importing and exporting capacity. The international price of crude oil is assumed to be about £45 per tonne in 1976 (at 1976 prices) and to rise

Table 4.9   *Operating[a] and Capital[b] Costs of Production Processes*

Production process	Operating cost (£/GJ)	Capital cost[c] (£/[GJ/year])
1 Coal extraction: tranche I	0.5	1.5[d]
2 Oil extraction	0.2	1.3[e]
3 Gas extraction	0.1	1.3[e]
4 Synthetic oil from coal	0.4	5.0[f]
5 Synthetic gas from coal	0.4	5.0[f]
6 Electricity from coal	0.2788	8.13[g]
7 Electricity from oil	0.1	6.0[h]
8 Electricity from gas	0.1	6.0[h]
9 Nuclear electricity	1.122[b]	13.0[g,i]
10 Electricity from gas turbines	2.6	5.4[h]
11 Coal extraction: tranche II	0.6	1.5[d]
12 Coal extraction: tranche III	0.7	1.5[d]
13 Coal extraction: tranche IV	1.0	1.5[d]
14 Coal extraction: tranche V	2.0	1.5[d]
15 Oil refinery output	0.026	0.097[i]
16 Petrol from naphtha	0.078	0.242[j]
17 Reforming output	0.071	0.236[j]

[a] Excludes fuel costs.

[b] Includes R & D and decommissioning costs but not interest during construction which is included by assuming that the capital cost is paid in 'leadtime + 1' equal instalments at the middle of each year starting 'leadtime' years before commissioning.

[c] £/[GJ/year] denotes the full capital cost of installing 1 GJ of capacity, that is, capacity which can then (subject to availability) produce up to 1 GJ of energy in each year of its life. (It does *not* denote an annualised equivalent of the capital cost.)

[d] NCB, private communication; NCB Annual Report and Accounts (1979); H. Boulter, 'Selby opens new horizons', *Financial Times*, 11 September 1975, p. 16.

[e] *Financial Times*, December 1 1979; Department of Energy (1978), *Development of the Oil and Gas Resources of the UK*, HMSO, London.

[f] Department of Energy, Principal Cost assumptions, SNG Production.

[g] Department of Energy (1977). (Based on cost estimates for AGRs. See Chapter 9 for a brief discussion on the pros and cons of AGRs and PWRs.)

[h] CEGB, private communication; Appendix 3 of the Annual Report (1979/80) of the CEGB.

[i] Includes fuel costs.

[j] Oil industry, private communication.

Table 4.10   *Operating and Capital Costs of Importing and Exporting*

		Imports	Exports
Operating Cost (£/GJ)	Oil	0.1	0.15
	Oil products	0.0	0.2
	Gas	0.4	0.7
Capital Cost (£/[GJ/year])	Oil	—	—
	Oil products	—	—
	Gas	2	3

Notes: (a) Capital costs for oil and oil products are included in operating costs.
(b) Above are rough approximations based on private communications.

at an average rate of 3 per cent per year in real terms in order to double
by the year 2000. The international gas price is assumed to be just under
13.5 pence per therm in 1976 and to rise at the same rate as the price of
oil. Prices of oil and gas are assumed to remain constant in real terms
after the year 2000, on the grounds that extensive international trade in
relatively cheap coal will (a) keep down oil and gas prices by virtue of
coal's competitiveness, and (b) allow the manufacture of synthetic oil
and gas to replace dwindling natural reserves. The effects of rising oil
and gas prices are considered in Chapter 6.

Table 4.11   *Operating (£/GJ) and Capital^a (£/[GJ/year]) Costs of
Distribution*

	Markets	Iron and			Commercial
Fuel	Domestic	Steel	Industrial	Transport	etc.
1 Coal	0.511	0.127	0.127	0.511	0.511
2 Crude oil	—^{b}	—	—	—	—
3 Gas (operating)	1.3	0.271	0.271	1.3	1.3
(capital)	3.091	1.546	1.546	3.091	3.091
4 Electricity					
(operating)	1.017	0.508	0.508	1.017	1.017
(capital)	9.445	4.647	4.637	9.445	9.445
5 Petrol	—	—	—	0.96	0.96
6 Naphtha					
(non-energy)	—	—	0.03	—	—
7 Kerosene	0.2	—	—	0.3	0.2
8 Gas/oil	—	0.2	0.2	0.5	0.2
9 Fuel/oil	0.03	0.03	0.03	—	0.03

Notes: ^{a}Capital costs are included separately for gas and electricity only. For other
fuels, they are included in operating costs since they are a relatively small
proportion of the total.
^{b}— indicates that distribution of the fuel to the market is inappropriate.

Sources: Annual Reports and Accounts of British Gas Corporation, National Coal
Board, CEGB and Electricity Area Boards. Total distribution costs divided by total units
supplied to obtain approximate cost per unit (Oil industry, private communication).

We have not included in the objective function any of the environmental and social costs of energy. This is not because they are insignificant: on the contrary, it is all too easy to produce an extensive list of external effects, many of them serious. Examples include the risks of injury and ill-health to workers in all energy industries, and in many cases to the general public; and the adverse effects on the ecology (e.g. oil spillage, air pollution from coal and thermal pollution of rivers) and on the scenery (unsightly coal tips and power stations). The problem with incorporating such considerations is that they are difficult to measure and evaluate. Certainly some progress has been made in this direction (Eden *et al.*, 1981, Ch. 9) but even economists who are sympathetic to social cost–benefit analysis recognise its limitations in dealing with such issues as the liberty of the individual and nuclear weapons proliferation (Pearce, 1979). Rather than use data which are the subject of serious contention, or which are adequate for some fuels but not for others, it seemed preferable to limit the model to the more tangible 'private' costs of investment and production. It would certainly be possible to incorporate external costs in the model, and at this stage we cannot say what difference they would make. It is worth noting, however, that, contrary to popular belief, nuclear energy is by no means the major source of external costs. 'Coal, closely followed by oil, carries the highest total risk ... The lowest risk fuel is natural gas ... Nuclear energy ranks second to gas in safety' (Eden *et al.*, 1981, pp. 235–6).

Appendix: BEM Mathematical and Computer Programme Notation

The mathematical notation used in describing the model in this chapter is set out in the first column below, and the corresponding notation used in the computer programme is set out in the second column.

Indices

i	I	fuel
m	M	market
t	T	period
b	BB	load–duration curve block
n_t	NYPP(T)	number of years in period t

Constants

P_{it}^m	CM(I, T)	import price of fuel i, in period t (CIF)
P_{it}^s	CS(I, T)	export price of fuel i, in period t (FOB)
C_{it}^{xm}	CXM(I, T)	imports operating cost for fuel i in period t
C_{it}^{xs}	CXS(I, T)	exports operating cost for fuel i in period t
C_{it}^{zm}	CZM(I, T)	imports capital cost minus terminal value

C_{it}^{zs}	CZS(I, T1)	exports capital cost minus terminal value
C_{jt}^{x}	CX(J, T)	operating cost of activity j, in period t
C_{jt}^{z}	CZ(J, T)	capital cost minus terminal value
d_t	DISFAC(T)	discount factor for period t
e_i	LOSS (I)	distribution losses of fuel i
ξ_i		$(1 - e_i)^{-1}$
a_{ij}	A(I, J)	$(0 < a_{ij} \leqslant 1)$, if fuel i is produced by activity j, zero otherwise
P_i	PM(I)	planning/safety margin for fuel i
g_j	AVML(J)	average availability of plant type j
h_{jvt}	HJVT(J, V, T)	fraction of capacity for process j, installed in period v, still effective in period t
φ_i	LDF(I)	demand load factor (gas and electricity)
$\bar{y}_{imt}$	YEXOG(I, M, T)	average annual exogenous demand for fuel i, in market m, in period t
w_{ib}	WB(BB)	level of demand for fuel i, in load block b as a fraction of peak
h_{ib}	HB(BB)	fraction of the year during which intensity of demand for fuel i is w_{ib}
Z_{jt}^{0}	ZCAP(J, T)	existing and/or contracted capacity for process j at the beginning of the planning period, still effective in period t
h_{ivt}^{m}		fraction of import capacity for fuel i, installed in period v, still effective in period t
h_{ivt}^{s}		same for exports
h_{ivt}^{w}		same for distribution capacity
ZM_{it}^{0}		existing and/or contracted import capacity for fuel i, at the beginning of the planning period still effective in period t
ZS_{it}^{0}		same for export capacity
w_{imt}^{0}		same for distribution capacity in market m
β_j	BFAC	oil and gas extraction depletion factor
R_j^{0}		reserves of fuel extracted by process j, proven at the beginning of plan period
ΔR_{jt}	DELTAR(J, T)	average annual discoveries during period t of fuel extracted by process j
D_j	DIFF(J)	maximum absolute difference in annual contraction activity for process j, from one period to the next
b_{ijt}	B(I, J, T)	input of fuel i required for the production of one unit of output of activity j, in period t

Variables

X_{jbt}	X(J, B, T)	average annual level of activity j during period t. b indicates the load–duration curve block and it is always equal to unity, except in the case of gas and electricity

Z_{jt}	Z(J, T)	capacity for process j installed in period t
M_{it}	M(I, T)	average annual level of imports during period t
S_{it}	S(I, T)	average annual level of exports during period t
W_{imt}	W(I, M, T)	distribution capacity for fuel i in market m, installed in period t
ZM_{it}	ZM(I, T)	import capacity for fuel i, installed in period t
ZS_{it}	ZS(I, T)	export capacity for fuel i, installed in period t

References

CEGB (1977), *Central Electricity Generating Board Corporate Plan*, London.

Department of Energy (1977), *Coal and Nuclear Power Station Costs*, Energy Commission Paper No. 6, Department of Energy, London.

Department of Energy (1978a), *Energy Policy: A Consultative Document*, Cmnd 7101, HMSO, London.

Department of Energy (1978b), *Energy Forecasts: A Note by the Department of Energy*, Energy Commission Paper No. 5, Department of Energy, London.

Department of Energy (1978c), *Energy Forecasting Methodology*, Energy Paper No. 29, HMSO, London.

Department of Energy (1979), *Energy Projections 1979*, Department of Energy, London.

Department of Energy (1980), *Development of the Oil and Gas Resources of the UK*, HMSO, London. (Also see 1978 and 1979 volumes.)

Eden, R., Posner, M., Bending, R., Crouch, E. and Stanislaw, J. (1981), *Energy Economics*, Cambridge University Press, Cambridge, UK.

Pearce, D. W. (1979), 'Social cost-benefit analysis and nuclear futures', *Energy Economics*, vol. 1, no. 2.

Pearce, D. W., Edwards, L. and Beuret, G. (1979), *Decision Making for Energy Futures*, Macmillan/SSRC, London.

Pearce, D. W. and Jones, P. (1980), 'Nuclear power and UK energy policy', *International Journal of Environmental Studies*, vol. 15, no. 4.

Robinson, C. and Marshall, E. (1981), *What Future for British Coal?*, Hobart Paper No. 89, Institute of Economic Affairs, London.

5

Base Case Results

5.1 Introduction

This chapter describes and discusses the solution to the BEM Base Case Model. Recall that the model chooses the pattern of energy production, investment and trade which minimises the cost of meeting specified levels of final demand for each fuel over a fifty-year horizon. In the Base Case, these levels of final demand are derived from projections made by the Department of Energy. The growth rates of demand for each fuel vary over time, but over the whole programme period they average out to about 2.4 per cent per annum for electricity, 2.1 per cent for coal and 0.6 per cent for gas. The final demand for oil is assumed not to increase at all.

Aggregating across the four fuels, total final energy demand increases by about two-thirds over the fifty years. More striking, however, are the changes in proportions of the total final demand accounted for by each fuel. Oil loses its dominant position (down from 46 per cent to 28 per cent) and gas falls also (23 per cent to 19 per cent). Coal and electricity become proportionately more important (18 per cent to 29 per cent and 13 per cent to 24 per cent, respectively). As Figure 4.7 showed, total final demand is spread much more equally among the four fuels.

The changing pattern of final demands is a matter of *assumptions*; in contrast, the model itself calculates how best to meet these demands, that is, what pattern of primary energy sources is least costly. The next few sections of this chapter describe in more detail the pattern of production and trade for each fuel taken in turn. Here and henceforth, the output of the model will generally be represented in the form of graphs, in order to highlight the significant features.

5.2 The Coal Industry

The total level of coal extraction over the fifty-year programme period, and the changing pattern of its allocation between various uses, are shown in Figure 5.1. There is a continually expanding programme of coal extraction throughout the period. It rises at about 1.8 per cent annually from 112m. tonnes in 1980 to 170m. tonnes in 2000 (which is the maximum level permitted by the constraints on the growth of coal extraction capacity), and then at 2.1 per cent annually to nearly 270m. tonnes in 2025.

This continued increase in output can largely be met by expanding

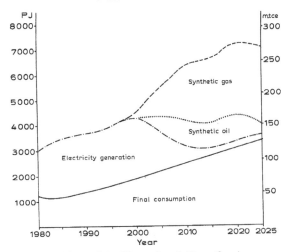

Figure 5.1   *Uses of coal (Base Case)*

capacity in the lower-cost pits (tranches I–III), although throughout the period it is necessary to utilise the high-cost tranche IV pits (see Figure 5.2). For the most part, tranche IV pits are used rather sparingly (at most 10 per cent of total output, usually much less), but after 2015 the exhaustion of the lower-cost pits requires a substantial expansion of tranche IV to account for over one-fifth of total output.

There are some striking changes in the use of coal over the pro-

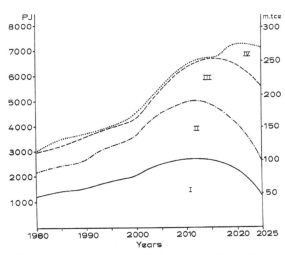

Figure 5.2   *Coal production by tranche (Base Case)*

gramme period. Until the turn of the century, essentially the only two uses for coal are (as at present) final consumption and electricity generation. The opening decade of the twenty-first century is one of rapid transition. During the final fifteen years of the programme (2010–25), coal is used predominantly for final consumption and producing synthetic fuels, with coal for electricity production at a very low level and declining even further. We examine these uses in turn.

(1) By assumption, coal for final consumption increases steadily at about 2 per cent annually throughout the period. As noted in the previous chapter, consumption in the Commercial and Domestic Sectors falls sharply (owing to the relative inconvenience of using coal), but this is more than offset by the rapid growth of consumption in the Industrial Sectors, including Iron and Steel (reflecting the growth in those sectors and a shift away from the relatively more expensive oil and gas). From 2000 onwards, final consumption is the most important single use for coal.
(2) Electricity generation is the most important use for coal before 2000, taking nearly 90m. tonnes of coal annually between 1985 and 2000. However, this high level of coal in electricity generation is maintained only because the expansion of nuclear electricity is constrained by capacity considerations in the nuclear supply industry. After the turn of the century a rapid expansion of nuclear capacity takes place, and coal consumption in electricity generation declines rapidly to 26m. tonnes in 2010 and 8m. tonnes in 2025.
(3) Production of synthetic gas and oil starts around the turn of the century. The consumption of coal in synthetic gas production rises tenfold in ten years, from about 8.5m. tonnes in 2000 to 85m. tonnes in 2010, and then at a slower rate of about 2.2 per cent per annum to 118m. tonnes in 2025. The consumption of coal in synthetic oil production reaches a level of about 38m. tonnes per annum throughout the decade 2010 to 2020, then falls to a third of this level in the final period.

The capital and operating costs of synthetic gas and oil are assumed to be identical in the model. Nevertheless, synthetic gas is produced slightly earlier, and on a larger scale than synthetic oil. Presumably this is because the import price of gas is higher than that of oil. Similarly, the fall in synthetic oil production in the first period reflects the exhaustion of coal reserves from the cheaper tranches, and the consequent need to extract coal from the most expensive tranche IV. At this higher marginal cost it is cheaper partially to replace synthetic oil by imported oil, although synthetic gas continues to be economically viable.

It should be noted that the above bright prospect for the UK coal industry, which is similar to the prospect envisaged by the Department of Energy (1978a, b), has been challenged by Robinson and Marshall (1981). They argue (1) that the department's projections of UK demand for coal are over-optimistic, (2) that if coal imports are allowed much of domestic production will not be competitive, (3) that if imports are not allowed, and there is no subsidisation of domestic production, coal is unlikely to retain a significant cost advantage over competing fuels, and (4) that domestic coal prices are likely to be closely linked to world oil prices. We shall explore the effects of lower demand, coal imports and rising production costs in later chapters.

Some would question the ability of the coal industry to raise output to 170m. tonnes in 2000 and 270m. tonnes by 2025. In the final chapter we reduce the end-of-century target to 150m. tonnes, which is probably more in line with current thinking. As regards the 2025 projection, it does not seem impossible for the coal industry to more than double output over 40 years, provided that profitable operation is envisaged, though organisational changes may be required to effect this. We also examine (in chapter 6) an assumption of higher gas reserves, which would reduce the need for synthetic gas and, consequently, the need for such large output of coal.

5.3 The Oil Industry

The sources and uses of oil are shown in Figures 5.3 and 5.4, respectively. Briefly, the main features are as follows: (1) By assumption, the final consumption of oil remains constant over the whole programme period. The use of oil in electricity generation and losses in refining and distribution are also roughly constant. Exports of oil products increase steadily. (2) Domestic oil extraction rises rapidly to a peak in 1985 and declines steadily thereafter. (3) Synthetic oil is produced on a modest

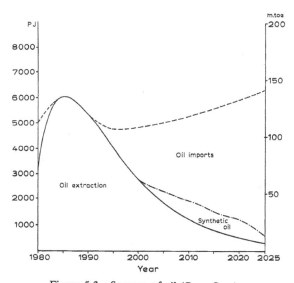

Figure 5.3 *Sources of oil (Base Case)*

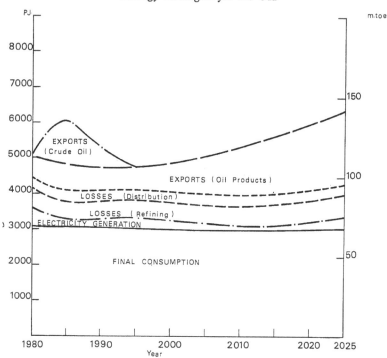

Figure 5.4 *Uses of oil (Base Case)*

scale from the turn of the century onwards. (4) During the 1980s crude oil surplus to domestic requirements is exported. However, the remainder of the programme period is characterised by ever-increasing oil imports. We shall examine each of these aspects in turn.

The amount of oil refined each year is closely related to the final consumption of oil products in the UK, which by assumption remains constant throughout the programme period. However, the two are not identical, since not all oil products refined in the UK are consumed within it: some trade takes place with other countries (mainly Western Europe) in order to balance out the excess supplies of and demands for these products. For example, the UK final demand for oil products in the first period (1977–81) averages about 70m. tonnes per annum, whereas the total amount of crude oil refined during that period is 113m. tonnes per annum. The difference between final demand and amount refined reflects physical losses in oil refining and distribution plus net balancing exports of oil products.

Next, consider the source of crude oil entering the refineries. At the beginning of the programme period, domestic extraction is the most important source, accounting for two-thirds of refining throughput. In the first two periods, oil extraction is limited by the lead time required to install capacity. Thereafter, oil reserves are developed as soon as they are discovered, and oil is extracted at the maximum possible rate, reaching a peak of 135m. tonnes in 1985. Extraction would be even faster if it were not for the technical constraints on the build-up of extraction capacity. These constraints are examined further in Section 5.10 below.

(Latest figures at the time of going to press suggest that the extraction rate in 1981 was about 1.85m. barrels a day, or 103m. tonnes per annum. The extraction rate was projected to rise to 2.26m. barrels a day (127m. tonnes) in 1984 and 1985 (*Financial Times*, November 25, 1981). It thus seems unlikely that an extraction rate of 135m. tonnes could be achieved by 1985. The revised versions of the model discussed in section 11.2 envisage lower 1985 extraction rates which are clearly feasible, however.)

Soon after 1980, the UK becomes a net operator of crude oil and oil products, and remains a net exporter for about a decade. Thereafter, net imports rise rapidly, building up to 29m. tonnes in 2000, 44m. tonnes in 2010 and 83m. tonnes in 2025. However, the precise pattern of extraction and trade does depend upon the assumptions about the level of oil reserves, and alternative assumptions are explored in the following chapter.

As remarked in the previous section, synthetic oil production starts in the year 2000, is maintained at about 16m. tonnes per annum until 2020, and falls slightly in the final period.

Some initial insight into oil production and trade policy can be obtained by comparing the relative costs of obtaining oil by different methods. Suppose the capacity costs of extracting oil and producing synthetic oil are annuitised over the lifetime of the capacity, and then added to the operating costs. The resulting 'long-run' costs are £17.00 per tonne to extract oil, and £74.50, £81.00, £87.50 or £106.50 per tonne to produce oil synthetically, depending upon whether the coal comes from tranche I, II, III or IV. The cost of importing oil depends upon the world price, and it rises steadily from £50.00 per tonne in 1980 to £105.00 per tonne in 2005, remaining constant thereafter (by assumption).

These calculations suggest that extracting domestic oil is by far the cheapest way of obtaining oil, as long as oil reserves are not exhausted, and will therefore be carried out first. (Actually, it is not quite that simple, since extracting oil today involves the sacrifice of oil revenue tomorrow. If the international price of oil is expected to rise faster than the discount rate, it would be profitable to postpone the exploitation of domestic reserves. This point is illustrated in the sensitivity analysis in the next chapter.)

Until 1995 it is cheaper to import oil than to produce it synthetically from tranche II, III or IV, whereas from 2000 onwards the cost of importing oil is above the cost of synthetic oil from tranche III but just below the cost of synthetic oil from tranche IV. The profitability of synthetic oil thus depends crucially upon the source of the coal – more precisely, upon the cost of the coal at the margin (i.e. the highest-cost tranche actually utilised).

Throughout the programme period tranche IV is in use except initially and from 2012–16. Why, then, is it profitable to produce oil synthetically throughout the period from 2000 onwards? Presumably the availability of tranche III coal during 2012–16 justifies the installation of synthetic capacity by that time, and once capacity is installed the relevant cost is the operating cost, without adding an allocation of capacity cost. Moreover, if capacity is to be made available in 2012–16, the cost of installing it earlier, so as to allow production in 2002–6, is merely the cost of *bringing forward* the investment. This cost is of the order of 5 per cent per year. Thus, taking into account the effects of cumulation, the cost of bringing forward capacity by ten years is about 60 per cent of capacity cost.

One would expect synthetic coal production to be profitable on a much larger scale if more extensive cheap coal resources were discovered in the UK, or if cheap imported coal were to be available. The latter possibility is explored in Chapter 7.

5.4   The Gas Industry

The modelling of the supply of natural gas in the BEM is almost identical to that of crude oil. The three sources of natural gas are extraction from indigenous reserves, imports and synthetic production from coal. The demand side, however, is less complex since natural gas is a single homogeneous product used in all sectors, while crude oil is required to go through a complex refinery process to prepare products appropriate for markets.

Figure 5.5 shows that extraction builds up to a peak of 19b. therms in 1985 and then declines steadily over the remaining programme period. With the exception of the first two time periods, in which extraction is

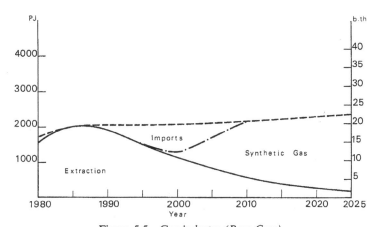

Figure 5.5   *Gas industry (Base Case)*

limited by the lead time required to develop newly discovered reserves, reserves are developed as soon as they are discovered and gas is extracted at the maximum rate permitted by the constraints on expanding capacity.

Between 1980 and 1990 the UK is almost self-sufficient in gas, with small amounts of imports making up the difference between consumption and extraction. After 1990, first imports and later synthetic production combine with extraction to meet total domestic demand.

In the year 2000 imports reach a peak of over 7b. therms or 38 per cent of total gas consumption. However, starting in 1995 synthetic gas production grows rapidly and completely replaces gas imports by 2010. By the end of the programme period, synthetic gas accounts for over 94 per cent of total gas consumption.

This policy reflects the changing relative costs of gas supply. As in the case of oil, extraction is the cheapest source, and consequently gas is extracted as rapidly as permitted by technical constraints and reserves. Until 1995, the import price of gas is below the cost of producing synthetic gas from tranche III coal, which is the highest-cost coal being extracted in substantial quantities. (The small quantities of tranche IV coal being extracted during these time periods are from extraction capacity that was available at the beginning of the programme period. It is not profitable to make any new tranche IV coal extraction capacity available until after the year 2015. From year 2000 onwards, however, the import price of gas exceeds the cost of synthetic production even from tranche IV coal.)

5.5 The Electricity Industry

The projected final consumption of electricity shows a faster growth than any other fuel. This projected growth is most rapid in the period 1980 to 2000, when it averages 3.2 per cent per year, compared to 2.1 per cent per year thereafter. Within this overall growth, nuclear electricity plays an increasingly prominent role (Figure 5.6), reflecting a cost advantage over its rivals coal and oil.

Although the capital cost of nuclear plant is substantially higher than that of coal-fired or oil-fired plant, the operating cost is much lower. By annuitising the capital costs it is possible to suggest the overall balance of costs per unit of electricity produced in each type of plant in base load production (see Table 5.1). The cost in 1976 prices is 0.88p per KWh for nuclear electricity, from 0.89p to 1.00p for coal-fired electricity depending on the coal tranche used, and 1.40p for oil-fired electricity. The model therefore selects nuclear electricity in preference to other forms, subject to capacity constraints and the relative magnitudes of base, medium and peak load demand.

In 1980 about 17 per cent of total electricity generation in the Base Case is nuclear but this increases to just over 48 per cent by 2000 and 94 per cent by 2025, a growth rate in the earlier period of 8.7 per cent per year and in the later period of 4.8 per cent per year. In the early period

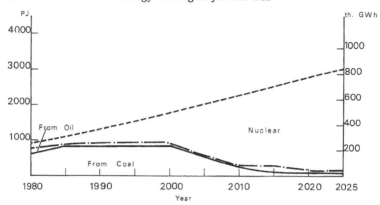

Figure 5.6　*Electricity generation (Base Case)*

even more rapid growth would have occurred in the absence of the capacity limitations of the nuclear power plant industry (which effectively constrain UK nuclear electricity production capacity to 40 GW until the year 2000).

We have already noted (in Section 4.3 above) the reservations expressed by Pearce and Jones (1980) and Pearce, Edwards and Beuret (1979) concerning the feasibility of attaining this 40 GW target. On average, two new stations a year will need to be constructed, requiring a new site every couple of years. Apart from the problems of construction there are likely to be severe problems of social acceptability. We note now that the Base Case not only requires a nuclear programme of this

Table 5.1　*Capital and Operating Costs of Electricity Production in BEM (1976 prices)*

Type of generating plant[a]	Capital cost[b]		Operating cost		Total cost[c]	
	£(GJ/yr)	£/KW	£/GJ	p/KWh	£/GJ	p/KWh
Coal-fired[d]	8.13	260	1.71–1.99	0.61–0.72	2.47–2.75	0.89–1.00
Oil-fired	6.00	192	3.29	1.20	3.85	1.39
Nuclear	13.00	416	1.12	0.40	2.43	0.88

Source: Department of Energy (1977) and coal costs by tranches in BEM.

[a]The model also includes gas turbine generators, but owing to their low capital cost and high operating cost these are used to meet peak demand only.

[b]Capital cost is the cost of providing 1 GJ of capacity which will be available for producing electricity throughout the plant life. Coal-fired and oil-fired stations have plant lives of thirty years while nuclear stations have a plant life of twenty-five years.

[c]Total cost of electricity for each type of plant is computed on the assumption that each plant is used in base-load generation and available for 70 per cent of the time.

[d]The range of costs for coal-fired stations reflects the range of coal extraction costs assumed in the model.

Table 5.2 *New Nuclear Capacity Construction and Reported Capital Expenditure*

	New construction (GW)	Capital cost (£m.)	Average capital cost per year (£m.)
1980–85	4.1	1,440	288
1985–90	9.6	3,374	675
1990–95	11.3	3,954	791
1995–2000	12.4	4,330	866
2000–05	43.3	15,160	3,032
2005–10	46.7	16,366	3,273
2010–15	40.1	14,058	2,812
2015–20	25.4	8,905	1,781
2020–25	26.1	9,139	1,828

Source: BEM Base Case.
N.B. Conversion factors are given in Table 5.2. All prices in 1976 terms.

magnitude up to the year 2000, but requires an even greater programme thereafter (Table 5.2). During the first fifteen years of the next century, an average of 8.66 GW new capacity will be required *per year*. At the previously assumed average size of station (1.3 GW), this means nearly seven stations per year, and if site capacity is about 2.5 GW then nearly three sites per year will be required. Technical progress may enable larger stations to be built, and more capacity to be accommodated on each site. Planning procedures may be speeded up. None the less, the nuclear programme envisaged by the Base Case is still a daunting one, and many would doubt its feasibility.

This growth in nuclear energy requires a substantial investment programme. Table 5.2 shows that between 1985 and 2000, the average annual investment expenditure in installing nuclear electricity plant will be about £655m. at 1976 prices. For comparison, during the financial year 1978–9, total capital expenditure in England and Wales by the CEGB was £515m. (£431m. at 1976 prices) of which £377m. (£315m. at 1976 prices) was spent on construction of new power stations. Thus, under the Base Case assumptions, annual investment in construction of new power stations between 1985 and 2000 would be over twice as much as for the financial year 1978–9. Furthermore, between 2000 and 2010 annual investment expenditure is about four times that between 1985 and 2000 (i.e. eight times the 1978–9 level).

Electricity generation from coal rises at 3 per cent per year up to 1985, but from then until 2000 growth is negligible, and the share of electricity from coal declines steadily from 64 per cent in 1980 to 47 per cent in 2000 as nuclear capacity builds up. The main reasons for the rise in coal-fired electricity in the earlier period are the long lead time on nuclear plant construction and the 40 GW constraint on new capacity. After the year 2000, electricity from coal declines rapidly at about 9 per cent a year, and by 2024 only 3 per cent of electricity is generated from coal. After the year 2004 all base load electricity generation is nuclear.

Oil-fired power stations and gas turbines retain a share of electricity generation in order to meet high peak demand, but their relative importance declines. Oil's share of electricity generation falls from 19 per cent in 1980 to 5 per cent in 2000, and becomes insignificant thereafter.

The Green Paper's assumed growth rate of 3.2 per cent for electricity is considerably higher than the latest CEGB forecast, and the nuclear programme originally envisaged is now no longer attainable. In section 11.2 we consider a revised version of the model involving lower electricity demand projections and a less ambitious nuclear programme.

5.6 Primary Energy and the Total UK Energy Bill

Total output of primary energy increases from 6,748 PJ (about 200m. tonnes of oil equivalent) in 1980 to 11,356 PJ (about 315mtoe) in 2025. The growth rate is somewhat lower than for final demand (50 per cent as opposed to 70 per cent). The most striking aspect is the changing composition of primary energy (Figure 5.7). Initially, oil accounts for about half the total output, coal for a third and gas for a fifth; nuclear power is negligible. By the year 2025, in contrast, coal has expanded to half the total output, nuclear has expanded to a fifth, and gas is negligible (Table 5.3). Britain is still dependent on three primary fuels, but

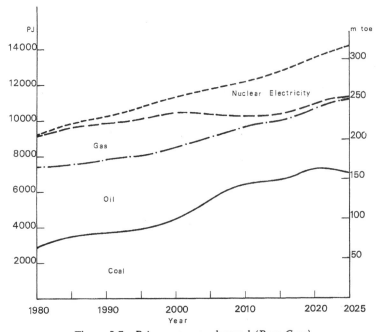

Figure 5.7 *Primary energy demand (Base Case)*

Table 5.3 Proportions of Final Demand and Primary Energy Accounted for by Each Fuel

Fuel	Final Demand						Fuel	Primary Energy					
	1980 (PJ)	(%)	2000 (PJ)	(%)	2025 (PJ)	(%)		1980 (PJ)	(%)	2000 (PJ)	(%)	2025 (PJ)	(%)
Coal	1,219	18	1,886	23	3,403	30	Coal	2,950	32	4,500	40	7,086	50
Oil	3,090	46	2,993	36	3,048	27	Oil	4,441	48	4,066	36	4,056	29
Gas	1,583	23	1,877	22	2,152	19	Gas	1,739	19	1,906	17	192	1
Electricity	857	13	1,625	19	2,753	24	Nuclear Electricity	160	2	866	8	2,844	20
	6,748	100	8,381	100	11,356	100		9,290	101	11,338	101	14,178	100

Source: BEM Base Case.

coal has replaced oil as the dominant source and nuclear energy has replaced gas as the third source. Thus the rather gentle shifts assumed in final demand have been met by a much more drastic transformation at the primary resource level.

The value of the objective function represents the present worth at 5 per cent discount rate of the minimum net cost (operating, capital, distribution and import costs less export revenues) of meeting the given levels of demand for the four fuels in the five market sectors. The value of the objective function in the Base Case solution is £214 billion. Since it is difficult to appreciate the significance of a present value figure over such a long time period, it may be helpful to express it as an annuity. A simple calculation shows that a present value of £214b. is equivalent to an average annual energy bill of £11.73b. at 1976 prices. This is roughly equivalent to 9 per cent of the Gross Domestic Product in 1978 (at 1976 prices). Of course, the actual energy bill implied by the model solution varies substantially from one time period to another. For example, coal extraction and nuclear production are both constrained before the year 2000. The costs of accelerating the expansion of capacity for these two activities will show up in higher energy costs in the period following the year 2000.

5.7   Comparison with the Department of Energy Reference Scenario

The final demand forecasts of the Department of Energy are embodied as constraints in the BEM. It is therefore of interest to compare the minimum-cost energy policy described in this chapter with the 'reference scenario' envisaged by the Department of Energy as accompanying its final demand forecasts. (See the 1978 Green Paper Annex I, pp. 85–8 and Energy Forecasts Charts 14–23.)

The Department of Energy envisaged a steady expansion for the coal industry, from 135m. tonnes in 1985 and 170m. tonnes in 2000 to 250m. tonnes in 2025. The BEM Base Case policy is very similar: 132m., 170m. and 270m. tonnes, respectively. As regards the markets for coal, the growth in final consumption is the same by assumption. From 1995 to 2025 the Department of Energy envisages a steady decline to zero in the use of coal for power stations, whereas BEM envisages a steady decline over a shorter period (from 2000 to 2015), with a consumption of some 10m. tonnes continuing to 2025. Both models envisage a dramatic switch to the use of coal for producing synthetic fuels beginning at the turn of the century, but whereas the Department of Energy envisages that this will be synthetic natural gas only, the BEM prescribes about two-thirds synthetic gas and one-third synthetic oil. Total production in BEM is initially faster, but levels out after 2015 instead of continuing to grow.

The Department of Energy envisages domestic oil extraction peaking at 125m. tonnes in 1982, then declining to 90m. tonnes in 2000 and 10m. tonnes in 2025. The BEM scenario is rather faster extraction: 134m., 61m. and 8m. tonnes, respectively. Both policies involve oil exports for the decade of the 1980s, and ever increasing imports thereafter, though BEM calls for a significant programme of synthetic oil production. The Green Paper warns that imports could reach 100 mtce by 2000; the BEM shows total fuel imports at precisely that level (of which nearly three-quarters are oil, just over one-quarter gas), and oil imports at double that level by 2025.

Gas is extracted at the same increasing rate up to 19b. therms in 1983 under the two policies, but whereas the Department of Energy scenario requires a continued increase in the rate of extraction to 22b. therms in 1995, followed by a rapid decline, the BEM envisages an earlier and steadier decline. As a result, BEM requires substantial natural gas imports from 1985 to 2010, until synthetic natural gas production is adequate to meet the balance of demand.

Both policies envisage a gradual switch from coal to nuclear energy as the major source of electricity production. The Department of Energy shows a 'gap' of some 50 mtoe in 2000, which the BEM meets by a slower decline in the consumption of coal and a faster and earlier nuclear build-up. The 'possible contribution from renewables' during 2000–2025 in the Department of Energy scenario is met by nuclear energy in the BEM.

To summarise, our results suggest that the Department of Energy 'reference scenario' is a close approximation to the minimum cost policy for meeting the forecast energy demand. It differs only in two major respects: the rate of domestic oil extraction is slightly too slow, while the rate of domestic gas extraction reaches too high a peak in 1995 (it would be cheaper to allow gas extraction to decline from 1985, and import natural gas from 1985 to 2010). Our results also suggest that the Department of Energy electricity 'energy gap' around the turn of the century could most cheaply be met, in about equal proportions, by a slower decline in the use of coal-burning plant and earlier and faster nuclear build-up. The results also suggest that nuclear energy would be the cheapest substitute if renewable energy sources were not available in the next century.

It should be remembered that these conclusions depend upon various assumptions in the model, notably the constraints on coal and nuclear capacity up to the year 2000, and the prohibition on coal imports. The effect of relaxing these assumptions is explored in Section 5.10 and Chapter 7.

5.8 Shadow Prices of Fuels

The unit cost of each production process for each fuel is specified as part of the input to the model. What is not known in advance, however, is which particular processes it will be optimal to use in each year, bearing in mind the changing world prices and the gradual exhaustion of domestic reserves. Consequently, it is generally impossible to specify in advance what will be the cost of any fuel 'at the margin', that is, the cost of a small increment in output. Such 'marginal costs' are relevant for a number of purposes – for example, in estimating the cost or saving of modifying output in order to meet a change in forecast demand, or in calculating the cheapest fuel with which to meet a prospective increase in demand for energy. Marginal costs are also relevant for pricing policy. In a free market, competition will tend to push price towards marginal cost (although monopoly power or government policy may restrict the operation of such forces). In Britain, the nationalised industries were required by the 1967 White Paper (Cmnd 3437) to set prices in relation to costs at the margin, subject to covering accounting costs. The desirability of such a pricing policy was endorsed by the 1978 White Paper (Cmnd 7131), although the individual industries were given more discretion in pricing.

The 1978 Green Paper also endorses this principle. It begins by noting that the function of energy policy is to influence the decisions of producers and consumers so as to ensure that the energy economy develops in accordance with the national interest, and points out that 'one of the most important instruments for exerting this influence is the level and structure of energy prices'. It then suggests, in effect, that prices should be related to marginal costs: 'Energy prices should give both producers and consumers reasonably accurate signals about the costs of energy supply . . . Since the object is to guide investment and other decisions that will affect future events, the relevant cost is the cost incurred or saved in expanding or contracting supplies at present or in the future, rather than an average of past costs' (p. 4).

We are therefore interested here in ascertaining what pattern of marginal costs over the next five years is implied by the model solution, and how these marginal costs relate to the pricing assumptions embodied in the Green Paper and the Department of Energy forecasts.

Associated with each constraint in a linear programme is a 'dual variable' or 'shadow price', which indicates the change in the value of the objective function that would be caused by a small incremental change in the constant on the 'right-hand side' of that constraint. For example, the shadow price associated with the constraint requiring coal output to be not less than coal demand in a particular year may be interpreted as the cost of meeting the demand for one extra PJ of coal in that year – in effect, this is the marginal cost of supplying coal. This calculation of marginal cost, it should be noted, is based upon the cheapest way of meeting the additional demand, taking into account whatever changes are appropriate in production and investment patterns for other fuels also. The shadow prices on the oil, gas and electricity demand constraints may be interpreted likewise.

Figure 5.8 shows how the shadow prices, or marginal costs, of each fuel change over the programme period. Shadow prices are also available for medium- and peak-load electricity, but for simplicity these are omitted. The shadow price of coal is fairly constant in the range £24–£32 per tonne, with a brief peak at £37 per tonne around the year 2000. Oil and gas shadow prices approximately double over the programme period, reflecting the rising world price and the gradual exhaustion of domestic resources. The shadow price of base-load electricity rises from

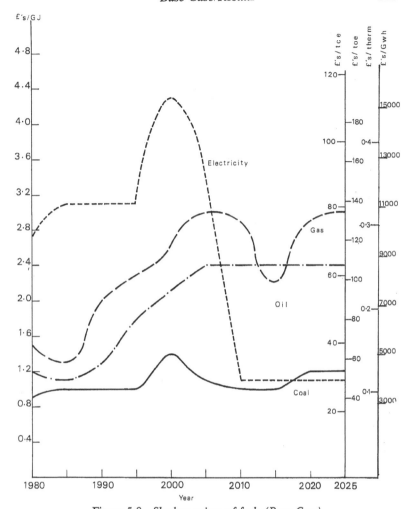

Figure 5.8 *Shadow prices of fuels (Base Case)*

£9,700 per GWh (0.97p per KWh) to £15,480 per GWh (1.55p per KWh) over the period 1980–2000, as coal- and oil-fired stations become more expensive to run, but then drops rapidly and severely to £3,960 per GWh (0.4p per KWh) from 2010 onwards, as cheap nuclear power becomes available.

The next task is to compare these marginal costs with the prices upon which the Department of Energy forecasts are based. This turns out to be a difficult task, since these assumed prices are not made clearly explicit. The Green Paper assumes that the world oil price will stay roughly constant in real terms until 1985 (p. 8), and that world oil and energy prices will rise gradually to around £20–£25 per barrel of oil equivalent (in 1977 terms) by the year 2000 (p. 10). This is at least double the 1978 level (p. 85). With respect to the UK, it is noted that coal needs a price advantage of 1p to 4p per therm, depending upon the market in question, if it is to be competitive with other fuels and meet the target output (p. 29). UK gas prices are expected to rise to reflect marginal costs rather than historic costs (p. 43). Nothing is said about the price of electricity, although it is indicated that 'unrestricted electricity supplies are likely to be expensive and limited to premium uses while for space heating requirements it is off-peak electricity which is likely to be competitive with other fuels' (p. 87).

The shadow prices in the Base Case Model suggest that marginal costs are not inconsistent with these assumptions. The marginal costs of oil and gas both roughly double by 2000. The marginal cost of coal does not increase substantially, so that its competitive advantage is preserved. The marginal cost of base-load electricity does increase substantially by 2000, though it falls steeply thereafter. The main question which these results suggest is how far the price of electricity will adjust to reflect the dramatic changes in marginal cost, and in the light of this whether the demand for electricity will grow as steadily as assumed over the whole fifty-year programme period.

5.9 The Value of Additional Reserves

Coal, oil and gas reserves are assumed to be finite in extent, but it is recognised that further exploration could discover new sources and convert some 'possible' reserves into 'probable' or 'proven' reserves. What would be the value of such additional reserves? How much money is it worth spending on such exploration? And in which periods would discovery be most useful? Here, again, the shadow prices on the fuel reserves constraints provide useful information.

The dual variables corresponding to the set of constraints (8) on available reserves are shown in Table 5.4. We shall comment on them in order.

(a) Coal
The dual variable on the tranche I coal reserves indicates that if one additional tonne of coal were available in tranche I, the present value of the cost of meeting UK energy demands would be reduced by £1.87. This is the saving net of any capacity and extraction costs that might be incurred. It suggests, for example, that it would be worth paying up to £1.87 per tonne in 1976 for the right in future to mine coal known to be of this lowest-cost character, if for some reason such reserves were not under the immediate control of the NCB (e.g. if the land were presently used for industrial or agricultural purposes). This figure represents the value of the land for coal-mining purposes, and may be compared with the value of the land for other purposes – in particular, it might represent one side of the equation in an environmental cost–benefit exercise.

Table 5.4 *Shadow Prices in the Base Case*

Constraint	Shadow Price (£ per PJ)	(£ per Natural Unit)
Coal Reserves		
Tranche I	71,060	1.87 per tonne
Tranche II	54,300	1.43 per tonne
Tranche III	37,920	1.00 per tonne
Tranche IV	0	0
Tranche V	0	0
Oil Reserves		
Period 1	0	0
Period 2	0	0
Period 3	6,660	0.30 per tonne
Period 4	55,670	2.50 per tonne
Period 5	85,740	3.84 per tonne
Period 6	68,520	3.07 per tonne
Period 7	91,260	4.09 per tonne
Period 8	64,680	2.90 per tonne
Period 9	77,230	3.46 per tonne
Period 10	61,610	2.76 per tonne
Gas Reserves		
Period 1	0	0
Period 2	0	0
Period 3	99,660	0.0105 per therm
Period 4	105,640	0.0111 per therm
Period 5	124,180	0.0131 per therm
Period 6	134,550	0.0142 per therm
Period 7	117,250	0.0124 per therm
Period 8	55,810	0.0059 per therm
Period 9	89,980	0.0095 per therm
Period 10	96,850	0.0102 per therm
Maximum Coal Extraction Capacity (170m. tonnes before 2000)		
Period 3	2,020	0.05 per tonne
Period 4	259,480	6.84 per tonne
Period 5	1,237,580	32.64 per tonne
Maximum New Nuclear Capacity (35 GW by 2000)		
Period 5	6,594,760	£208m. per GW

The Vale of Belvoir would probably fall in tranche I: the question is therefore posed whether it is worth sacrificing £1.87 per tonne of extractable coal for the sake of preserving the present rural amenities of this area. (If the coal is likely to be extracted in 1990, say, the relevant future value is $1.87 \times (1.05)^{14} = £3.70$.)

The other coal variables for the coal reserve constraints indicate that reserves of tranche II coal (which has higher extraction costs than tranche I) are worth £1.43 per tonne at the margin, and reserves of tranche III coal £1.00 per tonne. Tranche IV coal is not fully extracted by

2025, and hence additional reserves have no value within this fifty-year time period.

These variables may be used to assess the value of unexplored coal reserves. Suppose a coal seam is known to exist but its precise quality is unknown (i.e. it is characterised as tranche V in our model). If it is equally likely to be of tranche I, II, III or IV, its present expected value is simply 0.25 × (£1.87 + 1.43 + 1.00 + 0) = £1.08 per tonne, whereas if there is a 60 per cent chance of it being tranche I and 40 per cent chance of tranche II, its expected value is 0.6 (£1.87) + 0.4 (£1.43) = £1.69 per tonne, and so on.

(b) Oil

The oil reserves constraint is more difficult to analyse because it involves a pattern of discovery over time, by which possible reserves are gradually transformed into proven reserves. The shadow price in period t may be interpreted as the value of having an additional increment of oil available in period t rather than in period t +1. It represents, in effect, the value of bringing forward the discovery (more precisely, the proving) of oil. Thus discovering oil in period 1 that would otherwise be discovered in period 2 has zero value (since capacity expansion constraints preclude extracting it sooner), but oil discovered in time for extraction in period 4 rather than 5 is worth an additional £2.50 per tonne in present value terms, and oil discovered in period 7 rather than 8 is worth an extra £4.09 per tonne. From period 4 onwards it is worth on average £3.23 per tonne for each year by which the discovery of oil is brought forward.

In view of this, is it worth investing more resources in oil exploration? Exploration costs are not known with certainty. They depend on the mix of successful and unsuccessful wells drilled, and hence vary widely by company and area and over time. Historical experience suggests that they average about 10 per cent of the capital development costs of successful oil fields. From the model the capital development cost is £58.30 per tonne, which provides capacity for extracting 1 tonne per year over a lifetime of twenty years. But output is not in fact constant at 1 tonne: typically it reaches the peak capacity of 1 tonne in the third year after installation, remains at that level for about five years, then declines gradually to zero. Total output might be about 10 tonnes, hence average capital cost per tonne (not annuitised) is about £5.83. Thus exploration costs might be of the order of £0.58 per tonne.

These rough calculations suggest that expected exploration costs are significantly less than the value of exploration. But there are two additional complications. First, the calculations refer to *average* exploration costs, whereas what is in question here is the cost at the margin – whether it is worth *increasing* exploration above the levels assumed in the specified discovery pattern. If the most plausible locations are explored first, marginal costs are likely to exceed average costs. Second, additional exploration might well lead to discoveries being made more than a year before they otherwise would have been. In this case, their value is given by the sum of the shadow prices over the relevant period.

Whether these two considerations balance out is not clear. The only conclusion we can draw at this stage is that the case for additional exploration is finely balanced.

(c) Gas
The gas reserves constraint is identical in mathematical form to the oil reserves constraint and therefore the shadow prices corresponding to this constraint may be interpreted in a similar way to the oil reserves shadow prices. Discovering gas in period 1 that would otherwise have been discovered in period 2 has zero value owing to capacity expansion constraints. If discovery of a therm of gas is brought forward from period 4 to period 3, it would be worth 10.5p more in present value terms. The same interpretation applies to all the other gas reserves shadow prices. From period 3 onwards, a therm of gas would be worth 10.9p more on average if its availability for extraction can be brought forward by one time period.

5.10 Constraints on the Build-up of Capacity

Recall that constraints (8) in the model reflect the government's view (expressed in the 1978 Green Paper) that the maximum attainable output of coal before the year 2000 is 170m. tonnes per annum. There is no doubt, however, that a larger output could be secured at a price – for example, by installing more or better equipment, hiring more men, prolonging the life of older pits, etc. But precisely what price is worth paying? The shadow prices on the 170m. tonnes capacity constraints reveals by how much the present value of total energy cost could be reduced if the capacity constraints could be relaxed. The value of the shadow price for period 5 (1997–2001) is £33 per tonne of coal. The shadow prices for periods 3 and 4.are more positive but much smaller, at 5p and under £7 per tonne, respectively. Note that these prices are *net* of the capital and operating costs of coal extraction. They reflect the additional costs of using other fuels to meet energy demands which could more cheaply be met by coal *if* there were no constraint on total output in the years up to 2000. They also represent present (1976) values: to obtain values for 1990 (when construction costs will be incurred) these values should be doubled.

The 1978 Green Paper indicated that to achieve the target of 170m. tonnes would require the creation of an additional 4m. tonnes capacity per year at a cost of some £400m. per year, or £100 per tonne (p. 28). Assuming that this cost is roughly comparable to the capacity costs embodied in the present model, the question now posed is whether it would cost more than £166 per tonne to increase available capacity in the year 2000 still further (from 170m. to 171m. tonnes). If the Green Paper appraisal is valid, it does not seem at all implausible that efforts to exceed the 170m. target would be worthwhile, but on the other hand it should be recalled that some critics have in fact doubted whether the Green Paper target of 170m. is even attainable.

The final constraint limits new nuclear capacity in the year 2000 to a maximum of 35 GW, as suggested in the Green Paper. But at the same time it was acknowledged that 'a larger nuclear programme would not necessarily be ruled out in industrial terms, if in the light of experience it became clear that such a programme was needed and publicly acceptable' (p. 55). Does the BEM suggest that the 35 GW constraint will be binding and, if so, how severe a constraint is it?

The constraint is indeed binding (i.e. the solution involves new nuclear capacity equal to 35 GW in the year 2000), and its shadow price is £208m. per GW (£6.59m. per PJ). The Green Paper assumed that nuclear stations of size 1.25 GW would be built during the 1980s. Their capital cost would be of the order of £512m. each (using the BEM assumptions in Table 5.2). Thus, if the constraint were relaxed to allow an additional 1.25 GW nuclear station in the year 2000, the reduction in the (present value of the) UK energy bill (net of the capital and operating costs) would be about £260m. ($= 1.25 \times £208m.$), which is about half the capital cost of such a nuclear station. It would, in fact, be worth one third *more* than the present value of the cost of a nuclear station installed in the year 2000 (£512m. $- (1.05)^{20} = £193m.$). In other words, if the additional nuclear station were 'publicly acceptable', it would be worth paying over twice the normal price to get it installed by the year 2000.

References

Department of Energy (1977), *Coal and Nuclear Power Station Costs*, UK Energy Commission Paper No. 6, London, 1977.

Department of Energy (1978a), *Energy Policy: A Consultative Document*, Cmnd 7101, HMSO, London, 1978.

Department of Energy (1978b), *Energy Forecasts: A Note by the Department of Energy*, UK Energy Commission Paper No. 5, London, 1978.

Pearce, D. W. and Jones, P. (1980), 'Nuclear power and UK energy policy', *International Journal of Environmental Studies*, vol. 15, pp. 271–278.

Pearce, D. W., Edwards, L. and Beuret, G. (1979), *Decision-making for Energy Futures: A Case Study of the Windscale Inquiry*, Macmillan, London.

Robinson, C. and Marshall, E. (1981), *What Future for British Coal?* Hobart Paper, No. 89, Institute of Economic Affairs, London.

6

Base Case Sensitivity Analyses

6.1 Introduction

The purpose of this chapter is to test the robustness of the energy policy implied by the Base Case BEM solution set out in the previous chapter. As noted earlier, there is considerable uncertainty about a number of crucial assumptions. This chapter focuses mainly on those relating to oil and gas. Sensitivity analyses evaluate the effects on energy production and trade of the following variations in data assumptions:

(a) higher and lower levels of UK oil and gas reserves;
(b) world oil and gas prices rising at slower and faster rates up to the year 2000;
(c) world oil and gas prices rising after the year 2000;
(d) terminal values on domestic oil, gas and coal reserves;
(e) higher and lower discount rates.

In addition to the above, there are a number of other assumptions which need to be examined by sensitivity analyses. Different assumptions concerning the costs of producing nuclear energy and extracting coal, and the possibility of importing coal, are examined in Chapters 7 and 9.

There is not space to include here all of the seventy or so graphs that could be presented (six per case times twelve cases analysed). In most cases the main differences from the Base Case are briefly noted, and graphs are provided to illustrate the more dramatic differences from Base Case policy.

6.2 Oil Reserves

In the Base Case, the total UK crude oil recoverable reserves are assumed to be 150,000 PJ (about 3,345m. tonnes). As noted in Chapter 4, this figure is approximately the mid-point of the latest range of official estimates of UK oil reserves on the Continental Shelf (2,300–4,300m. tonnes) but a little lower than the oil reserves of 3,500m. tonnes assumed for the Department of Energy (1978b) projections. The width of the range is an indication of the uncertainty about the reserves. The actual UK recoverable reserves may turn out to be substantially higher because (1) technological advances such as floating platforms can reduce the costs of exploration and extraction in much deeper waters,

(2) substantial on-shore discoveries may be made and (3) oil reserves may have been underestimated owing to the natural conservatism of the oil industry. A further consideration is the international price of oil, since a higher price will make it worthwhile to look for oil which is more expensive to extract and to develop more sophisticated recovery techniques. By the same token, however, the failure to make technical advances, a lack of on-shore discoveries and a falling world price of oil would lead to lower recoverable reserves. We explore in turn the effects of these two possibilities.

The *High* oil reserves estimate adopted for the sensitivity analysis is double the Base Case reserve assumption, that is, 300,000 PJ (about 6,700m. tonnes). This figure is well above the high end of the official reserve estimates and above most other independent estimates. It is based on estimates made by Odell and Rosing (1976), the leading critics of the oil companies' conservatism in estimating oil reserves. The *Low* oil reserves estimate adopted is 120,000 PJ (about 2,700m. tonnes). This is less than 400m. tonnes above the sum of proven, probable and possible recoverable reserves, as estimated in Department of Energy (1980), in fields currently in production, under development, or in which significant discoveries have not yet been fully appraised. The pessimistic assumption therefore is that recoverable reserves discovered from the current substantial exploration programme (including on-shore reserves) will be merely 400m. tonnes, compared with the Department of Energy's estimated upper limit on new discoveries on the UK continental shelf of 1,800m. tonnes.

(a) Higher Oil Reserves
The main effects of higher oil reserves are as follows (see Figures 6.1 and 6.2).

1. More domestic oil is extracted, and at a faster rate. Extraction rises to a peak of 181m. tonnes in 1990 (compared to 135m. tonnes in 1985) and falls more slowly to 49m. tonnes (compared to 8m. tonnes) by the end of the programme period.
2. Exports of crude oil and oil products are much greater. They rise to a peak of 89m. tonnes in 1990 (compared to 44m. tonnes in 1985) and decline more slowly.
3. Oil imports are resumed fifteen years later (in 2010 compared to 1995) and rise to a lower level by the end of the programme period (83m. tonnes compared to 129m. tonnes).
4. Synthetic oil is manufactured at a lower but more consistent rate: a maximum of 11m. tonnes compared to 15.7m. tonnes.
5. The effects on oil refined and oil used in electricity generation are negligible.
6. The lower production of synthetic oil in 2005 means that less coal is required, and the expensive tranche IV coal is not mined in that period. This in turn makes it profitable to use the cheaper coal which is now available to increase production of synthetic gas by about 25 per cent in 2005 alone; gas imports are reduced correspondingly.

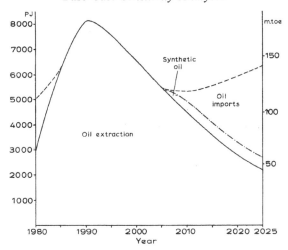

Figure 6.1   *Sources of oil (high oil reserves)*

7. In other respects the effects on other fuel industries are negligible.
8. The total energy bill is greatly reduced, from £214b. to £162b. present value, that is, by about 24 per cent. This is an average saving of £15.60 per additional tonne of oil reserves. That may seem quite small compared to current oil prices of the order of £100 per tonne, but such a comparison would be misleading. The figure of £15.60 is not the *gross* value of the oil reserves but the *net* value after deduct-

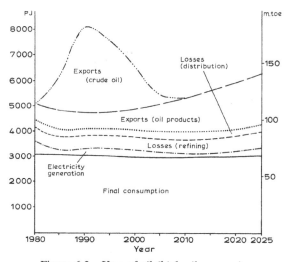

Figure 6.2   *Uses of oil (high oil reserves)*

ing costs of extraction, refining and distribution. In addition, it is expressed in 1977 prices (at which time the price of oil was around £45 per tonne) and is furthermore the present value (discounted at 5 per cent) of a saving accruing over fifty years. It is, therefore, a substantial saving.

(b)   Lower Oil Reserves
The effects of lower reserves can be summarised even more briefly: not surprisingly, the effects are essentially the opposite of those for higher reserves.

1. Less domestic oil is extracted, extraction rises to 108m. tonnes by 1985, about 20 per cent lower than in the Base Case and about 13 per cent lower than in the Department of Energy (1978b) projections. Thereafter it is about two-thirds of the Base Case level.
2. There is no 1985 peak in oil exports, and during the 1980s as a whole oil exports are down to 40 per cent of the Base Case level.
3. Oil imports are resumed five years earlier and are considerably higher, especially in the 1990s.
4. In other respects energy policy does not differ significantly from the Base Case.
5. The total energy bill is increased to £230b. present value, that is, by about 7 per cent above the Base Case. Each tonne of oil reserves 'removed' thus has an average present value of £23.10. The proportionate effect on total cost is actually greater than when reserves are doubled: here total cost increases by 7 per cent in response to a 20 per cent cut in reserves (elasticity of $7/20 = 0.35$) whereas a 100 per cent increase in reserves yielded a 24 per cent reduction in cost (elasticity of $24/100 = 0.24$). This is in fact to be expected, since the marginal value of reserves decreases as the size of total reserves increases.

6.3   Gas Reserves

In the Base Case, total UK gas reserves are assumed to be 53 trillion cubic feet (approximately 57,600 PJ). This is the central estimate of gas reserves in the 1978 Brown Book, and in subsequent years the central estimate has remained more or less the same. However, there is still considerable uncertainty about this figure. Table 2 in the 1980 Brown Book suggests that the ultimately recoverable reserves of natural gas on the UK Continental Shelf (including those already recovered) may lie within the range 39 to 85 tcf. In its energy projections made for the Green Paper (1978), the Department of Energy uses a central reserve estimate of 55 tcf remaining. This is close to our Base Case assumption.

In conducting our sensitivity analysis, we have taken as a *high* estimate of reserves the figure of 77 tcf. This is based on an estimate made by George (1974) using the ratio of structures already tested to structures remaining to be tested. The *low* estimate of reserves is the figure of

35 tcf which is the sum of proven, probable and possible reserves in present discoveries. We examine the two cases in turn.

(a) Higher Gas Reserves
Under this assumption, energy policy has the following main features compared to the Base Case.

1. Domestic gas extraction is significantly higher from 1990 onwards (Figure 6.3). The level of peak production is not significantly higher, but it continues for about fifteen years, and from 2010 onwards is more than double the Base Case rate. Despite this, almost 30 per cent of total gas reserves remain in the ground in 2025, compared to 10 per cent in the Base Case. In Department of Energy (1978b) energy projections, the gas supply profile for high gas reserves (75 tcf. remaining, i.e. slightly below our high reserves assumption) shows a broadly similar pattern to our high reserves case in that the peak level is not raised substantially above the Base Case. Instead, more gas is extracted in later years and consequently less substitute natural gas is required later. Peak gas extraction in the Department of Energy high gas and reserves projection is 20 per cent higher than in our high reserves case, partly because more gas is used for electricity production and partly because the Department of Energy projections assume that the additional gas will substitute for oil (a residual fuel which meets demand not met by the other fuels).
2. Gas imports are reduced to a negligible level: only 1.8b. therms in 2000 and none in other periods, compared to a peak of 7.3b. therms in 2000 and imports spread over a twenty-year period.
3. Production of synthetic gas is also reduced: to two-thirds the base level in 2010, 85 per cent in 2025. The net effect is that synthetic fuel accounts for 75 per cent rather than 92 per cent of domestic gas consumption, with the balance of 25 per cent rather than 8 per cent being met by domestic production.
4. Substantially less coal is required to produce synthetic gas, but the pattern of total coal production is essentially unaltered: identical up to 2000, slightly lower from 2000 to 2015, slightly higher thereafter. The coal hitherto used to produce synthetic gas is diverted to produce synthetic oil instead.

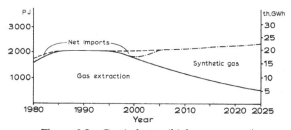

Figure 6.3   *Gas industry (high gas reserves)*

5. The production of synthetic oil is about half as high again as in the Base Case. Oil imports are correspondingly reduced. Both these effects are felt after the turn of the century.
6. Electricity production from coal is slightly increased, reflecting the lower cost of coal at the margin, and electricity production from oil is slightly reduced. Nuclear energy is virtually unaffected.
7. The total energy bill is reduced from £214 to £203.5b. present value, a reduction of about 5 per cent. Each of the additional 24 tcf is worth an average of £590m. (about 59p per thousand cubic feet or 5.8p per therm).

(b)   Lower Gas Reserves
Once again, the effects are in the opposite direction, and are less severe in magnitude.

1. Gas extraction is noticeably lower. The 1985 peak is about 10 per cent lower, at the turn of the century extraction is less than half the Base Case rate, and by 2025 it is about 30 per cent of it.
2. The gap between gas consumption and domestic production is met mainly by a vast increase in imports of gas over a thirty-year period. At their peak in the year 2000, imports are nearly double their Base Case level.
3. After the turn of the century, synthetic gas gradually replaces imports. Production is about 10 per cent higher than in the Base Case. By 2025, extraction of natural gas accounts for only 2 per cent of consumption (compared to 8 per cent).
4. Total coal extraction is virtually unaffected, but coal is switched from the production of synthetic oil to synthetic gas. Oil imports are increased to compensate. The electricity industry is scarcely affected.
5. The total energy bill is 6.7 per cent higher at £228.5b. present value. This values the last 24 tcf at an average of £650m. per tcf (65p per thousand cubic feet or about 6.4p per therm).

6.4   World Oil and Gas Prices

International oil and gas prices have been assumed to rise by 3 per cent per year up to the end of the century, by which time they would be double their 1977 levels, and to remain constant after the year 2000. (All calculations are in real terms.) Preliminary runs of the model showed that if the 3 per cent rise in the international prices of oil and gas were continued throughout the programme period, it would be worthwhile for the UK to convert domestic coal into synthetic gas and oil and export these fuels. In practice, this would be unlikely, since there are other countries (notably Australia and the USA) which can mine coal on a larger scale at a much lower cost than the UK can. These low-cost coal producers could presumably produce synthetic gas and oil for export at a lower price than the UK or, more probably, could export the coal for conversion into synthetic oil and gas by the importing countries themselves. It follows that competition from synthetic fuels is likely to keep down the rises in the prices of oil and gas once they reach levels comparable with the costs of producing synthetic fuels. For the same reason, it is unlikely that the UK will be a substantial exporter of synthetic fuels. Our assumption that international prices remain constant after the year 2000 is based on this argument.

In the sensitivity analysis carried out in this section, two alternative assumptions are examined in turn. The 'optimistic' assumption is that world oil and gas prices will rise at the lower rate of 1.5 per cent per annum to the year 2000. At this point they will be 41 per cent higher than in 1977, or 28 per cent below the Base Case level for the year 2000. The 'pessimistic' assumption is that world oil and gas prices will rise at the higher rate of 5 per cent per annum to the year 2000, by which time they will be just over three times the 1977 level, or 58 per cent above the Base Case level for 2000. In both cases, constant prices are assumed from 2000 onwards, and all calculations are in real terms.

(a) Low Increase in World Prices

1. Domestic oil extraction is completely unchanged (Figure 6.6). There is no production at all of synthetic oil. The deficiency is made up by increased imports of oil (up about 15 per cent from 2000 to 2020) and decreased exports (down about 16 per cent over the same period) (Figure 6.7). A rough calculation suggests that, in response to the 28 per cent oil price decrease after 2000, the own-price elasticity of demand for imported oil is about -0.54 and the own-price elasticity of supply of exported oil and oil products is about 0.57. Fifty per cent more oil is allocated to electricity production, although this accounts for less than one-tenth of total oil refined.
2. Similarly, the pattern of gas extraction is unaffected, there is no production of synthetic gas, and imports of gas are increased to compensate (Figure 6.8).
3. Since there is no production of synthetic fuel, coal extraction is substantially reduced throughout the programme period (Figure 6.4). In

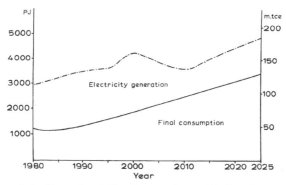

Figure 6.4 *Uses of coal (low increase in world oil and gas prices)*

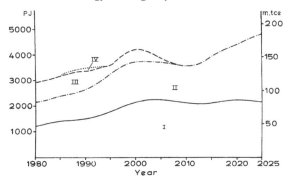

Figure 6.5   *Coal extraction by tranches (low increase in world oil and gas prices)*

the year 2000, total extraction is below the limit set by the constraint
on expansion of capacity. No tranche IV coal is extracted after 1990,
and no tranche III coal is extracted after 2005 (Figure 6.5). Only 2
per cent of available tranche IV coal and 25 per cent of available
tranche III coal are extracted within the programme period, compared to 53 per cent and 100 per cent, respectively, in the Base Case.
There is, however, a very substantial increase in the amount of coal
used for electricity generation after the turn of the century (up by 11
per cent in 2005, nearly double in 2010, over four times as high in
2015 and nearly seven times as high in 2025).
4. The general policy of a switch from oil and coal to nuclear energy as
   a source of electricity is continued, but the availability of cheaper oil
   and coal reduce the speed and extent of the changeover. Thus, in the
   year 2010 the proportions of nuclear, coal and oil change from 88,

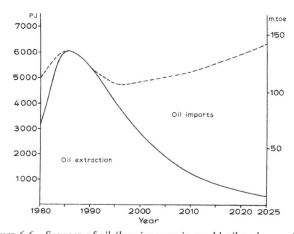

Figure 6.6   *Sources of oil (low increase in world oil and gas prices)*

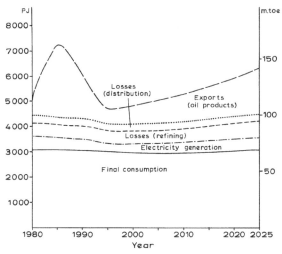

Figure 6.7   *Uses of oil (low increase in world oil and gas prices)*

10 and 2 per cent, respectively (in the Base Case), to 77, 17 and 6 per cent.

5. The total energy bill is 6.3 per cent lower at £201b. present value.

(b)   Higher Increase in World Prices

1. The rate of extraction of domestic oil reserves is slowed down. The 1985 peak rate is reduced from 135m. tonnes to 108m. tonnes but extraction is increased from 1995 onwards. As a consequence, exports of oil are substantially reduced during the 1980s (to about half the previous level), but are about 6 per cent higher thereafter. The production of synthetic oil is increased about two and a half times during the second decade of the next century (although it is reduced in the last period, when the exhaustion of tranche IV coal makes it too expensive to produce). The combined effect of higher

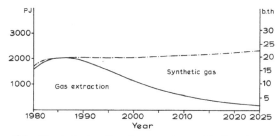

Figure 6.8   *Gas industry (low increase in world oil and gas prices)*

extraction and higher production of synthetic oil makes it possible to reduce imports by about 24 per cent from 1995 to 2020.

2. We may thus calculate that, in response to the 58 per cent price increase after the turn of the century, the own-price elasticity of demand for imported oil is about -0.41 and the own-price elasticity of supply of exported oil and oil products is about 0.11. Comparing these figures with those for the price decrease suggests that oil imports respond in roughly the same way to a price increase or decrease, whereas it is much easier to cut back oil exports when world price falls than to expand them when world price rises.

3. The pattern of gas extraction is unaffected. Production of synthetic gas is 57 per cent higher, which allows gas imports to cease one year earlier, and gas is exported on a substantial scale from 2010 onwards. (As noted above, it may be unrealistic to assume that the UK can profitably export gas, which in turn implies that it may be unrealistic to assume an annual increase in world gas prices of 5 per cent up to the year 2000.)

4. The increase in production of synthetic oil and gas require substantially greater production of coal after the turn of the century. All reserves of tranches I to IV are exhausted and tranche V is utilised from 2005 onwards.

5. The electricity industry is less affected than in the case of lower world price increases. After 1990 some of the electricity from oil is replaced by nuclear and (to a small extent in the last three periods) by coal.

6. The total UK energy bill is 6.7 per cent higher at £229b. present value.

6.5 Optimistic and Pessimistic Cases

We have so far examined separately the effects of different sizes of domestic resources of oil and gas and different levels of world prices of these fuels. However, these cases are not unrelated. If Britain discovers greater exploitable reserves, it is likely that other countries will do so too, and the world price is likely to be lower. Conversely, lack of success for Britain may well be associated with higher world prices. It is therefore appropriate to consider the implications of an 'optimistic' scenario (with oil and gas reserves at the High levels and world prices rising at the Low rate discussed in Sections 6.2–6.4), and a 'pessimistic' scenario (assuming Low oil and gas reserves and world prices rising at the High rate).

There is no need to describe the effects of this scenario in detail, since they correspond closely to particular aspects of the scenarios already discussed. A few notes will suffice.

(a) Optimistic Scenario

1. The oil industry behaves essentially as it does with High oil reserves, except that no synthetic oil is produced and slightly more oil is used

to generate electricity (as with Low world prices), and oil imports are slightly higher in 2025 (not substantially higher as with Low world prices).
2. The gas industry also behaves as it does with High gas reserves, except that gas is imported instead of produced synthetically (as with Low world prices, although imports do not need to be so high).
3. The electricity and coal industries behave essentially as with Low world prices, except that the small volume of tranche IV coal is eliminated.
4. Shadow prices are low and more or less constant throughout, as with Low world prices.
5. The total energy bill falls by just over a quarter to £158b. Note that this is only £4b. less than with High oil reserves alone.

(b) Pessimistic Scenario
The total energy bill rises by over 20 per cent to £260.31b. In contrast to the optimistic case, this is substantially higher than the energy bill associated with any single variation. In fact, the increase is almost exactly equal to the *sum* of the cost increases associated with Low oil reserves, Low gas reserves and High world price scenarios taken separately.

6.6   Interim Conclusions

At this stage, a summary of the results so far may be helpful. The sensitivity analyses described above yield the following broad conclusions and policy implications.

1. Doubling the available UK oil reserves (from 3345m. to nearly 6700m. tonnes) has considerable effect on the oil industry (faster and greater extraction, higher exports, lower imports and production of synthetic oil), but negligible effects on other industries. There is a very significant (24 per cent) reduction in the total energy bill. Reducing oil reserves has opposite effects on the oil industry.
2. Increasing available UK gas reserves by nearly 50 per cent has an analogous effect on the gas industry (prolonged extraction at peak rate yet leaving almost 30 per cent in place in 2025, negligible imports, reduced production of synthetic gas) and an indirect effect on the oil industry (increased production of synthetic oil, using coal no longer required for synthetic gas, hence a reduction in oil imports), but negligible effect on electricity and coal. The total energy bill is reduced by only 5 per cent. Reducing gas reserves has opposite effects.
3. Halving the rate of increase in world oil and gas prices (1.5 per cent per annum until 2000 instead of 3 per cent) does not affect oil and gas extraction, but synthetic production of these fuels is cancelled and replaced by higher imports. Coal production is very much lower, and the rate at which nuclear substitutes for coal and oil in electricity

Table 6.1 *Effects of Sensitivity Analyses on Total Energy Bill*

Assumption (Base Case value)	Scenario (Details)	NPV Cost (£b.) (% Base Case)	Scenario (Details)	NPV Cost (£b.) (% Base Case)
UK oil reserves (150 b. GJ)	High (300 b. GJ)	162.20 (75.5%)	Low (120 b. GJ)	229.70 (107.2%)
UK gas reserves (53 tcf)	High (77 tcf)	202.20 (94.5%)	Low (35 tcf)	228.50 (106.7%)
Increase in world prices of oil and gas to 2000 (3%)	Low (1.5%)	200.70 (93.7%)	High (5%)	228.60 (106.7%)
Combine above three items	Optimistic	158.00 (73.7%)	Pessimistic	260.00 (121.4%)

Note: Base Case NPV is £214.25 b.

generation is somewhat reduced. The energy bill is only slightly (6 per cent) lower.

4. A higher rate of increase in world prices (5 per cent) delays the extraction of oil but leaves gas extraction unaffected. Production of synthetic fuels is much higher in order to replace imports, and oil and gas exports are increased. Coal production is much increased, exhausting tranches I–IV and necessitating use of tranche V after 2005. The energy bill is slightly (6.7 per cent) higher.

5. An optimistic scenario (higher oil and gas reserves and lower increase in world prices) yields a combined policy of faster extraction of oil and gas plus imports instead of no synthetic fuels, slower shift from coal and oil to nuclear, and much reduced coal production. The energy bill is only slightly lower than with High oil reserves alone.

6. A pessimistic scenario (low oil and gas reserves and higher increase in world prices) yields a combined policy of low extraction of oil and gas, high and increasing imports of oil, high gas imports gradually replaced by high synthetic gas with some exports in 2015, large-scale coal production exhausting tranches I–IV and necessitating V. The energy bill is increased by the *sum* of the increases generated by each variation taken separately (i.e. about 20 per cent).

The minimum cost energy policy is thus quite robust with respect to the levels of UK oil and gas reserves but more sensitive with respect to rate of increase of world prices of these fuels. The total energy bill, on the other hand, is more sensitive to UK reserves than to world prices (Table 6.1). Finally, it is worth noting that the effects of any change in assumptions are generally not felt until around the turn of the century.

6.7 Rising World Prices after 2000

The Base Case assumes that world oil and gas prices rise at 3 per cent per annum up to the turn of the century, after which time they remain

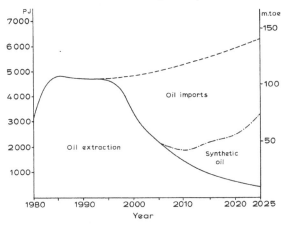

Figure 6.9   *Sources of oil (rising oil and gas prices after 2000)*

constant. This reflects the assumption that oil and gas will gradually be supplied synthetically (from coal) as the reserves of natural oil and gas are exhausted. It is arguable, however, that the ever increasing demand for synthetic fuels will drive up the world price of coal, which will in turn raise the world prices of oil and gas. To explore this possibility, we modify the Base Case by assuming that world prices of oil and gas continue to rise after the year 2000, but at the slower rates of 2 per cent and 1 per cent per annum, respectively. The assumption of no coal imports is retained for the present.

The most immediate and dramatic effect is that oil extraction is severely reduced over the first fifteen years (Figure 6.9). Instead of a sharp peak of 134m. tonnes in 1985, there is a plateau of about 106m. tonnes for the decade from 1985 to 1995. As a result of this initial conservation, domestic oil extraction is about 17 per cent higher over the remainder of the programme period. Less oil is used to generate electricity. The production of synthetic oil is delayed by five years, but then increases rapidly to account for nearly half of oil consumption by 2025. These changes make it possible to lower oil imports significantly from 2015 onwards.

Significant changes are necessitated in other fuel industries. There is a great increase in coal extraction from 2010 onwards, rising to a peak of 356m. tonnes by 2025 (Figure 6.10). This is achieved partly by lowering extraction from the cheaper pits over the first decade of the century, and partly by utilising tranche IV pits on a larger scale after 2015. Imports of gas are actually increased in later periods, with a corresponding reduction in synthetic gas: the purpose of this is presumably to reduce the demands on the coal industry. In effect, gas imports are substituted for oil imports (or, indeed, for coal imports which are not permitted).

The total energy bill is increased by £3.72b. present value (about 1.7 per cent). Compared to the effects of changing reserves examined

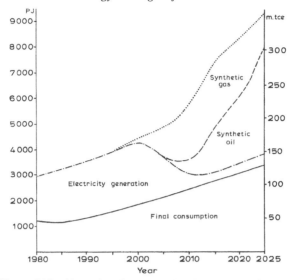

Figure 6.10   *Uses of coal (rising oil and gas prices after 2000)*

earlier, this is a negligible increase. What is much more important, however, is that one policy change – the reduction in oil extraction – needs to be implemented immediately if the increase in the total energy bill is to be kept to this level.

Since the optimal energy policy (particularly depletion policy) is clearly sensitive to the pattern of oil and gas prices after the year 2000, we shall carry out this sensitivity analysis in several different contexts in the next few chapters.

6.8   Terminal Values for Fuel Reserves

In the Base Case, capital equipment in place at the end of the fifty-year programme period is valued according to the length of its remaining useful life, but no value is attached to domestic fuel reserves remaining in the ground. Many people would argue that a positive value ought to be attached to such reserves. However, it is by no means clear what that value should be. The value of fuel reserves depends upon technological developments and energy requirements more than 50 years ahead, which are necessarily extremely uncertain, and also based upon ethical judgements about the weight to be attached to the welfare of future generations.

In order to obtain some rough idea whether this question is important, we explored the effects of valuing terminal reserves of coal, oil and gas at their world prices less domestic extraction cost. (Where these figures were negative, zero value was attached.) Using Base Case data (i.e. assuming no rise in world fuel prices after the year 2000), these values are as follows: coal £29.80 per tonne (tranche I), £26.60 (tranche II), £24.00 (tranche III), £16.90 (tranche IV), £0 (tranche V); oil £68.50 per tonne and gas £0.24 per therm. Of course, it is the present value of these prices which enters the objective function, with a term being subtracted of the form

$$\sum_j TV_j \left[R_j^0 - \sum_{t=1}^{T} X_{jt} \right]$$

where recall R_j^0 is the total reserves of fuel j, X_{jt} is the amount of reserves extracted in period t, and TV_j is defined as the terminal value of fuel j at the end of period T (where $T = 10$ in this run).

The main effect of introducing these terminal values is that the rate of domestic oil extraction is severely slowed down, to almost exactly the same pattern as in the previous section (Figure 6.11). This means that oil is conserved in the first fifteen years, but in fact total extraction over the whole fifty-year programme period is only 4 per cent lower than in the Base Case. Production of synthetic oil is increased by about 60 per cent, and oil imports are reduced. Less oil is used in electricity generation in the final decade, although slightly more is used in the 1980s. In order to meet the increased production of synthetic oil, coal extraction is increased by nearly 20 per cent mainly in the last two decades (Figure 6.12). However, the gas and nuclear industries are virtually unaffected.

Terminal values of the magnitude explored here thus do have an effect on energy policy, and this effect is by no means immediately obvious. In broad terms, there is more conservation of domestic oil within the fifty-year horizon, leading to increased output of coal and

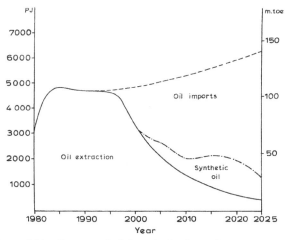

Figure 6.11 *Sources of oil (terminal values of reserves included)*

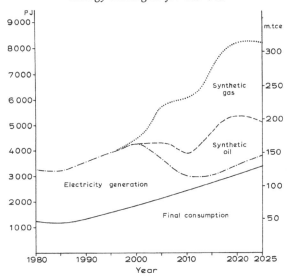

Figure 6.12   *Uses of coal (terminal values of reserves included)*

synthetic oil, but there is no large-scale hoarding of fossil reserves to *beyond* the horizon. Energy policy does not need to be dramatically redesigned, but greater conservation of oil is called for as an immediate modification of present policy.

The model was rerun with both terminal values and rising oil and gas prices after the year 2000. The only additional effect of rising prices was to replace the increase in oil imports over the last fifteen years by increased production of synthetic oil. This was made possible by a reduction in synthetic gas and corresponding increase in gas imports. The relative price increase of oil over gas prices leads, in effect, to the substitution of gas imports for oil imports after 2010. Nothing else is changed.

6.9   The Discount Rate

The Base Case uses a discount rate of 5 per cent per annum (in real terms). This rate is commonly used in government project appraisals. For example, it is the required rate of return (RRR) prescribed by the White Paper *The Nationalised Industries* (Department of Trade and Industry, 1978). However, there are differences of opinion concerning the appropriate rate. Some would argue that discounting undervalues the preferences and interests of future generations, and that it would be preferable to weight benefits and costs equally, regardless of the time at which they are incurred. In effect, this is a zero discount rate. Others would argue that a much higher discount rate is appropriate, to reflect not merely the opportunity cost of (risk-free) capital, but also the risks and uncertainties implicit in long-term investments. Indeed, a standard defence for the popular 'payback period' is that benefits and costs occurring beyond the specified period are too uncertain to be worth considering at all.

To explore the effects of different assumptions, we here examine the policies implied by a zero discount rate and then an 8 per cent discount rate.

(a) Zero Discount Rate

As remarked above, a zero discount rate weights costs equally, regardless of the period in which they are incurred. But world oil and gas prices are assumed to rise at 3 per cent per annum until the turn of the century. Thus, a tonne of oil now is worth less in money terms than a tonne of oil later. More concretely, a saving in imports in the early periods is less valuable than the same saving in imports after the turn of the century. This provides the key to understanding the consequent change in energy policy. The aim is to defer maximum production of oil and gas until around the turn of the century so as to minimise imports thereafter, if necessary by increasing imports in the early periods. The result is a rather dramatic change in policy (Figures 6.13, 6.14).

1. No domestic oil is extracted until 2000! Extraction reaches a peak of 163m. tonnes in 2005; it declines quite rapidly, but is still at 31m. tonnes per annum in 2025. The demand for oil before the turn of the century is met by imports, necessarily on a large scale. Imports begin again in 2010, but never subsequently account for more than a

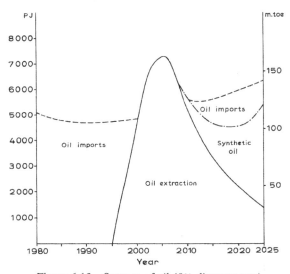

Figure 6.13   *Sources of oil (0% discount rate)*

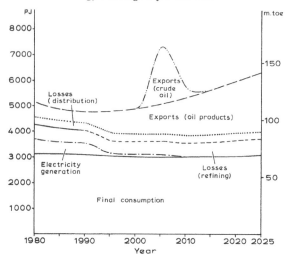

Figure 6.14   *Uses of oil (0% discount rate)*

quarter of total oil refined, since synthetic oil is built up rapidly to compensate for declining extraction. Synthetic production reaches nearly 89m. tonnes in 2025.

2. A similar response is observed in the gas industry. Extraction is deferred completely until 1990 and replaced by imports. Peak gas extraction is not reached until 2005, and the annual rate is still 4.6b. therms in 2025. Imports tail off by 2000, and extraction does not fall short of consumption requirements until 2005, when it is supplemented by synthetic gas. This is produced at a rapidly increasing rate, though not on quite the same scale as before. By 2025 synthetic gas accounts for three-quarters of requirements, compared to about 90 per cent in the Base Case.

3. Oil generation of electricity is virtually phased out by 2000, being replaced by coal-fired plants, but otherwise the electricity industry is unaffected.

4. The coal industry operates on a substantially lower scale for the first half of the programme period. Total extraction increases from 109m. tonnes in 1980 to only 164m. tonnes in 2010 (compared to 243m. tonnes). However, in order to cope with the synthetic fuel production, it then increases dramatically to 466m. tonnes in 2025 (compared to 269m. tonnes) – a threefold increase in fifteen years. All four tranches of coal are utilised reasonably evenly, and in fact all are completely exhausted by the end of the programme period.

(b)   Eight per cent Discount Rate

A higher discount rate provides a greater incentive to take benefits earlier and postpone costs. One would expect natural resources to be exploited more rapidly, with less concern for future consequences, and capital intensive projects to be delayed. As it happens, however, the 5 per cent discount rate provides sufficient incentive to extract oil and gas as fast as technically possible, so that a higher discount rate (at least, an 8 per cent rate) has no effect on these extraction patterns. The main changes are (i) that synthetic oil and gas do not replace imports to as great an extent in the last few periods – in fact, in the last period synthetic gas is about half the Base Case level – and (ii) that nuclear capacity (being more capital intensive) does not replace oil- and coal-fired equipment so rapidly in the generation of electricity – but even this change is very slight: nuclear still accounts for 86 per cent (as opposed to 88 per cent) of electricity generation in 2025.

To summarise, an 8 per cent (as opposed to 5 per cent) discount rate slows down the replacement of imports by synthetic fuels, and very slightly reduces the shift from coal-fired to nuclear plants, but the over-all effects are not large. In contrast, a zero discount rate leads to a drastic change in policy: complete postponement of oil and gas extraction for twenty years, meeting consumption entirely by imports for that period. The coal industry hardly grows at all until 2010, but then trebles in size by 2025 in order to produce synthetic oil on a large scale.

There is presumably some discount rate between zero and 5 per cent at which the drastic change in policy occurs. The critical rate is probably around 3 per cent, which is the rate at which world oil and gas prices are assumed to grow until the year 2000. It might be of interest to locate this critical rate more precisely, in so far as the real rate of return in the private sector is currently believed to be below 5 per cent. On the other hand, it is difficult to believe that such a low rate of return will continue to hold for very long (relative to the fifty-year time scale of the present model). The policy implications of a zero or low discount rate are of mainly academic interest rather than practical importance.

References

Department of Energy (1978a), *Energy Policy: A Consultative Document*, Cmnd 7101, HMSO, London.

Department of Energy (1978b), *Energy Forecasts*, Energy Commission Paper No. 5, London.

Department of Energy (1980), *Development of the Oil and Gas Resources of the UK*, HMSO, London. (Also 1978 and 1979 volumes.)

Department of Trade and Industry (1978), *The Nationalised Industries*, White Paper, Cmnd 7131, HMSO, London.

George, W. J. (1974), 'North Sea – recent activity in the British sector', paper presented at the *Financial Times Conference on Scandinavia and the North Sea*, Oslo, April.

Odell, P. R. and Rosing, K. E. (1976), *Optimal Development of the North Sea's Oil Fields*, Kogan Page, London.

7

International Trade Policy Considerations

7.1 Introduction

The model results discussed in the last two chapters describe the patterns of energy investment, production and trade that will achieve the objective of cost minimisation. But while cost is an important consideration, it is by no means the only consideration that influences public policy. Other relevant considerations include (1) the avoidance of disruptions in supply (as a result of international conflict, or domestic industrial disputes), (2) the effects on the balance of payments, (3) the employment effects of UK energy policy, (4) the conservation of non-renewable natural resources, (5) the preservation or enhancement of the environment, (6) the effects on health and safety, and (7) developing or keeping up with the 'state of the art' in science and technology (especially nuclear engineering).

In the present chapter we shall use the Birmingham Energy Model to trace out and evaluate in turn the effects of three specified policy measures related to the control of foreign trade, which are designed with a view to the first three considerations listed above (viz. security of supply, balance of payments and domestic employment). These policy measures are

(1) a restriction on the maximum net volume of imported oil (as a percentage of total oil processed in the UK),
(2) a restriction on the maximum balance of payments deficit on energy commodities, and
(3) the removal of present restrictions on coal imports into the UK.

The next two chapters (8 and 9) will explore the effects on the remaining four considerations (viz. resource conservation, the environment, safety and technological progress) of the conservationist and non-nuclear proposals of the 'soft energy' advocates. This separation of treatment is purely for convenience of exposition. It will soon become evident, for example, that the soft energy policy measures have important implications for imports and employment as well as for conservation and technical progress.

7.2 Concern for Security of Supply

To illustrate the considerations that affect public policy on energy, it will be useful to outline the growing concern for security of supply, and the various measures proposed to deal with it.

Until recently, the bulk of Europe's oil came from the Middle East. For several reasons this was thought to raise problems of security of supply: (1) other fuels are imperfect substitutes for oil, and renewable sources of energy such as hydroelectricity are not available in Britain in great quantities; (2) oil imports are militarily and politically insecure, and the growing government participation in the oil industry increases the likelihood of supply disruptions for political reasons; (3) the formation of OPEC has increased the monopoly power of oil producers and the likelihood of this power being exercised; (4) the USSR possesses extensive oil reserves of its own, and is thought to have imperialist objectives in the Middle East.

As early as 1965, potential risk to the security of energy supplies and an increasing cost to the balance of payments were seen to be the most serious problems associated with an increasing dependence on oil (Ministry of Fuel and Power, 1965). The 1967 White Paper (Ministry of Fuel and Power, 1967) made explicit reference to efficient resource allocation but also included security of supply, balance of payments and social and human consequences (presumably referring to the problem of falling coal consumption and employment). Some trade-offs between minimising the cost of meeting specified levels of energy demand and other policy objectives were envisaged. As early as 1968 the EEC Commission suggested that security of the oil supply was of paramount importance (EEC Commission, 1968), and proposed that member states should maintain stocks of oil sufficient for sixty-five days supply. A more comprehensive approach to EEC Energy Policy has been developed since then.

Following the Arab–Israeli war of 1973 there was a fundamental change in the world energy situation which gave particular emphasis to the dangers of economic overdependence on the Middle Eastern oil supply. Up to 1973 relatively cheap oil was in adequate supply, whereas coal was apparently in decline, owing to its cost disadvantage as well as the environmental consequences attached to its continued use. The future was perceived in terms of cheap and apparently environmentally clean nuclear power. The proximate cause for change was the Sinai war of 1973–4 which, together with the subsequent embargoes and supply disruptions, gave the OPEC producers the opportunity to control the oil supply, and to enforce price increases in the supply of crude oil. (However, see Robinson and Morgan, 1978, Ch. 2 and Odell (1981) for a discussion of the economic factors underlying the OPEC producers' ability to raise prices, control production and increase the benefit to them from the exploitation of oil, an exhaustible resource.) In addition it was becoming clear that, despite the inherent environmental disadvantages of buring coal, the public attitude towards the risks of nuclear power, combined with the growing international concern about nuclear weapon proliferation, was causing delays in the nuclear power programme throughout the Western Alliance. These delays were exacerbated by unforeseen and widespread construction and technological problems which incidentally do not appear to have been finally resolved (Tombs, 1980).

One result of this fundamental change in the perception of the energy future was a rapid development of international co-operation within institutions such as the EEC and the OECD whose objective was to identify, implement and monitor member states' energy programmes within the constraints of internationally agreed objectives.

Generally, international objectives since 1974 have shown concern for the problems arising out of dependence on imported oil. The basic idea has been to treat oil (particularly OPEC oil) as a balancing source of energy required to make up the 'energy gap'. To this end official objectives included the reduction of oil imports in physical terms, and the adoption of conservation measures in order to limit the expansion of energy demand. More specifically, there were international obligations to (1) restrict the use of oil and gas in electricity generation, (2) restrict the conversion of existing power stations to oil burning capacities, (3) maintain oil stocks at ninety days supply, and (4) share available oil supplies in the event of an emergency. Recently, rather more comprehensive oil sharing arrangements have been proposed (OECD, 1980, p. 25).

The main conservation measures recently recommended for EEC members (EEC Commission, 1980) relate to the utilisation of waste heat produced in electricity generation, the insulation of buildings and automobile efficiency. There are also pressures to increase conventional energy supply. These mainly take the form of recommending the advancement of coal extraction and nuclear power programmes, and the rapid advancement of the programme of exploitation and exploration for oil and gas on the UK Continental Shelf. Finally, a programme of investment in alternative energy is recommended.

Over the period 1974–8 the reduction in economic growth rates, a succession of mild winters, the imminence of North Sea oil, and an emerging surplus of oil at OPEC controlled prices, all combined to reduce both the demand for oil imports and the perceived importance of achieving the specified international objectives. However, the reduction in the level of Iranian oil production following the downfall of the Shah, and the outbreak of war between Iran and Iraq in 1980, once again highlighted the implications of insecurity of Middle East oil supplies.

Since the UK is relatively well endowed with indigenous oil and gas reserves, the constraints imposed by international energy policy agreements can be easily met without substantial policy adjustments. (Tzoannos *et al.*, 1979 have used the BEM to demonstrate this point.) Furthermore, a degree of conservation is being enforced by the current economic depression. Nevertheless the UK does have an international obligation to expand its coal and nuclear programmes, with the latter being the more favoured long-term option, and to expand the rate of development of North Sea oil reserves. There is also a suggestion that coal imports and the use of coal should be increased (at the expense of environmental standards, if necessary) (OECD 1980, p. 18).

The general problem of supply disruption may be associated with internal as well as external events. For example, there is the threat of the politico-economic power of coal miners in primary energy production, of power workers in secondary energy production, and of oil road tanker drivers in energy supply distribution. The downfall of Mr Heath's government has been associated with the miners' strike of 1974, and the power of oil tanker drivers to generate economic disruption was made clear during the severe winter of 1978/9. These experiences are not unique to the UK. The Irish Republic experienced the effects of a 'petrol famine' following the overthrow of the Shah's regime in Iran (external disruption) and the road tanker drivers' strike in September–October 1980 (internal disruption). Such petrol famines may cause severe public order problems, as is well illustrated by recent experience in Continental Europe and in the USA.

There are, of course, certain costs as well as benefits attached to reducing dependency on imported oil. If more expensive domestic substitutes are used, or even if conservation measures are adopted, then the costs of industrial production may rise. A country which is rapidly reducing its dependency on relatively cheap imported oil will be at a competitive disadvantage compared to countries which proceed more slowly – hence the concern of the Western European countries, expressed forcibly at the international summit meeting in Tokyo in 1979, at the failure of the USA and Japan to make a satisfactory contribution to the implementation of energy conservation measures since 1974. Or, to take another example, the expansion of domestic coal extraction to replace oil imports has the secondary effect of increasing the politico-economic power of the National Union of Mineworkers. As Robinson and Marshall (1981, p. 83) point out, 'Indigenous supplies are also subject to interruption, and it is by no means clear that British coal is a more secure source of fuel than imports'. There is thus a trade-off between the dangers of external and internal disruption.

7.3 Oil Import Dependency Constraints

Recall from Chapter 5 that the BEM cost-minimising solution for the Base Case involves net exports of oil for the period 1980–95 but an ever increasing dependence on imported oil thereafter. As will be shown shortly, imports accounted for nearly 43 per cent of oil refined at the turn of the century, and over 90 per cent by 2025. To reduce Britain's vulnerability to external supply disruption, it has often been suggested that oil imports should be limited, leading to the substitution of other fuels for oil (e.g. in electricity generation), an increase in the production of natural or of synthetic oil, and possibly a decrease in the domestic final consumption of oil. In this section we explore the effects of imposing constraints on oil imports, calculating the least-cost methods of adapting to such constraints and assessing the net cost to the economy.

The oil import constraints employed here state that, for each five-year period during the fifty-year horizon of the BEM, the average net imports of crude oil (i.e. gross imports less exports) must not exceed 40 per cent of the total volume of crude oil passing through UK refineries. The model was in fact run several times, with different percentages of maximum oil import dependency, and the 40 per cent level proved to be the lowest level feasible throughout the programme period.

Trade in oil products (as opposed to crude oil) is not included in these constraints, since it is largely intra-European rather than with the Middle East, but synthetic oil produced from coal in included in the total amount of crude oil going into domestic refineries.

The mathematical form of the constraint is:

$$M_{2t} \leqslant 0.4 \, (1.11 \, X_{15,t}) \qquad \text{for all } t,$$

where M_{2t} represents imports of oil in time period t, and $X_{15,t}$ represents the total amount of oil entering the UK refining process. The coefficient 0.4 represents the 40 per cent specified limit on net import dependency. The coefficient 1.11 reflects the fact that, owing to refinery consumption and distribution losses, a crude oil supply of approximately 1.11 tonnes of oil is required for each tonne of refined output.

In all other respects the model is as described for the Base Case. Thus, the model calculates the least costly way of adapting to the oil import constraints.

In the cost-minimisation model which we have examined so far, the final demands for each fuel are assumed to be fixed. The effects of oil import constraints (or indeed, any of the trade constraints considered in this chapter) are restricted to the methods of production and the extent of trade in energy products. In Chapter 10 we consider the additional possibility of meeting import constraints by modifications in the levels of final demands.

The effects of the oil import constraints can most easily be understood by comparing the time patterns of production and trade for each fuel with the analogous graphs for the unconstrained Base Case solution. The following brief account highlights and explains the most significant features.

As shown in Figure 7.1, in the Base Case, oil import dependency is negative in 1985 and 1990 (implying net exports) but thereafter rises rapidly to almost 43 per cent in 2000, 63 per cent in 2010 and over 90 per cent in 2025. Under the oil import dependency constraint, net exports in 1985 and 1990 are eliminated, import dependency rises to the maximum permissible 40 per cent in 2005 and remains at that level up to the end of the programme period.

Recall that the Base Case solution involves a rapid increase in North Sea oil extraction to 1985 (so as to achieve the benefits as early as possible), followed by a gradual decline thereafter (Figure 5.3). There is a net export of crude oil until the early 1990s and increasing net imports thereafter. Compared to this, the direct effects of the oil import constraints are (1) to slow down the rate of North Sea oil extraction, from a 1985 peak of 135m. tonnes to a ten-year plateau of 108m. tonnes (just as described in Section 6.7 above), and (2) to bring forward and greatly increase the scale of UK synthetic oil production (Figure 7.2). As a

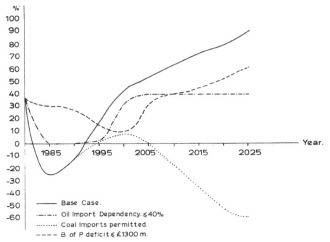

Figure 7.1 *Oil import dependency comparison (40 per cent oil import dependency)*

result of these measures, (3) gross oil imports rise to only 57m. tonnes by the end of the horizon, instead of 128m. tonnes.

The increase in production of synthetic oil is met partly by (4) an increase in coal production (Figure 7.3), especially in tranche IV from 2010 onwards, and partly by (5) a severe decrease in UK production of synthetic gas (never exceeding 6.3b. therms instead of increasing steadily to nearly 21b. therms), which leads in turn to (6) a vast expansion in the import of gas (Figure 7.4).

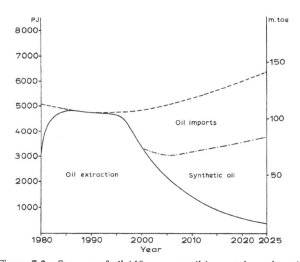

Figure 7.2 *Sources of oil (40 per cent oil import dependency)*

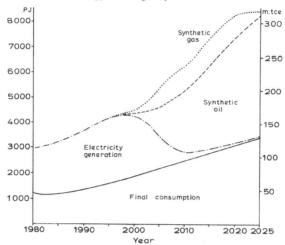

Figure 7.3 *Uses of coal (40 per cent oil import dependency)*

One surprising feature of the solution is that the imposition of the oil import constraint leads to a slightly *greater* use of oil-burning capacity to generate electricity (for peak loads), and less coal-burning capacity. The explanation is presumably that, at the margin, it is cheaper to use coal to produce synthetic oil than to substitute coal for oil in the production of peak-hour electricity.

Some indication of the increasing scarcity of oil is given by its shadow price (Figure 7.5). As in the Base Case, it rises steadily from £5.4 per tonne in 1980 to £94 per tonne in 2000. In the absence of import constraints the price levels off at £108 from 2005 onwards. In contrast, the oil import constraint raises the price to £155 in 2005, from which it falls to £112.10 in 2010 then rises steadily to £148 by 2025. Thus, after the turn of the century, when the oil import constraints begin to bite, the

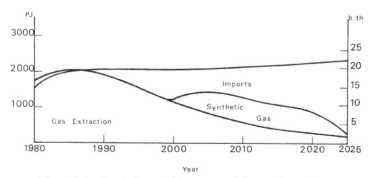

Figure 7.4 *Gas industry (40 per cent oil import dependency)*

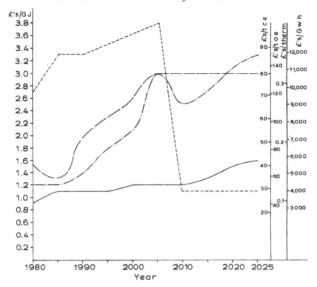

Figure 7.5 *Shadow prices of fuels (40 per cent oil import dependency)*

shadow price of oil is on average about 25 per cent higher than it otherwise would have been. The shadow price of coal also rises by about 25 per cent by the end of the period, reflecting the increased output from tranche IV pits.

The overall cost of the 40 per cent import constraints, as measured by the increased costs of the modified methods of production, is about £2b. present value (£108m. annual equivalent), or about 1 per cent higher than the Base Case cost. Further calculations reveal, however, that a 50 per cent oil import dependency can be achieved at a cost of only £1b. present value (£56m. annual equivalent). Thus, the last 10 per cent of independence (from 50 per cent to 40 per cent) costs as much as the first 50 per cent. By implication, some small reduction in oil import dependency could be achieved at a rather low cost.

7.4 Energy Balance of Payments Constraints

The balance of payments – or the lack of it – has been a perennial source of concern in postwar Britain. The dramatic increases in OPEC oil prices since 1974 appeared to exacerbate the problem. There has therefore been considerable pressure to extract UK oil resources as quickly as possible in order to reduce the outflow of foreign exchange on oil imports – and, indeed, to make a positive contribution by enabling the UK to become, temporarily at least, a net exporter of oil. However, there is little point in reducing imports of oil if this leads directly to increased imports of, say, gas or coal. It is therefore necessary to take a broader, sector-wide, view of the balance of payments problem. We have examined the balance of payments effects of visible trade in oil, gas and coal (where applicable). As Figure 7.6 shows, the energy sector is predicted to (1) start with a net deficit of £1300m., (2) move rapidly to a net surplus of £2500m. as North Sea oil reaches peak extraction (and export) rate, (3) decline over the next fifteen years to a deficit of about £5000m. and remain at approximately that level for the first fifteen years of the next century, then (4) finally fall even further to a deficit of about £8900m. by 2025. It can also be seen from Figure 7.6 that imposing the 40 per cent maximum oil import dependency constraint smooths out slightly the fluctuations in energy balance of payments. Both surpluses and deficits are lower in absolute terms but still the deficit grows to £8000m. by 2025.

Accordingly, constraints were imposed upon the model requiring that, for each five-year period within the horizon, the average annual deficit on the balance of payments for all energy products should not exceed £1300m. This figure of £1300m. proved to be the smallest deficit that it was feasible to impose, given the specified pattern of energy demands.

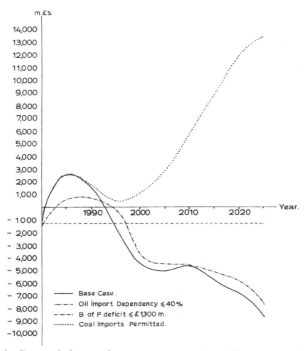

Figure 7.6 *Energy balance of payments comparison (40 per cent oil import dependency)*

Formally, the constraints read:

$$\sum_{\substack{i=\text{coal} \\ \text{gas} \\ \text{oil}}} (cs_{it} S_{it} - cm_{it} M_{it}) \geq -£1300\text{m.} \qquad \text{for all } t,$$

where S_{it} and M_{it} are, respectively, the levels of exports and imports of fuel i in period t, and cs_{it} and cm_{it} are the per unit export and import prices. (Actually, coal imports are not allowed in the model so far; their effect is explored in the next section.) It turns out that the cost-minimising solution is to have the energy balance of payments deficit at precisely £1300m. for the whole of the programme period. The constraint eliminates the surplus in earlier periods in order to keep the deficit down to the maximum permissible level in later years.

Once again, the results of imposing the energy balance of payments constraints are illustrated in cumulative graphs of production which should be compared with those for the unconstrained Base Case (Figures 5.1–5.7). The major features are as follows:

(1) The initial rate of oil extraction is substantially *reduced*, peaking at the turn of the century instead of in 1985 (Figure 7.9). Crude oil is imported throughout the programme period, even at peak domestic extraction rate. At first sight this is surprising, but the purpose is to reduce the pressure on the balance of payments in later years.

(2) Synthetic oil is not produced until the turn of the century, but is then produced on a larger scale (though not as extensively as when oil import constraints are imposed).

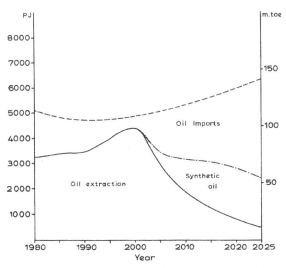

Figure 7.7 *Sources of oil (maximum balance of payments deficit, £1300m.)*

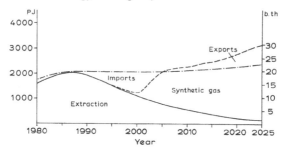

Figure 7.8   *Gas industry (maximum balance of payments deficit, £1300m.)*

(3) The pattern of North Sea gas extraction is unchanged, but the scale of synthetic gas production is dramatically increased, to the extent that gas is exported by 2005 and on an increasing scale thereafter (Figure 7.8).

(4) Coal production is substantially increased in later years, reaching an annual extraction rate of nearly 417m. tonnes by 2025 (Figure 7.9). Coal has to be mined in the most expensive tranche V, whose quality or location is as yet unknown (Figure 7.10). There must be considerable doubt whether it would even be feasible (let alone desirable) to expand employment in coal mining to the level necessary to achieve such an extraction rate.

(5) The amount of electricity generated from oil declines steadily to zero by 2025, being replaced by coal-fired capacity.

(6) As the balance of payments constraints take effect, and more costly methods or fuels have to be adopted in order to reduce

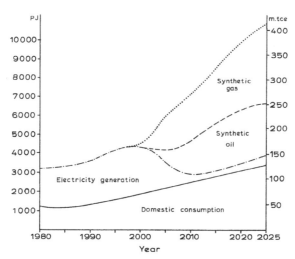

Figure 7.9   *Uses of coal (maximum balance of payments deficit, £1300m.)*

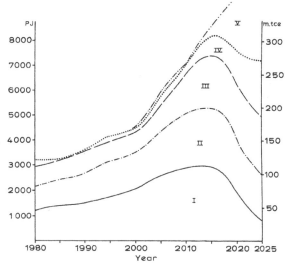

Figure 7.10   *Coal production by tranche (maximum balance of payments deficit, £1300m.)*

imports, the marginal costs (shadow prices) of the primary fuels rise much higher than they otherwise would (Figure 7.11). Instead of fluctuating around £26 to £32 per tonne, the price of coal gradually doubles. Instead of merely doubling (from £54 to £108 per tonne), the price of oil trebles (from £60 to £210 per tonne). Gas behaves quite similarly, nearly trebling from £0.20 to £0.60 per therm instead of doubling from £0.16 to £0.32 per therm. These prices do fluctuate, however, reaching a peak around 2000–2005, falling substantially in 2010, and rising even higher thereafter.

(7) The total cost of these import substitution methods amounts to £9.18b. present value over the fifty-year horizon of the model, an increase of about 4.4 per cent on the total energy costs that would otherwise be incurred. It has thus cost £9.18b. to reduce the maximum deficit on the energy balance of payments from £8500m. to £1300m., an average cost of £127.5m. for every £100m. by which the maximum deficit is reduced. (It is probably more appropriate to convert these present values to the future years when the reduced deficits will be experienced. The average cost of £127.5m. per £100m. would be about £411m. per £100m. at the turn of the century – a very much higher cost!)

(8) The shadow prices on the energy balance of payments constraints, after adjusting for the discount factor, rise steadily to the turn of the century, fall slightly, then rise to an even higher level by 2025. The constraints are therefore most severe around 2000 and again

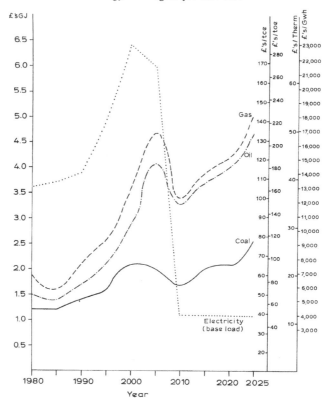

Figure 7.11 *Shadow prices of fuels (maximum balance of payments deficit, £1300m.)*

around 2025. In general the severity of the constraint is proportional to the level of the deficit that could otherwise be experienced (cf. Figure 7.6).

(9) The sum of the shadow prices over the ten periods is equal to £5.11m. This implies that, if the allowable deficit on the energy balance of payments were relaxed from £1,300m. to £1,400m., the present value of the reduction in costs would be about £511m. Thus, the last £100m. reduction in the maximum allowable annual balance of payments deficit costs about four times the average cost of the reduction from £8,500m. to £1,300m.

(10) Exploitation of the most expensive coal reserves (tranche V) in the next century and substantial exports of gas after the year 2005 are required to satisfy the balance of payments constraint. However, gas exports are unlikely to be feasible unless they are subsidised, since UK gas production will increasingly depend upon high-cost UK coal. UK synthetic gas is unlikely to find a market abroad

when other countries can also produce gas synthetically from cheaper imported coal.

7.5 Allowing Coal Imports

The Base Case model makes no provision for coal imports, since these have rarely occurred in substantial quantities in the UK, and the National Coal Board is strongly opposed to the idea. None the less, the CEGB and the British Steel Corporation have at various times applied to the government for permission to import. At the time of writing, it has just been revealed that imports of coal reached nearly 8m. tonnes in 1980, mainly by these two organisations. There must be other firms that would consider importing coal if the opportunity were available. Certainly, imports would become increasingly viable if, as the base case results suggest, it would otherwise be necessary to extract an ever increasing volume of coal from high-cost (tranche IV) UK pits (and to employ an ever increasing labour force). There is thus a strong case for allowing coal imports in order to reduce natural energy costs.

A second reason for allowing coal imports, as discussed briefly in Section 7.2, would be to temper the political and economic power of the UK coal miners to disrupt production in order to achieve higher wages, resist pit closures or further other political aims. A third and not unrelated reason would be to provide some competitive pressure for efficiency in the operation of the NCB.

In this section, we explore the effects of making coal imports available in each period at a price of £22.30 per tonne estimated by the International Energy Agency (1978). The results are shown in Figures 7.12–7.16, which may be compared with Figures 5.1–5.7 for the Base Case.

The main features are as follows:

(1) Domestic coal production is no longer economic in the most expensive (tranche IV) pits (Figure 7.12). Production in the cheaper pits (tranches I–III) is virtually unaffected until the year 2015, and actually increases in the subsequent decade (i.e. declines at a less rapid rate).

(2) Coal is imported on a very modest scale (under 14m. tonnes annually) until the late 1980s, but thereafter on a substantial scale, rising steadily to over 530m. tonnes per annum by 2025, which is more than double the level of domestic extraction. Naturally, there is an enormous increase in the use of coal throughout the British energy sector (Figure 7.13).

(3) A massive production of synthetic oil becomes economic, rising steadily to 212m. tonnes per annum by 2025 (Figure 7.14). Oil imports are cut to a maximum of 9m. tonnes in 2000, and by 2005 crude oil is exported once more, rising eventually to 78m. tonnes by 2025 (Figure 7.15).

(4) Synthetic gas production also becomes economic on a large scale

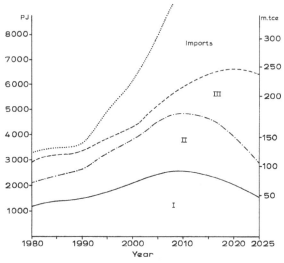

Figure 7.12   *Coal production by tranche and imports (coal imports at fixed prices)*

(Figure 7.16). There is a brief decade of imported gas from about 1987, but by the turn of the century synthetic gas plus natural gas meet the whole of UK requirements. There are no gas exports, however.

(5) Slightly more coal is used in the generation of electricity, especially in the last few periods, when oil-fired capacity is essentially elimi-nated and nuclear output is slightly reduced. But apart from that the electricity industry is unaffected – in particular, it is not economic to make a significant reduction in the nuclear programme.

Allowing coal imports thus causes drastic changes in energy policy, but are these changes in fact feasible? Probably not. Importing coal on such a scale would probably drive up the world price of coal. Admittedly the world coal market is potentially enormous, with several large and low-cost suppliers able to cope with even these substantial British requirements (Robinson and Marshall, 1981, pp. 36–7, 77–9). On the other hand, as discussed in Chapter 6, other countries could be increas-ing their coal imports at the same time. A substantial proportion of imported coal is used to produce synthetic oil which is then exported. This is an implausible scenario since producers of cheap coal will have a cost advantage in synthetic oil production over the UK and synthetic oil consumers are likely to find it cheaper to import the coal and undertake their own synthetic oil production.

Before exploring the effects of a rising world coal price, there is one aspect of the above results that is worth emphasising. Allowing the import of coal does eliminate the highest cost (tranche IV) pits, but

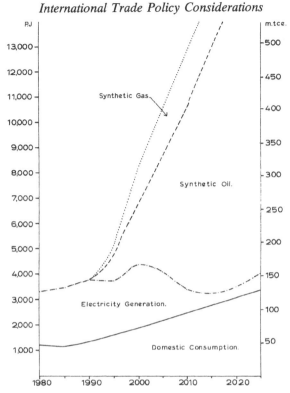

Figure 7.13   *Uses of coal (coal imports at fixed prices)*

these would not in any case be economic for more than 10 per cent of total production up to the year 2015. Domestic coal production from the vast majority of the pits remains unaffected. The main results of allowing coal imports are to replace other fuels (e.g. oil in the generation of electricity), and more especially to replace imports and increase exports of oil and gas by making it economic to produce synthetic fuels both earlier and on a larger scale. Coal imports provide a new source of employment in synthetic fuel production; they do not constitute a serious threat to the British coal mining industry or to the majority of the miners employed by it.

The model was rerun with the world coal price assumed to rise at the rate of 1 per cent per annum. The effect is quite startling: coal imports are worthwhile in only four periods, and then on a very small scale – about 11m. tonnes in 1986, less in 1990 and a maximum of 19m. tonnes in 2000 (Figure 7.17). Domestic coal production is essentially unaffected, except that pits in tranche IV are no longer utilised in the 1980s. The coal imports are used to increase the production of synthetic gas around the turn of the century, but otherwise energy policy is essentially

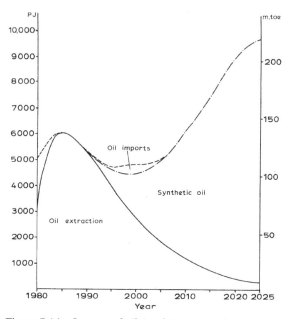

Figure 7.14   *Sources of oil (coal imports at fixed prices)*

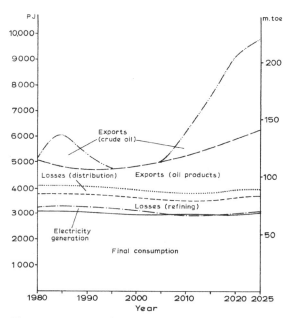

Figure 7.15   *Uses of oil (coal imports at fixed prices)*

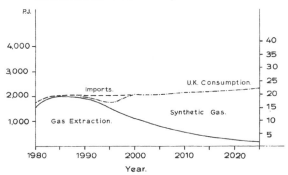

Figure 7.16   *Gas industry (coal imports at fixed prices)*

unchanged. This result clearly indicates that energy policy is extremely sensitive to the world price of coal.

It was pointed out in Chapter 6 that an increasing world price of coal might well drive up the world prices of oil and gas in so far as these prices will increasingly come to reflect the costs of synthetic production. We therefore ran the model with world coal price rising at 1 per cent per annum and also world oil and gas prices rising after the year 2000 at the rates of 2 per cent and 1 per cent per annum, respectively.

Once again there is a dramatic programme of coal imports and synthetic oil production and export, though not quite as large as when coal prices are assumed constant. Coal imports are maintained at a low level

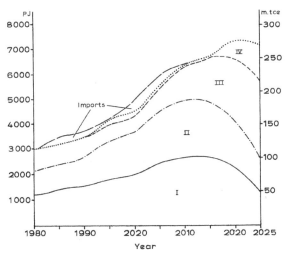

Figure 7.17   *Coal extraction by tranche and imports (coal imports at price rising by 1 per cent, domestic coal production cost constant)*

until the turn of the century, after which they rise steadily to 466m. tonnes by 2025. Synthetic oil production rises eventually to 187m. tonnes, with oil imports at a maximum of 34m. tonnes in 2005 and exports of crude oil rising eventually to 53m. tonnes. Gas imports last for two decades before being eliminated.

These results illustrate an interesting and important aspect of future energy markets. Although there are limits to the extent that coal can be substituted for oil and gas in consumption, the fact that coal can be used to produce these fuels synthetically means that imported coal is a perfect substitute for imported oil and gas. UK energy policy is therefore extremely sensitive, not only to the absolute world price of coal, but also to its price relative to the world prices of oil and gas.

Finally, the model was used to explore an allegation that is often put forward, to the effect that UK miners' wages, and costs generally, tend to rise concomitantly with any rise in the market price of other fuels. 'Given the semi-monopolistic position of the industry, however, and the very strong bargaining power of the NUM, it would be surprising if workers and managers in the coal industry did not succeed in capturing much of the market surplus (or rent) resulting from higher oil prices. Non-labour costs also seem likely to rise substantially because the NCB will have a reduced incentive to be cost-conscious as competitive pressures are lifted by the rise in price of other fuels' (Robinson and Marshall, 1981, p. 57). The model was run with domestic coal extraction costs rising at 1 per cent per annum, that is, at the same rate as the world coal price rises. The effect is a slight increase in imports to replace the extraction of coal from pits in tranche IV. (With constant oil and gas prices after 2000, this replacement is limited to a decade around the turn of the century; with rising oil and gas prices it affects production in the quarter century, 2000–2025.) In other respects, however, domestic coal extraction and energy policy as a whole are largely unaffected. This suggests that if coal imports are allowed, and if the NCB is not required to continue extraction from uneconomic pits for social reasons, without explicit subsidy, then the future of the British coal industry (or at least the potentially profitable bulk of it) may not be so sensitive to concomitant wage increases as some commentators have suggested. (But see Section 10.8, part (v) below.)

References

EEC Commission (1968), 'First guidelines for a Community energy policy', Memorandum, Brussels.

EEC Commission (1980), 'Energy policy in the European Community', Com (80) 397 Final, Brussels.

IEA (International Energy Agency) (1978), *Steam Coal: Prospects to 2000*, OECD, Paris.

Ministry of Fuel and Power (1965), *Fuel Policy* (White Paper), Cmnd 2798, HMSO, London.

Ministry of Fuel and Power (1967), *Fuel Policy* (White Paper), Cmnd 3438, HMSO, London.

Odell, P. (1981), *Oil and World Power*, (6th edn), Pelican, London.

OECD (1980), *Energy Policies and programmes of IEA Countries, 1979 Review*, Paris.

Robinson, C. and Marshall, E. (1981), *What Future for British Coal?* Hobart Paper 84, Institute of Economic Affairs, London.

Robinson, C. and Morgan, J. (1978), *North Sea Oil in the Future*, Macmillan, London.

Tombs, F. (1980), 'Nuclear energy: past, present and Future', Anniversary Lecture, Institute of Nuclear Engineers, 1980.

Tzoannos, J., Vaidya, K. G. and Soldatos, P. G. (1979), 'EEC energy policy and the UK: the Birmingham Energy Model', *Energy Economics*, vol. 3, no. 3.

8

Conservation

8.1 Soft Energy Paths

A number of students of the energy problem believe that energy consumption and reliance on exhaustible resources can be substantially reduced, partly by active pursuit of various conservation strategies and partly by increasing energy production from renewable sources. In particular, nuclear power can be curtailed substantially and even dispensed with altogether. Strategies of this kind have been referred to as 'soft energy paths' by their foremost advocate Amory B. Lovins (1977). In contrast to the 'hard path', with its reliance on the rapid expansion of centralised high technologies to increase energy supplies to plug the inevitable energy gap, the soft path proposes a phased, orderly transition to technologies based on 'energy income' rather than depletable 'energy capital'. Reliance on energy income means the development of renewable energy flows that are continuously available and replenishable, such as the sun, wind and vegetation, rather than oil, coal, gas and uranium which are depletable energy capital. Soft energy advocates also argue for a prompt and serious commitment to efficient use of energy via conservation, and the matching of energy sources to end-use needs in terms of their quality, scale and geographical distribution. The end-use orientation, as opposed to one which focuses on primary fuel supply, concentrates on determining how much of what kind of energy is needed for each task and supplying exactly that kind of energy. This matching of energy quality and scale to end-use needs, it is argued, can largely eliminate the costs and losses of secondary energy conversion and energy distribution. It is emphasised that the hard path uses premium fuels, particularly electricity, for many tasks for which their high energy quality is superfluous, wasteful and expensive.

Lovins argues that the main difference between the 'hard' and the 'soft' path is not in terms of how much energy is used, but in the technical and socio-political structure of the economic system. The soft path relies on diverse, flexible and relatively low technology systems entailing shorter development and construction times, and on smaller less sophisticated management systems, and is thought less likely to generate centralised and uncompetitive bureacracies. Above all, the soft path is seen as more democratic, depending on pluralistic consumer choice in deploying a myriad of small devices and refinements which are easily comprehended because they are physically and conceptually closer to end-uses. Consequently, they offer scope for participation since they are accessible rather than arcane. The hard path, in contrast, is seen as depending on unfamiliar and esoteric large-scale technologies requiring a major social commitment, and managed by central compulsory resource diversion. Such technologies depend on 'elitist technocracy' and offer minimal scope for consumer participation (Lovins, 1977, p. 148). Hard technologies, it is argued, also encourage industrial clustering and urbanisation, concentrate political and economic power, allocate costs and benefits inequitably and are alienating because of the remoteness and unapproachability of the central bureaucracy. Moreover, high technologies have attendant risks of error, accident and sabotage and require stringent control and some abrogation of civil liberties. (For a more extensive survey of the views of soft energy groups in the UK, see Rouse, 1979. A recent application of their views to energy modelling is provided by Lovins, 1979.)

One of the main components of the soft energy strategy is to increase energy efficiency through the application of conservation measures. It is the purpose of this chapter to analyse this component in the context of the BEM, indicating the sorts of policy issues that are raised. The next chapter will focus on the nuclear power debate. Whether 'hard' paths are necessarily more bureaucratic than soft ones, and less able to relate energy sources to end-uses, are debateable questions; for the most part they lie beyond the scope of this book, but some brief comments are made in the final section of this chapter.

8.2 Modelling Conservation

Conservation can be defined as the strategy of adjusting and optimising energy-using systems and procedures so as to reduce energy requirements per unit of output, while holding constant, or reducing, total costs of providing the output from these systems. Conservation techniques could improve the delivery of useful energy from a fixed stock of fuel, reduce the specific energy requirements of processes or energy consuming systems, or even modify the uses to which energy is put. The first two types of measure are referred to by soft energy groups as 'technical fixes' while the third is classified as 'social change' (Lovins, 1977). From an economic point of view, conservation strategies substitute other economic resources for energy, whilst from an engineering point of view conservation can be regarded as increased efficiency, allowing energy to be saved at no sacrifice in the goals of energy use.

A number of groups argue that there is immense scope for saving in all energy-using sectors of the economy, so much so that it may be possible to obtain an increased standard of living and still obtain significant savings in fuel consumption. (In recent years, the Department of Energy itself has repeatedly revised upwards the conservation allowance used in official forecasts. The latest forecast (Department of Energy, 1979) incorporates a conservation allowance which approximates to a reduction of some 20 per cent in useful energy demand up to the year 2000.) Moreover, advocates such as Leach *et al.* (1979) claim that such measures would be considerably cheaper than investing in nuclear power or any other source of energy. It is claimed that the real problems are not technical, or even economic in so far as many of the measures are cost-effective: the problem lies in the behaviour of consumers. Doyle and Pearce (1979) and Pearce, Edwards and Beuret (1979) have examined the problem of designing an incentive structure that will induce energy users to adopt cost-effective conservation measures. We return to this point later.

The approach adopted here is to concentrate on modelling conservation of the 'technical fix' variety. We shall not examine in any detail individual conservation measures such as insulation, lighting, heat pumps and the like, since cost data are not sufficiently reliable at present for such measures to be incorporated directly into the model. (For a review of the available evidence, see Rouse, 1979.) Instead, we shall be concerned with evaluating a recent empirical study by Gerald Leach and associates at the International Institute for Environment and Development (Leach *et al.*, 1979). This study involves a conservation strategy incorporating a package of individual measures which are claimed to be cost-effective. We shall incorporate the IIED final energy demand projections into the BEM in order to examine the implications of a low energy–high conservation scenario in the UK. The results will then be compared with those obtained in the Base Case, which (it will be recalled) is based on official projections of the Department of Energy. The main questions to be explored are the effects of the IIED strategy on the levels of production and use of the four main fuels, the present value of the total costs of the strategy and the policy implications raised.

8.3 The IIED Low Energy Strategy

The report by Gerald Leach and associates at the IIED entitled *A Low Energy Strategy for the United Kingdom* (henceforth referred to as the IIED Report) purports to show 'how the UK could have 50 years of prosperous material growth and yet use less primary energy than it does today'. It is claimed that the introduction of known conservation techniques at quite moderate rates could counterbalance all increases in energy use that would otherwise come about from growth in material standards.

In contrast to the econometric forecasting models used in the official projections of the Department of Energy, the IIED Report uses a physical model of energy use in the consuming sectors. It is conceded that econometric forecasting models are no longer based on crude extrapolation methods using a fixed energy–GDP linkage as in the past, but it is argued that distorting residuals of these techniques still remain. Because forecasts are still too heavily influenced by analyses of the past relationships between energy use and growth, they impart a 'hard energy' perspective or bias. Leach and associates favour a 'bottom-up' approach based on physical and engineering analyses, in preference to the 'top-down' methodology of official forecasts. In the bottom-up approach, the objective is to ensure that energy supply matches end-uses. It starts wherever possible with the ultimate purpose for which energy is used –

the useful energy demand – and works upwards from there to primary energy supplies, fuel by fuel and sub-sector by sub-sector. The Report examines each sub-sector in a great deal of detail: for example, in the industrial sector almost 500 separate categories of fuel end-use are specified. Such disaggregation, it is claimed, allows a close matching of energy supply to end-uses and facilitates the detection of saturation effects and important energy feedback effects. It also identifies which fuels cannot replace others in specific end-uses (such as electricity in transport or chemical feedstocks). Above all, it makes it possible to examine the large differences in opportunities for saving energy through conservation technologies.

The IIED Report assumes that Britain's economy grows healthily along conventional lines: the choices of future GDP growth rates are the same as those used in official Department of Energy forecasts as embodied in the BEM Base Case. A 'High' case and a 'Low' case are postulated. For the next ten to fifteen years GDP is assumed to grow at least as fast as in the 1960s. By the year 2025 it is assumed roughly to double (in the Low case) or treble (in the High case). Within these projections of economic growth, numerous detailed assumptions about improved living standards are made, all serving to emphasise that 'a future of material austerity' is not assumed. Fuel cost assumptions, very similar to those in the Base Case Model, are used to test whether conservation measures would be attractive for consumers and as policy options. It is stressed that the conservation assumptions are not 'implausibly rigorous', but merely involve the introduction of technologies that are already widely used or that should be available by the mid-1980s according to 'expert opinion'.

In the following discussion of the IIED Report's final energy demand data, we have chosen to concentrate on the High growth case since the GDP growth assumptions upon which its projections are based are most similar to those used in our Base Case. Such a comparison will enable us to examine the implications of the IIED conservation strategy *per se*. Reference will be made to the Low case only where its results differ significantly from the High case. For the most part the differences are quantitative rather than qualitative. (In the light of the present recession, however, the growth assumptions in the High IIED case now seem less plausible than those in the Low IIED case; we discuss this later.)

Projections of energy consumption by market sectors made in the IIED Report are shown in Figures 8.1–8.5. Comparison of these projections with the Base Case projections (see Figures 4.1–4.5) shows a wide divergence. In the Domestic Sector, the IIED Report projects a fall in total energy consumption from about 1,500 PJ in 1980 to about 950 PJ in 2000 and a further fall to under 800 PJ by 2025. This is in sharp contrast to the Base Case in which total Domestic Sector energy consumption throughout the programme period rises at an average rate of 0.68 per cent per year. In the IIED Report projection, coal and oil consumption fall sharply during the first three time periods but owing to the assumed conservation effects, gas and electricity consumption do not expand up to 2000 and indeed after that year gas consumption falls.

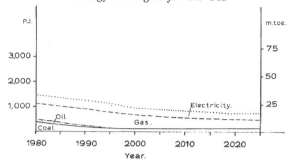

Figure 8.1 *Domestic Sector annual energy demand (IIED case)*

Energy consumption in the Iron and Steel Sector is projected to rise about 8 per cent between 1980 and 1990, then level off and later decline so that by 2025, consumption is almost 9 per cent below the 1980 level (see Figure 8.2). Coal retains the largest share of consumption throughout the programme period while oil consumption shrinks somewhat. Recall that in the Base Case energy consumption in this sector grows at an average rate of 1.8 per cent per year throughout the programme period and all fuels share in this growth.

Total energy consumption in the Industrial Sector (excluding iron and steel) rises at almost 1 per cent per annum up to 2000 but then levels off, presumably as conservation takes effect (see Figure 8.3). Coal consumption, however, rises rapidly throughout the programme period, electricity consumption rises somewhat but gas, gas oil and fuel oil consumption shrink over the programme period. In the Base Case, total energy consumption grows at about 1.5 per cent per year, coal and electricity consumption grow at a much more rapid rate while gas, gas oil and fuel oil consumption fall sharply.

In the Transport Sector (Figure 8.4), consumption of oil products rises to a peak in 1990 almost 20 per cent above the 1980 level. There is a continuous decline in consumption between 1990 to 2025 such that in

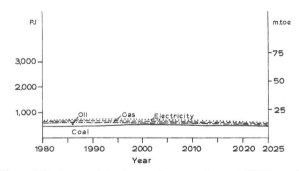

Figure 8.2 *Iron and Steel annual energy demand (IIED case)*

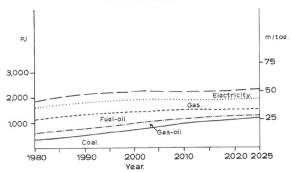

Figure 8.3   *Industrial Sector annual energy demand (IIED case)*

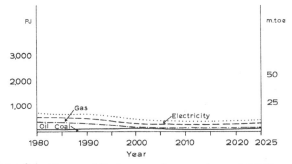

Figure 8.4   *Transport Sector annual energy demand (IIED case)*

the latter year consumption is only 77 per cent of the 1980 level. Most of this fall comes from the reduction of petrol consumption though aviation fuel is also somewhat reduced. In the Base Case, consumption of oil products in the Transport Sector grows throughout the programme period at 0.8 per cent per year. However, petrol consumption is projected to fall while aviation fuel and gas diesel oil rise substantially.

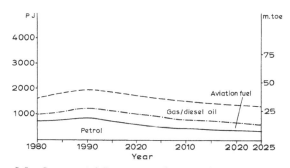

Figure 8.5   *Commercial Sector annual energy demand (IIED case)*

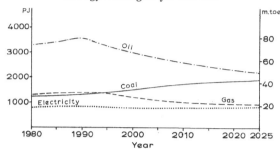

Figure 8.6a *Annual total final energy demand (IIED case)*

Energy consumption in the Commercial and Other Sector (Figure 8.5) shows a slow fall up to 1990, a rapid fall between 1990 and 2000 and then a relatively stable consumption level up to the end of the programme period. Most of the fall results from a fall in oil consumption. Coal consumption rises somewhat up to 2000 while gas and electricity remain at more or less the same level throughout the programme period. In the Base Case, total consumption in this sector rises at an average annual rate of 1.2 per cent per year. Within this overall growth, coal and oil consumption fall while gas and electricity rise substantially.

Figure 8.6 illustrates the IIED total final energy demand projections which form the basis for the subsequent comparative analysis. In contrast to the steady growth in total final energy demand assumed in the Base Case (Figure 5.1), the IIED Report projects a slight increase up to 1990 and then a fairly steady decrease to the end of the period. Con-

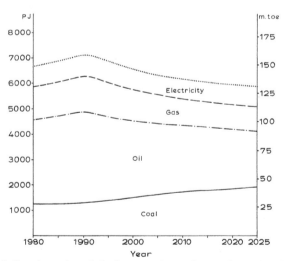

Figure 8.6b *Annual total final energy demand: cumulative (IIED case)*

sumption is projected to rise up to 1990 because this is assumed to be a period during which economic growth is fairly rapid and living standards are rising substantially, but some of the longer term conservation measures have not yet become effective. By 1990, projected total energy consumption is just over 7,100 PJ (158 mtoe) compared with almost 7,500 PJ (167 mtoe) in the Base Case. After 1990, the Report assumes the widespread application of conservation technologies, as well as increasing saturation effects in the use and ownership of energy-using goods. These enable a continued growth in material welfare together with a decrease in total energy consumption. By the year 2000, projected total energy consumption in the final consuming sectors has declined to 6,600 PJ (147 mtoe), and by the end of the programme period it is down to below 5,900 PJ (132 mtoe). In contrast, the Base Case projected consumption rises to 8,400 PJ (187 mtoe) by the year 2000 and reaches about 11,350 PJ (253 mtoe) by 2025. Thus, energy savings of 48 per cent are assumed possible by the end of the period as a result of the rigorous application of conservation technologies.

The striking differences between the Base Case and the IIED case are also reflected in the projected demands for the four major fuels. In the latter case, the projected consumption of oil and gas decline after 1990, coal consumption expands, while electricity consumption, after falling slightly to 2000, continues at a near-constant level to the end of the period. By the end of the programme period, coal, oil, gas and electricity consumption in the IIED case are respectively 56 per cent, 72 per cent, 44 per cent and 31 per cent of the consumption levels in the Base Case.

In the IIED case, oil, though of declining relative importance, remains the most important fuel in final energy demand throughout the period, still meeting 35 per cent of consumption requirements by 2025. This contrasts with the Base Case in which oil's share declines more rapidly, meeting 27 per cent of requirements by 2025, with its consumption falling below that of coal after 2015. The share of projected electricity consumption in the IIED case rises marginally from 12 per cent in 1980 to 14 per cent in 2025 while in the Base Case it rises to 24 per cent in 2025. Coal and gas shares in final energy demand in the IIED case are broadly similar to those in the Base Case (see Table 8.1).

Table 8.1   *Proportions of Final Demand Accounted for by Each Fuel*

			Final Demand			
Fuel	*1980*		*2000*		*2025*	
	(PJ)	(%)	(PJ)	(%)	(PJ)	(%)
Coal	1247	19	1521	23	1915	33
Oil	3306	50	3020	46	2208	38
Gas	1315	20	1228	19	933	16
Electricity	790	12	808	12	816	14
	6658	101	6577	100	5872	101

Scenario: IIED case in the BEM.

In order to examine the implications of the IIED Report's conservation strategy, we have incorporated the Report's final energy demand projections into the BEM. That is, we have rerun the model to calculate the minimum-cost policy for meeting the IIED demand projections given in Figures 8.1–8.5 rather than the Base Case projections of Figures 4.1–4.5. In the next few sections we examine the implications for the production and use of each of the four major fuel sectors taken separately. We then look at the implications for primary energy as a whole, and examine the effects of conservation on the total 'energy bill'.

8.4   The Coal Industry

Base Case results have already been discussed in Chapter 5; briefly, the coal industry expands vigorously throughout the whole period. By the end of the century coal output reaches 171m. tonnes, which is in line with the targets laid down in the NCB's *Plan for Coal*. Although the demand for coal for electricity generation declines rapidly in the next century, new markets for coal appear in the Industrial Sector (as improved combustion techniques are introduced) and in the synthetic fuel industry. Coal production peaks at 282m. tonnes in 2020, falling to 209m. tonnes by the end of the period.

The rapid build-up in coal demand to the end of the century, particularly for the decade after 1995 in which annual output is required to rise by 6.2m. tonnes per annum, means that in most periods the most expensive coal (tranche IV) is required to meet demand, albeit in small quantities. The less productive pits which comprise this tranche are concentrated in Scotland, South Wales and Kent. Jobs and prosperity will thus be maintained in areas where few alternative employment opportunities exist, thereby alleviating the problems associated with their eventual run-down. Furthermore, extensive new developments such as Belvoir and Selby, though environmentally contentious, will provide future employment and prosperity. On the whole, in spite of the rapid growth in nuclear electricity, the future of the coal industry seems assured in the Base Case.

The IIED scenario also requires an expanded coal sector, with average annual growth over the period at 2 per cent, slightly higher than the 1.9 per cent achieved in the Base Case. However, the time profile of this growth is quite different, with significantly less stability of employment and investment in the mining industry (Figure 8.7).

The demand for coal for final consumption is assumed to grow steadily but much more slowly than in the Base Case. The demand for electricity stays about constant and nuclear fuel gradually supplants coal, with the result that by 2010 the amount of coal used to generate electricity is less than one-tenth of the amount used in 1980. On the other hand, a new market opens up after 1995 for synthetic fuels. The synthetic gas market grows eventually to only just over one-third the size it attains in the Base Case. However, synthetic oil is first produced a decade earlier than in the Base Case, and eventually achieves about four times the

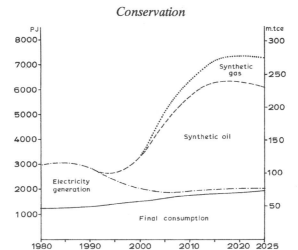

Figure 8.7   *Uses of coal (IIED case)*

annual production rate. The major reason for the greater expansion of synthetic fuel is that, at the margin, conversion from coal is now cheaper than imports. Because the annual output of coal is lower, production and investment can be concentrated in lower-cost mines. (The same logic explains why the growth in synthetic fuel production is even greater in the Low IIED case than in the High case. By the year 2015, over three-quarters of domestic coal production, about 225m. tonnes, is used for synthetic fuel. See Rouse, 1980.)

The net effect is that the coal sector grows to a slightly higher level of production by 2025 than in the Base Case. About three-quarters, rather than a half, of this production is eventually used for synthetic fuels.

There is, however, a lag between the decline in the market for electricity generation and the growth of the markets for synthetic fuels. Between 1985 and 1995 the total requirement for coal falls at an average annual rate of 1.6m. tonnes, then over the next decade it rises at an average annual rate of 9.6m. tonnes. Expansion continues thereafter, but at a more modest rate.

It is not clear how best to handle this instability of demand. A reduction in coal production during 1985–95 may make it difficult to expand rapidly during the next decade, and would certainly be resisted by the National Union of Mineworkers. Coal stocks could be substantially increased, but stocking capacity is limited. It should also be noted that, in spite of the rapid build-up in projected coal demand after 1995, the more expensive coal (tranche IV) is not required (Figure 8.8). Though this will generate financial savings, jobs will be lost in high-cost mining areas. In the IIED scenario, therefore, the future of the coal industry is in conflict with the Coal Board's *Plan for Coal*, which envisages a gradual expansion of coal output to the end of the century and beyond.

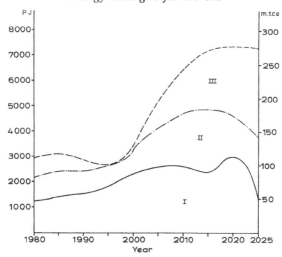

Figure 8.8   *Coal extraction by tranches (IIED case)*

The IIED coal output profile will have serious implications for stability and employment in some parts of the mining industry. This raises questions about the viability of such a strategy both economically and politically.

A further point is worth commenting on. The IIED Report claims that its coal strategy would 'have strong bearing on the need for opencast mining in environmentally sensitive areas'. In fact, however, opencast mining is likely to be the cheapest coal source, and therefore the last to be relinquished.

The BEM enables us to compare the capital costs of the coal extraction requirements of the two energy strategies. In the Base Case, the capital cost of coal extraction to the year 2000 is £2.3b. in 1976 prices. This is based on the NCB estimate of a capital cost of £38.58 per tonne of coal extracted. In the IIED case, the capital cost up to the year 2000 is £1.4b., a saving of 40 per cent. In the next century, however, the IIED coal programme is *more* costly, at £6.7b. compared with £4b.

One final point should be appreciated here. If fluctuations in output and employment generate costs which have not been incorporated into the model, such costs will be ignored in calculating an efficient solution. The model can easily be modified by introducing costs associated with (rapid) changes in output, or by imposing constraints on the rate of change. The result would be a smoother time profile of coal output, achieved by delaying the replacement of coal by nuclear energy in electricity generation and/or by bringing even further forward the production of synthetic fuel. Of course, this modified pattern of output would be achieved only at a cost. It is therefore important to ascertain whether the costs of instability of output are likely to be greater or less than the costs of avoiding it. The model could be used for this purpose, but we have not had time to do so.

8.5 The Oil Industry

In the Base Case, final consumption of oil is assumed to remain more or less constant. Oil reserves are exploited as fast as possible, with the result that oil extraction grows rapidly to peak in 1985 at 135m. tonnes, then gradually declines to less than 8m. tonnes by 2025 (Figure 8.9). There is a net export surplus over the initial period 1980–95, but imports increase rapidly thereafter. Net imports reach 83m. tonnes (about 91 per cent of consumption requirements) by 2025. The oil import bill is kept down by the production of synthetic oil from coal on a limited scale after the turn of the century: in its peak production year (2010), synthetic oil provides only 13 per cent of consumption requirements.

In the IIED case, final consumption of oil is projected to remain more or less constant up to the turn of the century, but to decline significantly thereafter. By 2025, oil consumption is assumed to be 70m. tonnes, only half the level in the Base Case.

The pattern of oil extraction is practically identical in the two cases. This means that, after the turn of the century, domestic oil accounts for a significantly higher proportion of final consumption than in the Base Case: 69 per cent versus 57 per cent in the year 2000, 26 per cent versus 20 per cent in 2015, and 11 per cent versus 5 per cent in 2025.

The major difference between the two cases lies in the production of synthetic oil, which takes place a decade earlier and on a much larger

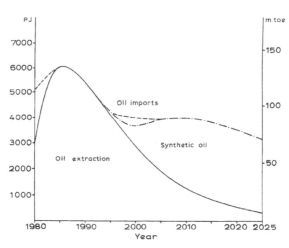

Figure 8.9 *Sources of oil (IIED case)*

scale in the IIED case: output rises to 60m. tonnes (compared to a maximum of 16m. tonnes in the Base Case), and by 2025 accounts for 89 per cent of oil consumption (Figure 8.9). In fact, so great is the output of synthetic oil that the UK is a net importer of oil for only five years in the early 1990s, and for almost all the programme period crude oil is exported, albeit on a small scale after the turn of the century (Figure 8.10). (As noted earlier, the production and export of synthetic oil are even greater in the IIED Low case.)

As pointed out in the previous chapter, in the Base Case the high import dependency of the oil supply strategy could be a cause for concern, given the uncertainties surrounding international relations. In the IIED case, the projected zero imports and high exports will avoid these potential problems. On the other hand, to the extent that a strong energy balance of trade maintains a high value for the pound sterling, British manufacturing industry may – as at the time of writing – find it difficult to compete internationally.

The implications of the IIED future for the oil refining industry (and the manufacture of petrochemicals) may also cause concern. In the Base Case, refining capacity is calculated to remain fairly stable during the present century but to expand in the next century, peaking at 142m. tonnes in 2025. By contrast, oil refining in the IIED case is a contracting activity throughout the period, as a result of the declining oil demand and supply and the high export of crude oil. By 2025 only half as much oil is refined as in the Base Case, so that employment would be lower (especially in coastal areas). However, these effects will be partly offset by the opportunities created in the rapidly expanding synthetic oil industry.

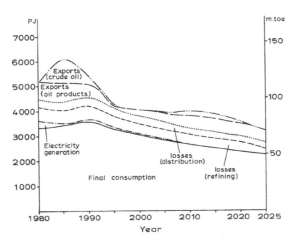

Figure 8.10 *Uses of oil (IIED case)*

8.6 The Gas Industry

In the Base Case, the final demand for gas is assumed to rise steadily from 16.5b. therms in 1980 to 22b. therms in 2025. As in the case of the oil industry, gas extraction from the North Sea takes place as fast as the reserves and depletion constraints allow. Domestic gas extraction is just sufficient to meet demand in 1985, but by 2025 it meets only 8 per cent of requirements. To meet the increasing demand for gas, imports rise rapidly, peaking in the year 2000 at over 7b. therms, some 40 per cent of gas requirements in that year. Thereafter, as the price of imported gas rises, the demand for gas is progressively met by the production of SNG. Gas imports decline sharply after the turn of the century, ceasing altogether by 2005.

In the IIED case (Figure 8.11), projected gas consumption rises slightly up to 1990 and then contracts steadily to the end of the programme period, by which time it is a mere 40 per cent of the Base Case level. North Sea gas reserves are extracted and consumed much less rapidly than in the Base Case. By the year 2000 North Sea gas still provides 95 per cent of gas requirements, compared with only 55 per cent in the Base Case; by the end of the period these figures are 25 per cent compared with 8 per cent. As a consequence, there is less need for synthetic gas and no need for imports. In fact, the lower projected demand actually permits an export surplus until the turn of the century. The synthetic gas industry is much smaller than in the base case: 8b. therms as opposed to 21b. therms by the end of the period.

The lower production of the SNG permits a considerable saving in resources. In the Base Case the capital investment required for synthetic gas production between the years 2000 and 2025 is over £14b., and the operating cost is £1.2b. (1976 prices). In the IIED case these figures are £5.5b. and £0.5b., respectively. Hence, the application of cost-effective conservation measures in the gas consuming sectors will permit considerable resource savings and impose less strain on the balance of payments at the end of this century.

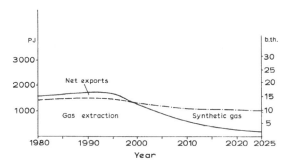

Figure 8.11   *Gas industry (IIED case)*

8.7   The Electricity Industry

The IIED Report has described as 'controversial and crucial' the changes in the electricity industry resulting from its future energy strategy. The controversies concern the future of nuclear power and the appropriateness of using electricity to meet end-use demands. The future role for electricity is crucial because of the large energy conversion and distribution losses which accompany its use and which substantially influence primary energy demand.

In the Base Case, the projected consumption of electricity grows faster than for any other fuel, averaging 2.6 per cent per annum over the period. Within this overall growth, nuclear electricity plays an increasingly prominent role because of its cost advantage over its rivals coal and oil. In 1980 about 17 per cent of total electricity generated is nuclear; this increases to 48 per cent by the year 2000, and to 94 per cent by 2025. An even higher growth rate in the earlier period is prevented by the capacity limitations in the nuclear power plant industry, which limit nuclear capacity to 40 GW by the year 2000. These limitations, together with the long lead times on nuclear plant construction, explain why coal-generated electricity grows fairly rapidly up to 1990. Thereafter it declines continuously, its share falling to a mere 3 per cent by the end of the period. Oil-fired power stations and gas turbines retain a share of electricity generation but only in order to meet high peak demand.

The IIED Report uses lower electricity demand forecasts than those of the Base Case. (As noted earlier, the Department of Energy itself has repeatedly revised upwards the conservation allowance used in official forecasts. The latest forecast (Department of Energy, 1979) incorporates a conservation allowance approximately equal to a reduction of some 20 per cent in useful energy demand up to the year 2000.) The Report also considers a number of cases where electricity can be conserved and its use limited to meeting only the most appropriate end-use demands (viz. motive power, short-period intermittent heating and electronics). As a result, electricity consumption is projected to remain more or less static throughout the period (Figure 8.12). This means that it is half the Base Case level at the end of the century (at 246,640 GWh), and a mere one-third of the Base Case level by 2025 (at 249,000 GWh).

Capital and operating costs of electricity are the same in both scenarios, and the least-cost mixes of power stations and fuels are about the same. In both cases, nuclear electricity plays an increasingly prominent role. In the IIED case, however, nuclear electricity generation in the years 2000 and 2025 is 80 per cent and 30 per cent, respectively, of that in the Base Case. Coal-generated electricity in the IIED case declines even more dramatically to 23 per cent of the Base Case level in the year 2000 but is a higher proportion in later years. The absolute size and share of coal in electricity generation remains steady after 2010 due to the lower operating costs of coal-fired stations, which in turn results from the lower marginal costs of coal extraction since tranche IV coal is not required. (In the IIED Low case, in fact, electricity from coal

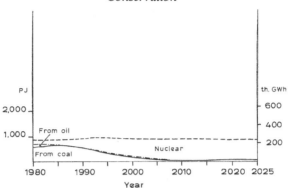

Figure 8.12 *Electricity generation (IIED case)*

increases both absolutely and relatively after 2010 since the much lower coal extraction costs make coal-fired stations competitive with nuclear ones.)

Though the relative importance of fuels in power stations is not substantially different, the scale of investment in electricity generating capacity is considerably reduced. In the Base Case, total installed generating capacity rises from 73 GW in 1980 to 139 GW in the year 2000 and peaks at 235 GW in 2025. Of this total capacity, 40 GW is nuclear in 2000 and 152 GW in 2025. In the IIED case, total installed generating capacity, is 71 GW in 1980; it increases slightly up to 1990, falls back to 71 GW at the end of the century, then rises to 78 GW by the year 2025. The nuclear component increases to 44 GW by 2005, and remains at that level to the end of the period.

On the basis of capital cost figures of £416/KW for nuclear, £260/KW for coal and £192/KW for oil and gas turbines (in 1976 prices), the annual investment expenditure requirements of the programmes can be determined. In the Base Case, annual investment expenditure on new capacity between 1980 and 2000 amounts to £905 million per year, of which some £655 million is for nuclear plant. The annual investment expenditure in the next century rises substantially to £2,890 million per year. This implies a very considerable commitment of resources over the twenty-five-year period. In the IIED case, by contrast, investment in new capacity is much reduced. The total capital cost of the IIED programme between 1980 and 2000 is £10b. compared with £18b. in the Base Case, the difference between the investment programmes representing a saving of £400m. per year up to 2000. (This annual saving exceeds the whole CEGB investment programme in new plant construction in the financial year of the 1978–79.) In the next century the average capital cost of the IIED programme is £255m. per annum, under one-tenth that of the Base Case. This represents an investment saving of over £2,635m. per year between 2000 and 2025.

(Investment savings in the Low IIED case are even more impressive at

£455m. per year up to the year 2000. However, this is still considerably less than the £1,000m. savings estimated in the IIED Report itself. The difference is partly explained by the Report's use of a capital cost figure of £560/KW for nuclear capacity compared with the BEM's £416/KW, but a considerable discrepancy remains.)

8.8 The Nuclear Programme

We noted in Chapter 5 the various problems likely to be associated with the Base Case nuclear programme. Pearce, Doyle and Common (1979) have estimated that the likely nuclear programme implied by the IIED energy projections up to the year 2000 requires only seven stations to be built between 1976 and 1990 (equal to the current construction programme plus AGRs at Torness and Heysham) and two more stations between 1990 and 2000. There would be no fast breeder reactors. These requirements for nuclear capacity will probably be politically acceptable. However, they may be insufficient to sustain an indigenous nuclear industry. It is argued within the industry that key personnel are likely to leave if the past commissioning programme is continued and there is no expectation of more rapid growth. Moreover, since the industry is predicted to decline after 2000, key personnel will be discouraged from entering the industry (see Pearce, Doyle and Common, 1979). Against this, it can be argued that the industry has survived with comparatively low rates of commissioning in the past, and that post-2000 expectations are no worse than those for the indigenous oil industry, where no such inhibition of labour entry has been noted.

Even if the indigenous nuclear industry is not sustained, this need not be an issue of major concern. Plant requirements could be met by imports. Any significant import programme would be costly in terms of the balance of payments, but the IIED nuclear programme would be modest in comparison with the Base Case, so the import bill would not be overwhelming, particularly as the IIED energy future does not require oil imports as does the Base Case. Furthermore, if it is felt that any future energy scenario should be 'low-risk', in the sense that it maintains a large number of feasible energy options, an additional constraint could be built into the BEM so as to maintain a 'tick-over' nuclear capacity in the IIED case. Of course, there are costs to maintaining such options in energy policy and these constraints would need to be evaluated carefully. Purchasing established technology from abroad (e.g. the pressurised light water reactor) and building power stations in the UK under licence could be one such option which arguably has the added advantage of avoiding the costs and uncertainty associated with developing a new technology. (See Cook and Surrey, 1977, for a discussion of these issues and recent UK experience.)

The nuclear programme implied by the BEM for the IIED energy demand projections is similar to that envisaged by Pearce, Doyle and Common (1979) for the period up to 1990 and after the year 2000. However, between the years 1990 and 2000, the BEM recommends construction of ten nuclear power stations and a correspondingly lower generation of electricity from coal.

The BEM has not incorporated directly into its cost assessment those items associated with the risks to the physical, social and political environment since relevant cost data are not sufficiently reliable at present. However, it is likely that the IIED scenario would reduce many of the environmental impacts of electricity generation in general, and nuclear generation in particular (especially the risks involved in fuel transportation, reactor safety, and waste disposal). The likely shelving of the fast breeder reactor in the IIED case is particularly significant in this respect.

8.9 Primary Energy

Figure 8.13 and Table 8.2 provide a summary of the combined changes in the four fuel sectors in terms of primary energy demand in the UK economy over the fifty-year period. Recall that the consumption of primary energy in the Base Case is projected to rise throughout the period, increasing at about 1 per cent per annum. By contrast, in the IIED scenario demand rises marginally up to 1990, since growth during this period is fairly rapid, but the scope for conservation is yet to be fully

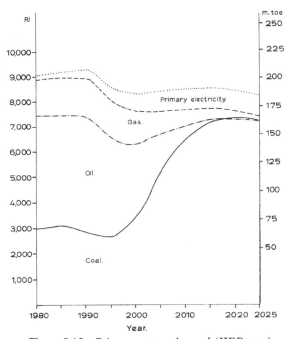

Figure 8.13 *Primary energy demand (IIED case)*

Table 8.2   *Proportions of Primary Energy Accounted for by Each Fuel*

Fuel	1980 (PJ)	(%)	Primary Energy 2000 (PJ)	(%)	2025 (PJ)	(%)
Coal	2950	33	3449	42	7234	87
Oil	4485	50	2893	35	0	0
Gas	1455	16	1280	15	208	3
Nuclear	160	2	683	8	843	10
	9050	101	8305	100	8285	100

realised. After 1990, widespread conservation becomes possible and it is assumed that important saturation effects appear in 'energy use'. By the year 2000, primary energy requirements are some 10 per cent lower than in the Base Case, and by 2025 the primary fuel requirement exhibits an energy saving of 42 per cent over the Base Case. (The Low IIED case provides even larger savings, reaching about 49 per cent of the Base Case by 2025.)

In both cases, primary electricity and coal are the expanding sectors throughout the period, though in the IIED case the growth rate of the primary electricity sector is much lower. Primary oil and gas both decline rapidly in the IIED case, whereas in the Base Case primary oil (mainly imported in the next century) continues to remain an important fuel throughout the period.

8.10   The Energy Bill

The value of the objective function (the energy bill) in the Base Case is £214b. at 1976 prices. This represents an annuitised energy bill of approximately £11.73m., which is about 10 per cent of GDP at factor cost in 1978 (at 1976 prices). The value of the objective function in the IIED case is £120b., only 56 per cent of the Base Case. The annuitised value is £6.6b., representing 5.6 per cent of GDP at factor cost in 1978 (at 1976 prices). Hence, an energy saving of 44 per cent is possible if the IIED energy demand takes place. (In the Low IIED case the total energy bill is £107b. This gives an annuitised value of £5.9b., some 5 per cent of GDP at factor cost in 1978. This represents an energy saving of nearly 50 per cent over the Base Case.)

Another way of looking at this information is to note that the lower cost of energy under the IIED scenario will mean a lower energy bill for each demand sector. To evaluate the consequences of this is a complex task involving the examination of the responses of demand to lower energy cost and the manner in which one sector's lower costs may be passed onto another. Suppose we make the simplifying assumption that members of the Domestic Sector will ultimately benefit from the reduction in the energy bill, either directly via the energy they consume or in the form of lower prices for the goods and services they buy as a result of the lower cost of energy in their production. The reduced cost of £5.13b. per year in the IIED case then amounts to approximately £92 per person per year. For an average household of two adults and 2.3 children the reduced bill is about £415 per year. (Comparable figures for the Low IIED case are £105 saving per person per year, and £450 saving for the average household.)

The lower demand in the IIED case means that the more expensive sources of fuels do not need to be utilised; consequently shadow prices of all fuels are generally lower than in the Base Case. It is not necessary to extract coal from the expensive tranche IV, and the coal shadow price is 30 per cent lower in the 1980s and 1990s. Cheaper coal means, in turn, that synthetic fuels can be produced more cheaply – in fact, more cheaply than imports. The shadow price of electricity (coal-fired at the margin) is also reduced during the first part of the programme period, but is identical during the second part when all base load electricity is nuclear.

8.11 Summary of Results

The IIED Report argues that conservation measures could be implemented which would lead to an eventual decrease in the total demand for energy over the period 1990–2075 without any significant reduction in the rate of economic growth. This claim stands in contrast to the Department of Energy projections embodied in the Base Case analysis, which envisages a substantial increase in all energy demands over the same period. In this chapter we have reported the results of incorporating the IIED projections in the BEM in order to calculate the minimum cost strategy for meeting the IIED demand projections.

The major *differences* in output patterns from the Base Case are as follows:

- total production of coal is more or less unchanged, but a greater proportion of output is used to make synthetic oil from 1995 onwards, and a lower proportion is used to make electricity;
- synthetic oil can be manufactured economically on a larger scale, and there are net exports instead of substantial net imports of oil after the turn of the century;
- natural gas can be exported until the turn of the century, no imports are required thereafter, and a smaller synthetic gas output suffices to meet domestic requirements;
- the proportions of electricity generated by nuclear and coal-fired stations are not significantly different but the total level of generation is significantly lower.

The main *advantages* of the IIED conservation programme are:

(1) net imports of gas and oil replaced by net exports for all or part of the period;

(2) cheaper production of synthetic oil and gas as a result of cheaper coal at the margin;
(3) lower costs of investment in the electricity generating industry;
(4) a lower nuclear building programme which is more likely to be within the industry's capacity and the availability of suitable sites;
(5) reduction in the risks to society and the environment associated with nuclear energy;
(6) a net saving in costs of providing energy, estimated at nearly £100 billion present value, which is about 44 per cent of the total energy bill, or about £415 per average household per annum.

The main *disadvantages* of the IIED conservation programme are:

(1) no output from the (most expensive) coal pits located mainly in depressed areas;
(2) less stability in the time profile of coal production, implying reduced output and employment over one decade followed by increased output and employment (or alternatively the financing of large coal stocks or other, perhaps more costly, measures to stabilise employment);
(3) doubt whether the reduced nuclear programme will sustain a domestic nuclear industry (or alternatively the higher cost of maintaining a viable programme);
(4) the costs, of unknown magnitude, of implementing the proposed conservation measures, and the possibility that these costs will be incurred unnecessarily if higher energy prices do not materialise.

As a result of implementing the IIED conservation measures, and meeting the resulting demands in the cheapest way, the British economy would be less dependent upon energy, but a greater proportion of its primary energy sources would be coal. This means that Britain would be less dependent upon imported fuels, but by the same token it would be much more dependent upon stable and efficient production in the domestic coal industry (assuming no coal imports). Whether the advantages of national self-sufficiency outweigh the disadvantages of dependence upon a single primary fuel is, to a large extent, a matter of opinion.

8.12   Some Problems of Conservation Policy

We have shown in this chapter that the least-cost energy policy for meeting the IIED demand projections, which reflect an extensive programme of conservation, would be substantially different from the least-cost policy for meeting the Department of Energy projections; in particular, the total cost would be about £100b. less in present value. This sounds an immense saving, which ought immediately to be aimed at. But should it? And what kinds of measures would be required? This final section considers briefly some of the difficult problems involved in designing or implementing a conservation policy. (For more extensive discussion see Eden *et al.*, 1981, Ch. 12.)

The first and most obvious point to make is that conservation is not an end in itself: it is adopted as a means of securing certain (further) goods or services that would otherwise be sacrificed. But conservation itself involves sacrifices: walking instead of driving a car, houses and offices heated at lower temperatures, resources devoted to insulation, and so on. The proper question is not whether there are savings to be made from conservation, but whether the savings, or benefits, outweigh the costs.

Who is to decide the answer to this question? One view is that consumers should make their own decisions in the light of their own circumstances. For example, they can decide whether the inconvenience of walking or car-sharing is worth, say, £5 per week, or whether the savings in their heating bill justifies the cost of the insulation.

Several objections to this view are often raised. (1) Because of the inadequacy of certain markets, fuel prices might not reflect true costs to society. For example, if oil companies doubt whether they will be allowed to store and sell oil reserves in, say, fifty years time, they may decide to extract and sell the oil as soon as possible, resulting in a lower price, excessive current usage and inadequate conservation. (2) Consumers may not have access to all available information concerning current developments and future price trends, so that decisions made on their own limited previous experience may be faulty. (3) Consumers may use wrong 'decision rules' for evaluating conservation opportunities – for example, they may be myopic and insist on 'payback' within a two-year period – which is against their own long-term interests.

On the other hand, the suggestion that governments should make or influence conservation decisions is also open to objections. (1) Governments, too, have limited information, particularly about the particular circumstances of individual firms and households. (2) Any government policy is necessarily 'broad-brush', and it is impossible to encourage all projects for which benefits exceed costs without at the same time encouraging some for which this is not the case (e.g. in subsidising house insulation). (3) Governments in practice are by no means as far-sighted and altruistic as some would believe: they too are myopic and concerned about the next election – in particular, they may well be concerned to be seen to be 'doing something'. (4) Any programme of subsidies involves a redistribution of income which may or may not be thought acceptable. (5) A conservation policy will have varying degrees of success – some may fail to conserve despite apparently attractive inducements (cf. Doyle and Pearce, 1979), while others will receive handsome payments for doing something they would have done anyway. (6) Governments may be more inflexible than individuals, and respond more slowly to changes in relative prices which make conservation more or less important. (7) Finally, the authoritarian element of government involvement may itself be considered undesirable.

In appraising any conservation policy, it is thus necessary to establish how far individuals are expected to respond of their own accord, and how far their choices are to be influenced by government policy. Further-more, it should be clear just what kind of government measures are envisaged, and why. The IIED proposals of Leach *et al.* have come in for some criticism on this score, most recently by Marshall (1980). (1) The report claims that the measures involved are cost-effective, but no details or evidence are provided. (2) There is no discussion of how far market forces alone will yield the envisaged level of conservation, or of what kinds of intervention will be required. (3) There is no acknow-ledgement that the widespread adoption of conservation will lead to lower energy prices (via lower demand) and thereby reduce the incen-tive to conserve. (4) It is arguable that energy is income-elastic, and the IIED growth targets would require higher energy demand than pro-jected. (5) It may be more difficult to eradicate energy-using habits and encourage energy thriftiness than the authors envisage. At the same time, it should be pointed out that the Department of Energy projec-tions have been criticised for substantially *understating* the market response to higher energy prices (Pearce, 1980).

Finally, we might note the recent change in US energy conservation policy reflecting President Reagan's free market philosophy. 'Enforced energy conservation and "indiscriminate subsidies" to develop costly substitutes for imported oil are rejected in the latest draft US National Energy Plan marking a significant reversal in US energy policies' (*Financial Times*, 15 July 1981).

It is beyond the scope of this book to appraise the merits of these arguments, let alone to design an 'optimal' conservation policy. Our task has been to calculate the physical and financial consequences of meeting two patterns of energy demand which reflect different degrees of con-servation, regardless of how that is achieved. Nevertheless, this book makes two further contributions to the question of conservation. Chap-ter 10 introduces demand functions for energy, which allow quantities demand to response to prices (i.e. embodying market-induced conserva-tion), and the postscript examines the implications of a revised (and lower) estimate of energy demand.

References

Cook, P. L. and Surrey, A. J. (1977), *Energy Policy: Strategies for Uncertainty*, Martin Robertson, London, 1977.

Department of Energy (1979), *Energy Projections 1979*, HMSO, London.

Doyle, G. and Pearce, D. W. (1979), 'Low energy strategies for the UK – economics and incentives', *Energy Policy*, vol. 7, no. 4.

Eden, R., Posner, M., Bending, R. Crouch, E. and Stanislaw, J. (1981), *Energy Econ-omics: Growth Resources and Policies*, Cambridge University Press, Cambridge, UK.

Leach, G., Lewis, C., van Buren, A., Romig, F. and Foley, G. (1979), *A Low Energy Strategy for the United Kingdon*, The International Institute for Environment and Development/Science Reviews, London.

Lovins, A. B. (1977), *Soft Energy Paths*, Penguin Books, Harmondsworth, 1979.

Lovins, A. B. (1979), 'Re-examining the nature of the ECE energy problem', *Energy Policy*, vol. 7, no. 3, September.

Marshall, Eileen (1980), 'Low energy strategies for the UK – an economic perspective', *Energy Policy*, vol. 8, no. 4, December.

Pearce, David (1980), 'Energy conservation and official UK energy forecasts', *Energy Policy*, vol. 8, no. 3, September.

Pearce, D. W., Doyle, G. and Common, M. (1979), *Comments on Reviews and Assessments of the IIED's Low Energy Scenario*, ABECON LEFA Paper 79/3, University of Aberdeen.

Pearce, D. W., Edwards, L. and Beuret, G. (1979), *Decision Making for Energy Futures: A Case Study of the Windscale Inquiry*, Macmillan, London.

Rouse, J. S. (1979), 'Soft energy paths and the Birmingham Energy Model', Occasional Paper, Department of Government and Economics, City of Birmingham Polytechnic, September.

Rouse, J. S. (1980), 'Energy conservation and the Birmingham Energy Model: low energy strategies for the UK', Occasional Paper, Department of Government and Economics, City of Birmingham Polytechnic, October.

9

Non-nuclear Futures

9.1 The Nuclear Debate

An important set of issues in the current debate on energy policy is associated with the contribution to be made by nuclear power to UK energy production. We begin by briefly summarising the arguments. (A detailed discussion appears in Rouse, 1979.) Proponents of nuclear energy point out the cost advantage that nuclear power has in electricity production over its main rival coal. They claim that cheap and abundant nuclear electricity will be a substitute for oil in space heating and electricity production. In the longer run, a larger share for nuclear power in the electricity industry will release coal for synthetic gas and oil production. Opponents of nuclear energy dispute the cost advantage of nuclear energy on a number of grounds. They claim that, even if there is a cost advantage, the substitution for oil is unlikely to occur and may be wasteful if it does. They point out that the risks of nuclear energy – with respect to health, large accidents, the environment, nuclear proliferation, sabotage and civil liberties – weigh heavily against it.

The purpose of this chapter is to use the Birmingham Energy Model to evaluate certain aspects of the nuclear debate, in particular, to assess the impact on the UK energy sector of different assumptions about nuclear costs and nuclear policy. Section 9.2 outlines the pattern of nuclear electricity production in the BEM under our Base Case set of assumptions. This is followed in Section 9.3 by a comparison between the Base Case solution and the BEM solution if a policy of not building any more nuclear power stations is pursued. Since there is some disagreement concerning the likely magnitude of future energy costs, Section 9.4 examines the implications for energy policy of alternative assumptions about nuclear and other costs. Section 9.5 examines the effects of a non-nuclear policy under the low energy demand projections of the IIED Report. This is followed in Section 9.6 by a brief discussion of the possible role of renewable energy sources. The concluding section summarises the issues that have been raised by both the non-nuclear debate and the conservation debate of the last chapter.

9.2 Nuclear Electricity in the Base Case

Recall from Chapter 5 that a cost-minimising policy implies a very prominent role for nuclear electricity. At the beginning of the programme period (1980) about 17 per cent of total electricity production is nuclear, but by the end of the period (2025) about 94 per cent is nuclear. Moreover, the growth rate of nuclear electricity production over the first two decades is slower than it otherwise would have been because it is assumed that capacity limitations in the UK nuclear power plant industry will limit UK nuclear electricity production capacity to 40 GW up to the year 2000.

This rapid growth in the production of nuclear electricity reflects two important factors: (1) the relative cost advantage of nuclear electricity over coal-fired and oil-fired electricity (Table 5.2), and (2) the above average growth in final demand for electricity (averaging 2.7 per cent compared to 1.2 per cent for total final energy demand). We have already seen (Chapter 8) that a lower final demand (resulting from conservation) would require a very much smaller nuclear programme, and we shall shortly examine (Section 9.4) the effect of higher capital costs of nuclear electricity.

An important policy consideration is the effect of an expanding nuclear programme on the coal industry. As we have noted in Chapter 5, electricity generation from coal rises up to 1985 (reflecting the lead time on nuclear plant construction), remains at about 225,000 GWh up to the turn of the century (while nuclear capacity is limited), and then declines sharply. However, total UK coal production and consumption continue to rise throughout the period, at just below 2 per cent per year, because the decline in the requirements of coal for electricity generation is outweighed by the increase in UK final consumption and by the use of coal for synthetic gas and oil production from 2000 onwards. Thus, a rapid expansion of nuclear electricity need not lead to a decline in the total demand for coal. In fact, the proponents of nuclear electricity have suggested that precisely this type of diversion of coal from electricity production to production of synthetic gas and oil would bring substantial benefits to the UK since nuclear energy is indirectly substituting for natural oil and gas.

9.3 A Non-nuclear Policy in the Base Case

Many members of the anti-nuclear lobby argue that, even if the production cost advantage of nuclear electricity is accepted, the environmental, social and political disadvantages and risks are so great that complete abandonment of the nuclear programme must seriously be considered.

In order to model such a non-nuclear policy we modify the Base Case assumptions to assume (1) that nuclear power stations currently under construction will be completed and will subsequently be available for electricity production as required, but (2) that no additional nuclear power stations will be commissioned and constructed. (Mathematically, this involves constraining the nuclear capacity construction variables to be equal to zero.) The effects on each fuel are shown in Figures 9.1–9.6 (to be compared with Figures 5.1–5.7 for the Base Case).

The direct effect of stopping the nuclear programme is to increase electricity production from coal, since this is the next cheapest alternative

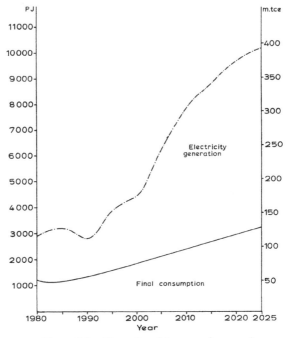

Figure 9.1   *Uses of coal (non-nuclear case)*

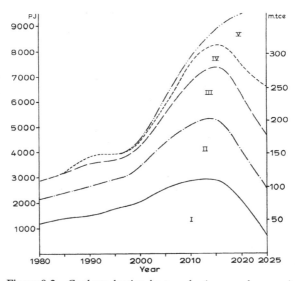

Figure 9.2   *Coal production by tranche (non-nuclear case)*

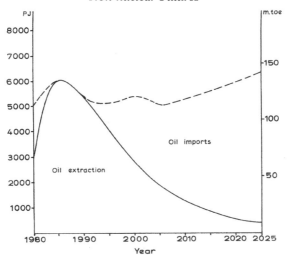

Figure 9.3 *Sources of oil (non-nuclear case)*

(Figure 9.5). In addition, electricity production from oil and even gas increases rapidly up to 2000, since the BEM incorporates the assumption that UK coal production capacity cannot be increased beyond 170m. tonnes per year by the end of the century. Even beyond the turn of the century, oil and gas retain a significant share of electricity production. The marginal opportunity cost of electricity rises steeply to £30,600 per GWh (3.1p per KWh) in 2005, dips, then rises to nearly the same level by 2025 (Figure 9.6). In contrast, when nuclear energy is available it rises to £15,480 per GWh (1.5p per KWh) by 2000 then falls to £3,960 per GWh (0.4p per KWh) thereafter.

Total coal extraction is substantially higher with the non-nuclear strategy, nearly half as high again by the year 2025 (Figure 9.1).

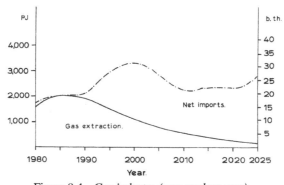

Figure 9.4 *Gas industry (non-nuclear case)*

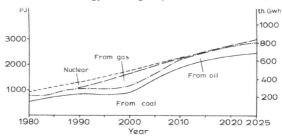

Figure 9.5 *Electricity generation (non-nuclear case)*

Tranches IV and V are mined extensively (Figure 9.2), with the result that the marginal cost of coal is nearly three times as high. At these relative prices, it is cheaper to increase imports of oil and gas than to produce oil and gas from coal (Figures 9.3 and 9.4). The increase in gas imports for two decades around the turn of the century is quite dramatic, reaching nearly 2lb. therms in 2000. Thus, during the first quarter

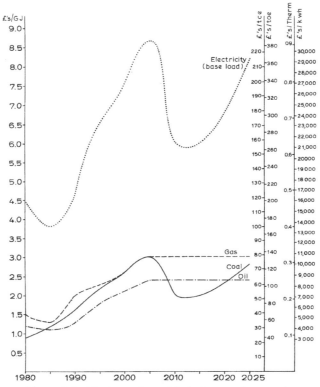

Figure 9.6 *Shadow prices of fuels (non-nuclear case)*

of the next century, the non-nuclear strategy leads to increasing reliance on imports of resources about whose prices and security of supply there is likely to be considerable uncertainty, and which may have serious implications for the balance of payments.

The value of the objective function in the Base Case solution is £214b. at 1976 prices. This is the net present value at 5 per cent discount rate of the total cost of meeting UK energy demand between the years 1976 and 2025. The value of the objective function in the non-nuclear case is £250b. or about 16.5 per cent higher than in the Base Case. The annuitised energy bill in the Base Case is approximately £11.73b., about 9.4 per cent of GDP at factor cost in 1978 (at 1976 prices). The annuitised energy bill in the non-nuclear case is £13.68b., or about 10.9 per cent of the GDP in 1978.

Suppose we make the simple assumption, as we did in Chapter 8, that the Domestic Sector will ultimately foot the increase in the energy bill, either directly for the energy it consumes or in the form of higher prices for the goods and services it buys. On this basis, the extra cost of £1.95b. per year under the non-nuclear strategy is approximately £35 per year per person. For an average household of two adults and 2.3 children the additional cost is about £150 per year.

Whether it is worth a 16.5 per cent increase in the energy bill in order to avoid relying upon nuclear power – or, more tangibly, whether the average household would be willing to pay £150 per year for this benefit – is at present unknown, and would in any case be exceedingly difficult to ascertain. The merit of our model, however, is that it provides a clear estimate of the order of magnitude of the monetary costs of adopting a non-nuclear policy, which can then be weighed against the various benefits which have been claimed for such a policy.

9.4 Sensitivity Analysis

The results reported above reflect the assumptions on relative costs, prices, demand projections and constraints incorporated in the BEM Base Case. In this section the implications of alternative assumptions on nuclear electricity costs are investigated.

In the Base Case of the model, costs of electricity production are taken from estimates made by the Department of Energy (Table 5.2). A number of critics of nuclear energy have argued that official cost estimates of nuclear energy (i.e. those made by the Department of Energy and the CEGB) are too low. It has been argued (1) that inadequate allowance is made for the costs of research and development, decommissioning, waste storage and interest costs during construction; (2) that the high load factors for nuclear power stations assumed in the official estimates are rarely attained in practice, and (3) that international experience shows a high degree of capital cost escalation, owing to improvements in design and to more stringent safety requirements. (See Pearce, 1979; Sweet, 1978; Ryle, 1977; Elliott, 1979; Shaw, 1979; and the summary by Rouse, 1979.)

Table 9.1   *Nuclear   Electricity   Capital   Cost   Estimates*
(Converted to 1976 Prices)

Source	
Department of Energy (1977)[a]	£416/KW
Leach (1977)	£560/KW
CEGB (1980)	£606/KW
Flowers Report (1976)	£750/KW
Energy 2000 (1977)	£1250/KW

[a]Excludes transmission and distribution capital costs which are included separately in BEM.

It is therefore appropriate to assess the effects of higher nuclear capital costs on the pattern of energy production and supply. Table 9.1 shows the wide range of estimates of nuclear capital cost that have been made recently. The Department of Energy estimate used in the BEM Base Case is at the low end, with other estimates ranging up to three times as high. However, the other estimates include distribution costs which are included separately in BEM (see Section 4.4 of Chapter 4). The model was rerun several times with different levels of capital costs over this whole range. The results of this sensitivity analysis are as follows.

(1) Increasing nuclear electricity capacity cost by 20 per cent has no effect on the fuel mix for electricity, since nuclear electricity still has a cost advantage over coal from higher cost tranches. The most significant change in the patterns of production and supply is lower synthetic oil production and higher oil imports than in the Base Case.

(2) At nuclear capacity cost 40 per cent higher, electricity from coal and nuclear electricity are at the same levels as in the Base Case up to the year 2005, but after that year there is more electricity from coal and less nuclear. However, even up to the year 2025, nuclear electricity remains at about 80 per cent of the Base Case level. There is less synthetic oil and marginally higher oil imports.

(3) At double the Base Case nuclear capacity cost, the switch from nuclear to coal electricity is greater, there is less synthetic oil and substantially more imports.

(4) At nuclear capital cost three times higher than in the Base Case, coal extraction is slightly higher. Electricity from coal is much higher, especially after 2000, although nuclear electricity is not totally eliminated. For example, in the year 2010, electricity from coal and nuclear energy are 435m. and 163m. MWh, respectively (compared to 66m. and 558m. MWh in the Base Case). With the higher nuclear capital cost, electricity from oil is about double the Base Case level throughout the period. Coal is too expensive to produce synthetic fuels, so oil imports are higher after 1999 and there are substantial gas imports as well.

The effect on the total energy bill is shown graphically in Figure 9.7. As the capital cost of nuclear electricity increases threefold, the energy bill rises steadily from £214b. to £243b. (an increase of about 13 per cent). As noted in the previous section, a complete moratorium on new nuclear construction would raise the bill to £250b.

The comparison of the nuclear and non-nuclear Base Cases, and the outcome of the sensitivity analysis reported above, indicate that it is not adequate to evaluate nuclear electricity simply by comparing generation costs for electricity produced by different fuels. It is true that nuclear electricity substitutes directly for coal in electricity production, but the total consumption of coal continues to increase over the entire period since coal also substitutes indirectly for imported oil and gas (whose prices are expected to increase rapidly over the next few years).

9.5 A Non-nuclear Policy with Low Energy Demand

Finally, we examine the effects of a non-nuclear policy under the IIED Report's Low energy demand forecasts, discussed in the previous chapter. (As before, we concentrate on the higher of the two IIED demand projections.) Figures 9.8–9.12 may be compared with Figures 8.7–8.13.

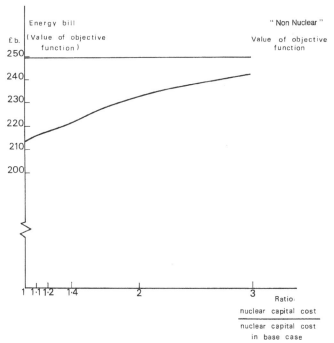

Figure 9.7 *Sensitivity of energy bill to nuclear capital cost (Base Case demand assumptions)*

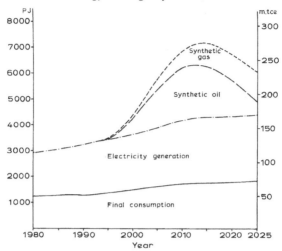

Figure 9.8   *Uses of coal (non-nuclear, IIED case)*

As in the previous analysis of the Base Case, the direct effect of
stopping the nuclear programme is to increase electricity production
from coal, since this is the next cheapest alternative (Figure 9.11). Oil-
generated electricity increases only slightly and there is no electricity
from gas. In order to meet the increasing demand for coal from the
electricity sector, coal extraction up to 2010 rises faster (Figure 9.8). In
the year 2000, for example, coal output (at 164m. tonnes) is 25 per cent
higher than in the IIED base case. The higher coal extraction requirements result in higher marginal costs of coal, since tranche IV coal is

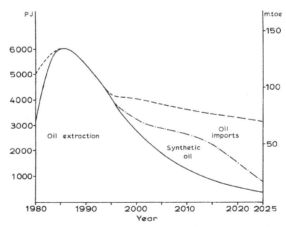

Figure 9.9   *Sources of oil (non-nuclear, IIED case)*

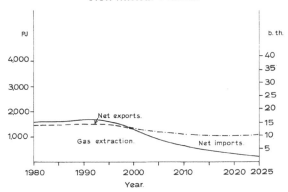

Figure 9.10   *Gas industry (non-nuclear, IIED case)*

required from 2000 until the end of the period. This more expensive coal is not required at all in the IIED base case. Higher coal extraction costs mean, in turn, that synthetic fuel production is far less economic. By 2010, synthetic oil production is only half as high, and continues to decline to the end of the period (Figure 9.9). Synthetic gas production is also lower (Figure 9.10). Eventually, the lower demand for coal in synthetic fuel production more than outweighs the increasing demand for coal for electricity production, so that coal extraction by 2025 (at 234m. tonnes) is below that of the IIED base case (at 274m. tonnes).

The higher cost of synthetic oil means that oil imports become a more cost-effective supply strategy. Oil imports, zero in the IIED base case after 2000, meet 20 per cent of oil requirements in the year 2000, and 77 per cent by 2025 (equivalent to 92m. tonnes of coal). Whereas the IIED base case permits a substantial surplus in the oil balance of trade in the next century, a non-nuclear policy involves rising net imports and an increasing strain on the balance of payments. A non-nuclear policy

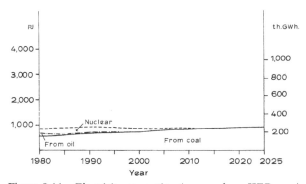

Figure 9.11   *Electricity generation (non-nuclear, IIED case)*

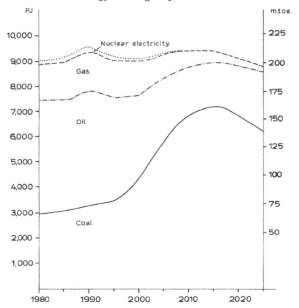

Figure 9.12 *Primary energy demand (non-nuclear, IIED case)*

has a similar effect in the Base Case, though here the burden is substantially less.

Figure 9.12, which should be compared with Figure 8.12 in the previous chapter, summarises the main changes in terms of primary energy demand. It can be seen that the gap resulting from the moratorium on nuclear electricity is filled first by coal then by primary oil via imports.

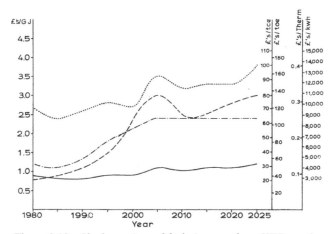

Figure 9.13 *Shadow prices of fuels (non-nuclear, IIED case)*

Table 9.2 *Proportions of Final Demand and Primary Energy Accounted for by Each Fuel: Non-nuclear Base Case*

Fuel	Final Demand						Fuel	Primary Energy					
	1980 (PJ)	(%)	2000 (PJ)	(%)	2025 (PJ)	(%)		1980 (PJ)	(%)	2000 (PJ)	(%)	2025 (PJ)	(%)
Coal	1219	18	1886	23	3403	30	Coal	2885	31	4500	35	10380	56
Oil	3090	46	2993	36	3048	27	Oil	4506	49	4772	38	5264	29
Gas	1583	23	1877	22	2152	19	Gas	1739	19	3325	26	2773	15
Electricity	857	13	1625	19	2753	24	Nuclear	160	2	115	1	0	0
	6749	100	8381	100	11356	100		9290	101	12712	100	18417	100

Source: Non-nuclear Base Case.

Table 9.3 *Proportions of Final Demand and Primary Energy Accounted for by Each Fuel: Non-nuclear IIED Case*

Fuel	Final Demand						Fuel	Primary Energy					
	1980 (PJ)	(%)	2000 (PJ)	(%)	2025 (PJ)	(%)		1980 (PJ)	(%)	2000 (PJ)	(%)	2025 (PJ)	(%)
Coal	1247	19	1521	23	1915	33	Coal	2950	33	4330	49	6171	71
Oil	3306	50	3020	46	2208	38	Oil	4485	50	3370	37	2399	27
Gas	1315	20	1228	19	933	16	Gas	1445	16	1323	14	212	2
Electricity	790	12	808	12	816	14	Nuclear	161	2	115	1	0	0
	6658	101	6577	100	5872	101		9041	101	9138	100	8782	100

Source: Non-nuclear IIED case.

After 1990 the total demand for primary energy is slightly above that of the IIED Base Case (by 9 per cent in the year 2000, 6 per cent in 2025).

The net present value of the cost of meeting UK energy demand is £120b. (at 1976 prices) in the IIED Base Case. With a non-nuclear policy it is 4.5 per cent higher (at £126b.). The annuitised energy bills are £6.6b. and £6.9b., respectively. Hence, the cost of a non-nuclear policy averages £300m. per year over the planning period. (With the IIED Low demand projection, the cost of a non-nuclear policy is only £104m. per annum.) This result poses a relevant policy question: though a nuclear programme combined with a conservative strategy will be £300m. per year cheaper than a non-nuclear conservation strategy, will this compensate for the additional risks which might be incurred by the nuclear programme? Once again the model alone cannot answer this question, but its great value is that it can pose it.

The total energy bill of the IIED non-nuclear case is still only half that of the BEM Base Case. We have seen in Section 9.3 that the energy bill in the BEM non-nuclear case is 16.6 per cent above the BEM Base Case bill (about £1950m. per year more). Hence, the cost of a moratorium on additional nuclear capacity in the high energy demand future of the Department of Energy (BEM Base Case) is considerably greater than it is in the case of a low energy (conservation) future as envisaged by the IIED Report. The increased cost of the non-nuclear strategy in the low energy future is only 15 per cent of the increased cost of such a strategy in the high energy (non-conservation) future. The magnitude of these figures seems to lend some support to the view, frequently expressed by soft energy groups, that the supposed indispensability of nuclear power stems largely from the high energy demand forecasts embodied in official scenarios. If conservation measures were vigorously adopted, it would be less costly to dispense with nuclear power.

9.6   Renewable Energy Sources

The role of renewable energy sources in future supply strategies is provoking increasing interest. This is due to the growing awareness of the problems associated with the exhaustion of fossil energy reserves and to the possibly adverse environmental, social and political impacts of their further development, using increasingly complex technologies.

Renewable energy sources can be divided broadly into two groups: those (including wind, wave and tidal) more suitable for generating electricity centrally; and those (including solar, geothermal and, again, wind) more suitable for provision of low grade heat on the consumer's premises. The problem that besets most renewable sources is that they tend to be dispersed and intermittent, so that their supplies are erratic, variable and unpredictable. Other than varying social and economic activities to accommodate varying supplies, some form of storage will be needed if renewables are to provide a large fraction of future energy requirements. If storage is not available then they could only be used in conjunction with an energy source that can be varied at will, such as nuclear electricity. The capital cost of the renewable sources would then be additional to that required for the back-up system, and would have to be justified by the savings in fuel consumption during periods when they make a significant contribution (Chapman, 1977).

The Green Paper recognises that 'the energy to be derived from alternative sources such as the sun, tides, waves, winds and geothermal energy will assume increasing importance and may ultimately play a considerable part in providing primary energy in the UK' (Green Paper, 1978). Renewable energy sources are not, however, expected to contribute significantly to supply before the end of the century. The Green Paper suggests that it would be technically feasible to produce in the UK up to 30–40 mtce per year from renewable sources by 2000, though it is recognised that the actual contribution is likely to be much less, probably under 10 mtce. The IIED Report (Leach *et al.*, 1979) is less optimistic: renewable energy sources are expected to contribute only the equivalent of 4–6m. tonnes of coal by 2000, rising to no more than 11 mtce by 2025. Several studies, however, see renewables playing a very significant role. The National Centre for Alternative Technology (Todd and Alty, 1977) expect renewables to contribute 105 mtce by 2025. Sir Martin Ryle (1977), Peter Chapman (1978) and the Centre for Alternative Industrial and Technological Systems (Elliot, 1979) are also optimistic, particularly if more money is devoted to serious research in the renewables field. The inadequacy of funded research is a common complaint among those who favour the renewables path (e.g. Fabian Society, 1980). Fur further discussion see Eden *et al.* (1981, Ch. 8).

It must be emphasised that the basis of all the above studies, official as well as unofficial, is intelligent speculation on the basis of the limited number of data sources available. At present, most renewables are at an early stage of development, and without substantial programmes of further work it is impossible to establish their feasibility and future costs and benefits. A survey of the available evidence (Rouse, 1979) indicates considerable variation in the estimates of the costs of renewable energy sources. Given this uncertainty we have not attempted to model them in the BEM, but with more accurate data there is no reason why the BEM could not include renewables as a supply strategy alongside the more conventional ones currently modelled. Alternatively, it would be possible to conduct a sensitivity analysis by rerunning the model several times, with different assumptions on cost of renewables, in order to ascertain the minimum cost at which they would be economically viable.

9.7 Soft Energy: A Summary

Proponents of 'soft energy' usually recommend a 'package' of measures including (1) reduced consumption of exhaustible resources via conservation, (2) a reduced reliance or complete ban on nuclear power and (3) the development of renewable energy sources. This is an appropriate place to set out an overall summary of the results obtained in the last two chapters.

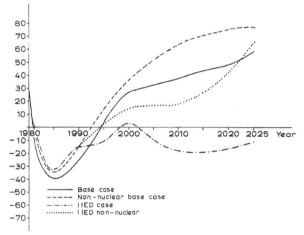

Figure 9.14 *Oil import dependency comparison (non-nuclear and IIED cases)*

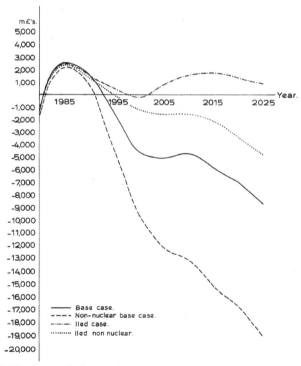

Figure 9.15 *Energy balance of payments comparison (non-nuclear and IIED cases)*

We have examined four alternative energy scenarios: (1) the Base Case (Department of Energy) demand projections, (2) the low energy (IIED) demand projections, (3) the non-nuclear Base Case, and (4) the non-nuclear low energy case. For each scenario, the BEM has calculated the strategy for meeting energy demand at minimum cost. Figures 9.14–9.16 set out the time pattern of three of the most salient long-term characteristics of each solution: the percentage dependence on oil imports, the energy balance of payments, and the volume of domestic coal production. Figure 9.17 gives the net present value of the total costs incurred in the energy sector from 1980 to 2025 (the energy bill).

The four strategies exhibit the following broad *similarities*. All involve a similar level of crude oil exports during the first fifteen years, followed by a steadily increasing dependence on imports. All strategies show a positive energy balance of payments over the first fifteen years, reaching about £2,000–£2,500m. in 1985, followed by a steadily worsening deficit. Finally, all involve increasing domestic coal production until about 2010.

The *differences* between the four strategies are as follows.

(1) In the *Base Case*, oil import dependency rises steadily to nearly 60 per cent by the end of the period, and the energy balance of payments falls to a deficit of nearly £9,000m. Domestic coal extraction

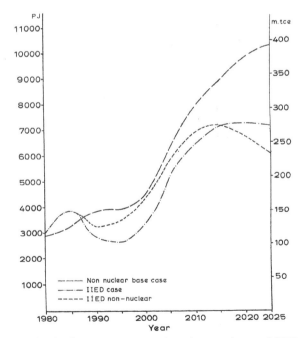

Figure 9.16 *Coal extraction comparison (non-nuclear and IIED cases)*

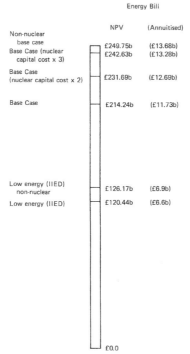

Figure 9.17   *Comparison of energy bills: Base, IIED and non-nuclear cases*

rises steadily to 275m. tonnes by 2020 before falling to 269m. tonnes over the next five years. The total energy bill is £214b. present value.

(2) In the *low energy case*, the oil import dependency rises to only 2.5 per cent in 2000 and is negative thereafter. The energy balance of payments stays in surplus of up to £2,000m. throughout the programme period with a brief exception around the turn of the century. Domestic coal extraction fluctuates quite severely rising from 114m. tonnes in 1980 to 147m. tonnes in 1985, falling to 100m. tonnes in 1995 then rising to 278m. tonnes in 2020, then finally falling slightly to 275m. tonnes by 2025. The energy bill is much lower, at £120b.

(3) In the *non-nuclear Base Case*, oil import dependency is higher throughout, rising to over 75 per cent by 2025, and the energy balance of payments is much more adverse, falling eventually to a deficit of £1,900m. Domestic coal production is much higher throughout, rising steadily to 389m. tonnes by 2025. The energy bill is £250b., nearly 17 per cent above Base Case cost.

(4) In the *non-nuclear low energy case*, oil import dependency follows roughly the same path as in the Base Case. The energy balance of

payments is stronger than in the Base Case, through still increasingly in deficit. The pattern of domestic coal production is again not unlike the Base Case, rising to 257m. tonnes by 2010 then falling to 231m. tonnes by 2025. The total cost is £126 billion, less than 5 per cent higher than the low energy case.

We thus have the following two broad conclusions.

First, if the future demand for energy in the UK follows the pattern described by 'soft energy' advocates such as Leach and the IIED, rather than that described by the Department of Energy in 1978, there will be very considerable savings in the costs of meeting energy requirements, energy imports will not be a drain on the balance of payments and the UK will be much more secure against disruption of foreign oil supplies. On the other hand, there may be difficulties in adjusting coal production to fluctuating demand (unless further constraints are imposed) and an unknown price will have to be paid to achieve the level of energy conservation envisaged.

Second, the costs and consequences of a non-nuclear policy depend crucially upon the assumed levels and growth of demand for energy. Assuming Department of Energy projections, a non-nuclear policy will slightly increase oil import dependency, substantially worsen the energy balance of payments, increase the output of domestic coal to perhaps a dangerously high level of dependence, and substantially increase the energy bill. If, instead, the IIED low energy projections are assumed, a non-nuclear policy substantially increases oil import dependency, converts the energy balance of payments surplus to a deficit, increases coal output but not to an unmanageable level, and increases the energy bill by only a trivial percentage.

One final point is worth noting. The estimates of the cost of going non-nuclear may well be underestimated if several other countries go non-nuclear too, which may be a more likely development than a unilateral moratorium. The more countries that switch from nuclear to coal, oil and gas, the higher the world market prices of these fuels are likely to be, and consequently the higher will be the costs of going non-nuclear.

References

Chapman, P. (1977), 'The economics of UK solar energy schemes', *Energy Policy*, vol. 5, no. 2.

Chapman, P. (1978), 'Alternative energy sources', in G. Foley and A. van Buren (eds), *Nuclear or Not*, Heinemann, London.

CEGB (1980), *CEGB Annual Reports 1979–80* (Appendix 3), London.

Department of Energy (1977), *Coal and Nuclear Power Station Costs*, Energy Commission Paper No. 6, London.

Department of Energy (1978), *Energy Policy: A Consultative Document*, Cmnd 7101, HMSO, London.

Eden, R., Posner, M., Bending, R., Crouch, E. and Stanislaw, J. (1981), *Energy Economics: Growth Resources and Policies*, Cambridge University Press, Cambridge, UK.

Elliot, D. (1979), 'Energy options and employment', Centre for Alternative and Industrial Technological Systems, North East London Polytechnic.

Energy 2000 (1977), *Energy Supply to the year 2000: Global and National Studies*, 2nd and 3rd Technical Reports, Workshop on Alternative Energy Strategies, MIT Press, Cambridge, 1977.

Fabian Society (1980), J. Goode, D. Roy, A. Sedgwick, 'Energy policy: a reappraisal', *Fabian Research Series No. 343*, London.

Flowers Report (1976), *Nuclear Power and the Environment*, Royal Commission on Environmental Pollution, 6th Report (Chairman: Sir B. Flowers), Cmnd 6618, HMSO, London.

Leach, G. *et al.*, (1977), 'Evidence to the Windscale inquiry', *Windscale Inquiry Report*, HMSO, London, 1978.

Leach, G., Lewis, C., van Buren, A., Foley, G. (1979), *A Low Energy Strategy for the United Kingdom*, International Institute for Environment and Development, Science Reviews, London.

Pearce, D. W. (1979), 'Social cost-benefit analysis and nuclear futures', *Energy Economics*, vol. 1, no. 2.

Rouse, J. S. (1979), 'Soft energy paths and the Birmingham Energy Model', Occasional Paper, Department of Government and Economics, City of Birmingham Polytechnic.

Ryle, M. (1977), 'The economics of alternative energy sources', *Nature*, vol. 267, 12 May.

Shaw, K. R. (1979), 'Capital cost escalation and the choice of power stations', *Energy Policy*, vol. 7, no. 4, pp. 321–8.

Sweet, C. (1978), 'Nuclear power costs in the UK', *Energy Policy*, vol. 6, no. 2.

Todd, W. and Alty, C. J. (1977), *An Alternative Energy Strategy for the UK*, National Centre for Alternative Technology.

10

Variable Demand

10.1 The Importance of Variable Demand

All the versions of the Birmingham Energy Model so far described assume that projections have been made of the levels of final consumption for each fuel in each period over the next fifty years, and the task is to choose a strategy for meeting those specified demands. This strategy includes extraction, depletion, import and export of the fossil fuels, synthetic production of oil and gas from coal, and the generation of electricity from coal, oil, gas or nuclear energy. But it does not allow variations in final consumption. In this chapter, we wish to explore the possibility that it may be advantageous to reduce or increase the final consumption of energy in general, or to switch consumption from one fuel to another. That is, we wish to make the levels of demand *endogenous* (to be determined within the model) rather than *exogenous* (specified from outside the model).

Of course, it is somewhat more difficult to build and operate a model with variable demands that are determined endogenously than one in which demands are fixed exogenously. At the very least, the model has to be extended in size and values have to be attached to final consumption in order that the advantages of changes in final consumption can be weighed against the costs. None the less, a strong case can be made for a more comprehensive model.

The main argument is that demand depends to a significant extent upon absolute and relative fuel prices. Any forecast of demand levels is implicitly assuming a future path of prices. But in so far as fuel prices reflect costs, prices will depend upon the policy that is adopted to meet demand, which is in turn determined by the model itself. Only by chance would the pricing structure resulting from the solution to a fixed demand model be the same as that implicitly used to forecast these fixed demands.

To illustrate, consider the different structures of marginal costs (shadow prices) resulting from the various runs of the cost model. In the Base Case, the shadow price of coal lies mostly in the range £24 to £32 per tonne while the shadow price of oil rises steadily from £54 to £108 per tonne then stays at that level. When the energy balance of payments constraint is imposed, the coal shadow price rises to £68 per tonne while the oil shadow price rises eventually to £211 per tonne. In contrast, when coal imports are allowed, the coal shadow price stays constant at £21 per tonne and the oil shadow price settles at £99 per tonne. Actual prices will not of course be precisely equal to these shadow prices but they are likely to move in the same general directions. Is it reasonable, then, to expect the demand for coal to be the same at £68 as at £21 per tonne, or the demand for oil to be the same at £211 per tonne as at £99 per tonne.

In considering situations where fuel prices can differ by a factor of two or three, attention clearly needs to be paid to price elasticities of demand. There are several possible effects to be considered. A general doubling of fuel prices will surely stimulate the adoption of conservation measures. A fall in the price of a fuel may stimulate completely new sources of demand. A rise in the price of one fuel relative to another will cause consumers to seek ways of substituting the relatively cheaper fuel for the relatively expensive one.

Price elasticity of demand also modifies the effects of imposing or re-laxing various policy constraints, since final consumption can be varied along with methods of production. For example, with fixed demands the balance of payments constraint has to be met by large-scale produc-tion of coal from tranches IV and V and by the manufacture and export of synthetic gas in order to compensate for the import of oil. With variable demands, however, the consumption (and hence import) of oil could be reduced, which in turn would not necessitate such high produc-tion levels of coal and synthetic gas. We explore this particular example in Section 10.7 below.

This added flexibility lowers the cost of imposing any given policy restriction, since the model has additional 'degrees of freedom' in seek-ing the cheapest way of accommodating any constraint. By the same token, the value of relaxing any restriction (e.g. allowing coal imports) is greater, since new opportunities (e.g. increased coal consumption) are available.

The remainder of this chapter describes a larger and more sophisti-cated version of the BEM in which final consumption is determined within the model (i.e. demand is endogenous). The policies it yields are compared with those of the fixed demand model, and the importance and usefulness of the two types of model are appraised.

10.2　Intuitive Structure of the Variable Demand Model

In the fixed demand model, the objective is to minimise the *cost* of meeting exogenously specified levels of energy demand, by appropriate choice of investment, production and trade policies. In the variable demand model, the objective is to maximise the *net benefit* generated by the energy sector as a whole. Net benefit is defined as total benefit from fuel consumption less costs of investment and production and net imports. The cost terms are identical to those in the fixed demand model, as are the various blocks of constraints. Here we need only discuss the nature of the benefits from consumption.

Figure 10.1 shows a hypothetical demand curve for some fuel, on the assumption that incomes and the prices of competing and complement-ary goods are held constant. The usual interpretation of the demand

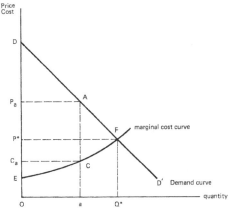

Figure 10.1 *Definition of net benefit*

curve is that it shows the quantity demanded by consumers at any price. However, it may alternatively be interpreted as showing the *value* to consumers of each successive unit of output, on the assumption that each successive unit is devoted to the highest value usage outstanding. Thus, the ath unit is worth p_a to some consumer, and the first Oa units of output are in total worth ODAa, which is the area under demand curve up to output a.

Similarly, the marginal cost curve represents the cost of successive units of output. Thus, the ath unit of output is assumed to cost c_a and the total cost of the first a units of output is given by OECa, which is the area under the marginal cost curve up to output a.

It follows that the net benefit of the ath unit of output is $p_a - c_a (=AC)$, and the net benefit of Oa units of output is EDAC.

It is now immediately obvious that if the objective is to maximise this net benefit, output should be expanded to q^*, at which point the net benefit of an additional unit of output is zero, and total net benefit of q^* units is EDF. In this simple model, the optimal (net benefit maximising) output would be demanded and supplied at a price equal to p^*, which is the marginal cost at optimal output.

An alternative interpretation of net benefit is possible. If price p_a is charged, the area p_aDA represents consumer surplus, defined as the value of output to consumers over and above what they actually have to pay. Similarly, area Ec_aC represents producer surplus (or net revenue), defined as the amount which producers get in excess of their actual costs of production. It may be verified that the sum of consumer and producer surplus is maximised at output q^*, and is in fact equal to net benefit as defined earlier. Thus, the objective in the fixed demand model might equally be described as the maximisation of consumer plus producer surplus.

10.3 Mathematical Formulation

The above analysis involving a single fuel with prices of other fuels held constant is inappropriate for the energy sector as a whole. In our model we wish to choose prices and output of all fuels simultaneously, bearing in mind that, in general, the demand for each fuel will depend on its own price and also on the prices of all other fuels. A graphical representation is no longer adequate, and a more formal mathematical model becomes necessary.

To represent the single-fuel model more formally, let $p(q)$ denote the inverse demand curve and $c(q)$ the marginal cost curve. Net benefit $B(q)$ is defined by

$$B(q) = \int_0^q [p(q') - c(q')] \, dq'$$

To maximise, set the derivative equal to zero

$$B'(q) = p(q) - c'(q) = 0$$

hence at optimality price equals marginal cost

$$p(q) = c'(q)$$

More generally, consider the system of demand functions

$$y_i = y_i(p_1, \ldots, p_n) \qquad i = 1, \ldots, n$$

where y_i denotes consumption of fuel i as a function of prices $p_1, \ldots, p_n$ of all fuels (for a specified level of national income). Write the inverse demand functions

$$p_i = p_i(y_1, \ldots, y_n) \qquad i = 1, \ldots, n$$

Net benefit associated with output vector $(y_1, \ldots, y_n)$ is given by the line integral

$$B(y_1, \ldots, y_n) = \oint \sum_{i=1}^n p_i(y_i') \, dy_i'$$

where the path of integration is from the origin $(0, \ldots, 0)$ to the point $(y_1, \ldots, y_n)$. This integral has a unique value if and only if the matrix of partial derivatives $Dp/Dy = [\partial p_i/\partial y_j]$ is symmetric. This is equivalent to symmetry in the matrix Dy/Dp of derivatives of the direct demand functions.

The requirement of symmetry is not as restrictive as it might seem. It is true that empirically estimated demand functions typically do not have this property, but these are uncompensated functions (i.e. demand for each product is not adjusted to compensate for changes in income resulting from changes in other prices). In principle, it is the compensated demand curves which should be used in our analysis, and these *do* satisfy the symmetry condition if they are derived from a suitable utility function.

(For discussion of the line integral as a measure of benefit and its mathematical properties, see Hotelling, 1938; Hicks, 1956; Willig, 1976; and Carey, 1977. On compensated demand functions, see Hicks, 1956, and Hurwicz and Uzawa, 1971.)

One of the few systems of demand functions with the symmetry property is the linear system

$$p = Ay + b$$

where A is a symmetric matrix and b is a vector of constants (incorporating the effects of other variables such as income). The corresponding benefit (or utility) function is the quadratic expression

$$B(y) = \tfrac{1}{2} y' Ay + by$$

This benefit function is strictly concave with a unique maximum if A is negative definite (Hadley, 1964, Chs 3, 7). This in turn requires the own-price derivatives $\partial p_i / \partial y_i$ (which form the main diagonal of A) to be negative and sufficiently large to outweigh the cross-price derivatives (which will be positive for fuels that are substitutes). This requirement is a generalisation of the requirement in the single fuel model that the demand curve be downward-sloping. If such a condition were not met, increasing consumption in some direction could yield ever increasing marginal benefits, which is economically implausible.

The quadratic element of the benefit function suggests that a quadratic programming algorithm be used to solve the model. However, such algorithms are not widely available and can only deal with problems of limited size. Since our model is predominantly linear, with several hundred variables and constraints, it was thought to be more convenient to linearise the benefit function in order to use a standard linear programming package. This would allow the model to be run repeatedly (e.g. to carry out sensitivity analyses and explore the implications of different assumptions).

One difficulty with linearising the benefit function $B(y)$ is that it is not separable, that is, it contains cross-product terms of the form $a_{ij}y_iy_j$ as well as terms of the form $a_{ii}y_i^2$. We therefore transformed the expression by introducing a new set of variables u defined by $y = Vu$, where V is the matrix of eigenvectors of A. We thus have

$$y'Ay = u'V'AVu = u'Du$$

It is well known (Lancaster, 1973) that if A is a real symmetric matrix then D is a diagonal matrix having the eigenvalues of A as diagonal elements. The result of the transformation is that the expression $\Sigma_i\Sigma_j a_{ij}y_iy_j$ is replaced by the simpler expression $\Sigma_i d_i u_i^2$, plus the addition of the linear constraints $y = Vu$. The negative definiteness of A ensures that all the d_i's are negative, so that $u'Du$ is concave and the objective function has a unique optimum.

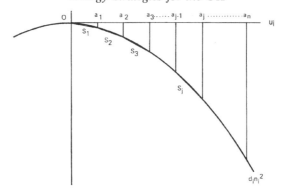

Note: The function has a negative value throughout since d$_j$ is negative.

Figure 10.2 *Piecewise linearisation of a separable quadratic function*

We used a standard procedure for obtaining piecewise-linear approximations to the expression $u'Du$ (Charnes and Cooper, 1961, Ch. 10; Dantzig, 1963, Ch. 24; Beale, 1968, Ch. 10). Each term $d_i u_i^2$ is approximated by a piecewise linear expression $\Sigma_j S_{ij} \Delta_{ij}$, which takes the same values as $d_i u_i^2$ at points $0, a_1, a_2, \ldots, a_n$ (see Figure 10.2). The variable u_i is replaced by the sum of variables Δ_{ij}, where $0 \leqslant \Delta_{ij} \leqslant a_j - a_{j-1}$. The coefficient of Δ_{ij} in the objective function is S_{ij}, which has approximately the slope of the original curve in the range (a_{j-1}, a_j).

By reducing the size of these ranges, and correspondingly increasing the number of approximating variables, the approximation may be made as close to the original function as desired. In the present model, we found after some experimentation that different levels of refinement in making linear approximations (ranging between ten and forty units) were required for different fuels in order to obtain adequately smooth results. Since the model was to be run a large number of times, it was more convenient to maintain the same approximation each time than to tailor the approximation to each set of data. This accounts for the 'ripple effect' in some of the graphs, which would presumably be eliminated if a finer approximation were used.

10.4 Fitting the Demand Functions

Recall that there are eight fuel products (coal, gas, electricity and five oil products) which might be consumed in each of the five market sectors. However, it was not thought appropriate to model demand for each fuel in each sector as a function of the price of all other fuels. Some simplification seemed possible. First, certain fuels are unsuitable for meeting certain demands (e.g. aviation fuel in the Industrial Sector), hence are omitted entirely from that sector. Second, the demands for certain fuels are thought to be less dependent on price than on other factors such as output or income; hence are assumed to be determined exogenously (e.g. requirements in the Iron and Steel Sector). Third, some fuels are not in effective competition with other fuels in certain sectors; hence their demand is largely a function of their own price (e.g. petrol in the Transport Sector). Finally, most fuels are in effective competition with some but not all fuel products (e.g. in the Domestic Sector gas, electricity and kerosene compete with each other for many uses but not with other fuel products).

The assumptions made are set out in Table 10.1. It should be emphasised that the aim is to simplify the analysis of a very complex situation by incorporating the most important interdependencies and eliminating the less important ones. Different assumptions could well be justified by subsequent experience, or under changed conditions, or with a view to more refined analysis.

A difficulty in modelling energy demand is that substitution between fuels is unlikely to respond immediately to changes in relative prices.

Table 10.1 *Demand Assumptions in the Variable Demand Model*

Market Sectors	Exogenous demand	*Demand Assumptions* Interdependent endogenous demand	Endogenous demand (own elasticity)	Fuels excluded from Market Sector
Domestic	Coal	Gas Electricity Kerosene[a]		Fuel oil Gas oil Petrol Naphtha[b]
Iron and Steel	Coal Gas Electricity Fuel oil			Gas oil Petrol Naphtha Kerosene
Other Industry	Electricity Naphtha	Coal Gas Fuel oil	Gas oil	Petrol Kerosene
Transport	Coal Gas Electricity		Petrol Kerosene[a] Gas oil[c]	Fuel oil Naphtha
Commercial and Other	Coal	Gas Electricity Kerosene[a]		Fuel oil Gas oil Petrol Naphtha

[a] Kerosene is a broad fuel category which includes heating oil in the Domestic and Commercial Sections and aviation fuel in the Transport Sector.
[b] Naphtha is by far the most important oil product in non-energy use though there are many others.
[c] Mainly diesel fuel in Transport Sector.

Table 10.2 Long-run Own-Price and Cross-Price Elasticities in BEM

Price	Domestic Sector								Industrial Sector (excluding Iron and Steel)							
Demand	Coal	Gas	Electricity	Fuel oil	Gas oil	Kerosene	Naphtha	Petrol	Coal	Gas	Electricity	Fuel oil	Gas oil	Kerosene	Naphtha	Petrol
Coal	0	0	0	—	—	0	—	—	−1.0	0.4	0	0.4	0	—	0	—
Gas	0	−0.5	0.4	—	—	0.17	—	—	0.4	−1.0	0	0.4	0	—	0	—
Electricity	0	0.4	−1.0	—	—	0.17	—	—	0	0	0	0	0	—	0	—
Fuel oil	—	—	—	—	—	—	—	—	0.4	0.4	0	−1.0	0	—	0	—
Gas oil	—	—	—	—	—	—	—	—	0	0	0	0	−0.2	—	0	—
Kerosene	0	0.78	0.89	—	—	−1.0	—	—	—	—	—	—	—	—	—	—
Naphtha	—	—	—	—	—	—	—	—	0	0	0	0	0	—	0	—
Petrol	—	—	—	—	—	—	—	—	—	—	—	—	—	—	—	—

Table 10.2 continued

Transport Sector

Price → Demand ↓	Coal	Gas	Electricity	Fuel oil	Gas oil	Kerosene	Naphtha	Petrol
Coal	O	O	O	—	O	O	—	O
Gas	O	O	O	—	O	O	—	O
Electricity	O	O	O	—	O	O	—	O
Fuel oil	—	—	—	—	—	—	—	—
Gas oil	O	O	O	—	-0.2	O	—	O
Kerosene	O	O	O	—	O	-0.2	—	O
Naphtha	—	—	—	—	—	—	—	—
Petrol	O	O	O	—	O	O	—	-0.5

Commercial and Other Sector

Price → Demand ↓	Coal	Gas	Electricity	Fuel oil	Gas oil	Kerosene	Naphtha	Petrol
Coal	O	O	O	—	—	O	—	—
Gas	O	-1.0	0.4	—	—	0.4	—	—
Electricity	O	0.4	-1.0	—	—	0.4	—	—
Fuel oil	—	—	—	—	—	—	—	—
Gas oil	—	—	—	—	—	—	—	—
Kerosene	O	0.4	0.4	—	—	-1.0	—	—
Naphtha	—	—	—	—	—	—	—	—
Petrol	—	—	—	—	—	—	—	—

Notes:

[a] The row for each fuel shows the price elasticities of demand for the fuel in the appropriate Market Sector. For example, in the Industrial Sector the own-price elasticity of demand for coal is -1.0 while the elasticity of demand for coal with respect to the price of gas is 0.4.

[b] The symbol, O, indicates an assumed zero own-price elasticity (exogenously determined demand) or an assumed zero cross-price elasticity (no substitution). The symbol, —, indicates that the fuel is excluded from the market.

This is partly because changing from one fuel to another generally involves the purchase of new energy-using appliances, and partly because consumers naturally base such decisions not only on current relative prices but also on expected future prices, and their expectations may in turn reflect past experience. These considerations are not explicitly included in the demand model. A modified version embodying time lags is discussed in Section 10.9 below from which it would appear that omitting time lags does not cause serious errors in such a long-term energy model.

We turn finally to the price elasticities incorporated in the model. There is no doubt that energy consumption *is* significantly responsive to price (Pindyck, 1979; Kouris, 1981; Uri, 1979). However, there is considerable variation in the estimated price elasticities, both for energy as a whole and for individual fuels and sectors (Department of Energy, 1977; Taylor, 1977). The elasticities we have used are shown in Table 10.2.

In the Domestic, Industrial and Commercial Sectors, where three fuels are assumed to compete, we have set own-price elasticities equal to unity (except for gas in the Domestic Sector set at –0.5). These elasticities, and the associated cross-price elasticities, are broadly in line with the long-run elasticities estimated by Pindyck. Own-price elasticities for gas oil in the Industrial Sector, and petrol, kerosene (aviation fuel) and gas oil in the Transport Sector were estimated by one of the authors from British consumption data using time series analysis. The low values presumably reflect the lack of close substitutes.

Since there is so much doubt about the magnitudes of price elasticities, and whether these magnitudes can be expected to remain constant over time, we have run the model with alternative assumptions, as reported in Section 10.7 below. A much more detailed sensitivity analysis could be worthwhile, and the model is well equipped to do this.

The effect of changes in national income on energy consumption is included in the model by specifying income elasticities of demand for fuels and a trend rate of growth of GDP of 2 per cent per year over the programme period. Recent estimates and assumptions of UK income elasticities of energy consumption have been in the range 0.5 to 1.0 (see e.g. Common, 1981 and Kouris, 1981). For all fuels whose demands are endogenously determined, other than kerosene and gas oil in the Transport Sector (for aviation and road haulage, respectively) the income elasticity (or more precisely, the GDP elasticity) of fuel demand is assumed to be at the low end of this spectrum (0.5), while for kerosene and gas oil in the Transport Sector GDP elasticities are assumed to be at the other end of the spectrum (1.0). The approach taken here, in which the demand for a fuel in a market is related to prices of fuels and income, is of course different from the approach used by the Department of Energy (1978), in which total energy consumption in a sector is assumed to be a function of GDP (or another measure of economic activity) and fuel shares in the sector are then determined by relative prices and other considerations.

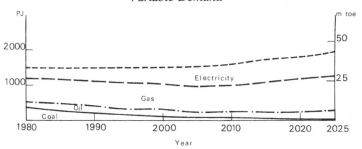

Figure 10.3 *Domestic Sector annual energy demand (variable demand)*

10.5 Changes in Final Consumption

As already explained, final consumption is now determined endogenously within the model instead of being specified exogenously. We consider in turn each of the five demand sectors (Figures 10.3–10.7), comparing them with the fixed Base Case (Figures 4.2–4.7). For brevity,
only the most significant differences are noted.

1. Domestic Sector: Oil consumption rises slightly over time instead
of falling to near zero; gas and electricity consumption do not rise so far
or fast. Aggregate energy demand falls to half the fixed demand level by
2025.
2. Iron and Steel Sector: Specified exogenously as before.
3. Industrial Sector: Coal consumption rises only half as high; gas oil
and fuel oil consumption are higher initially and do not fall significantly.
Aggregate energy consumption is initially three-quarters of the fixed
demand level, but eventually rises to about the same level.

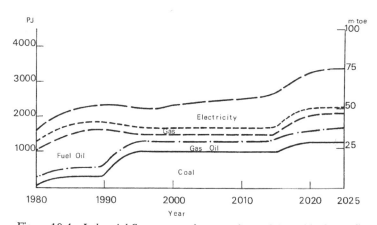

Figure 10.4 *Industrial Sector annual energy demand (variable demand)*

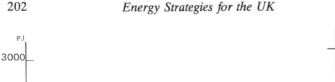
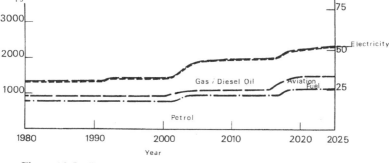

Figure 10.5   *Transport Sector annual energy demand (variable demand)*

4.   Transport Sector: Consumption of motor spirit rises instead of falling; diesel oil consumption rises more sharply; aviation fuel consumption increases to less than half the fixed demand level. Aggregate energy consumption is eventually nearly 20 per cent higher than the fixed demand level.

5.   Commercial Sector: Oil consumption falls then rises instead of falling throughout; gas consumption increases at a slower rate; consumption of electricity is much lower. Aggregate energy consumption eventually falls to three-quarters of the fixed demand level.

There are thus significant differences in the predicted patterns of energy consumption. When the five sectors are aggregated, these differences to some extent cancel out, and certainly the aggregate demand for energy as a whole is the same in 2025 as in the fixed demand model. (It is 6 per cent lower in 1980, but the elasticities of demand may overestimate the short-run possibilities of conservation and substitution.) Nevertheless, there are still substantial differences in the mix of fuels. By 2025 oil accounts for 44 per cent of the total instead of 27 per cent,

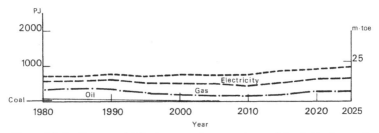

Figure 10.6   *Commercial Sector annual energy demand (variable demand)*

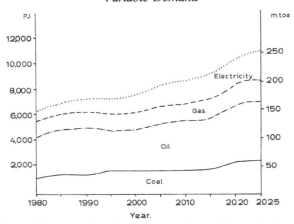

Figure 10.7 *Annual total final energy demand (variable demand)*

and the shares of the other three fuels are reduced about equally (Table 10.3).

The implications of the variable demand model may be appreciated by presenting these results in a different light, using them in order to evaluate the Department of Energy demand assumptions. That is, suppose (1) that the elasticities of demand and the world market prices incorporated in the demand model are accepted as reasonable estimates of what will happen, (2) that domestic fuel prices are allowed to reflect marginal costs (shadow prices), and (3) that there are no government restrictions on capacity or output other than those already embodied in the model. How close are the Department of Energy demand projections to those which the model suggests will maximise net value of output in the UK energy sector? The predicted aggregate demand for energy as a whole over the next fifty years tallies almost exactly. However, this conceals very substantial differences with respect to individual sectors and fuels. Aggregate energy demand is underestimated in the Transport Sector, overestimated in the Commercial Sector and severely overestimated in the Domestic Sector. Aggregate demand for coal, electricity and gas is overestimated, whereas the demand for oil is severely underestimated. The single most glaring difference is that the Department of Energy projections assume that by 2025 oil will mean a *lower* proportion of final demand than coal, whereas the BEM suggests that oil will still account for *over twice as much* final demand as coal.

Given the tentative nature of our elasticity assumptions, it would not be appropriate to interpret the above differences as criticisms of the Department of Energy but they do highlight the importance of price elasticities. (See, however, the criticism by Pearce, 1980, that the department has implicitly assumed energy elasticities which are too low, leading to an overestimate of total demand.)

Table 10.3 Proportions of Final Demand Accounted for by Each Fuel: Comparison of Fixed and Variable Demand

Fuel	Fixed base case						Variable base case					
	1980		2000		2025		1980		2000		2025	
	(PJ)	(%)	(PJ)	(%)	(PJ)	(%)	(PJ)	(%)	(PJ)	(%)	(PJ)	(%)
Coal	1219	18	1886	23	3403	30	1006	16	1878	24	2330	21
Oil	3090	46	2993	36	3048	27	3240	51	3181	41	5020	44
Gas	1583	23	1877	22	2152	19	1276	20	1362	17	1726	15
Electricity	857	13	1625	19	2753	24	799	13	1424	18	2232	20
	6748	100	8381	100	11356	100	6321	100	7845	100	11308	100

Source: BEM fixed and variable base cases.

10.6 Production and Extraction Policies

We now examine in more detail the implications for each of the four fuel industries, as shown in Figures 10.8–10.13 (to be compared with Figures 5.1–5.6 for the fixed demand case).

The total production of coal is about the same, but lower proportions are used for domestic consumption, synthetic gas production and electricity generation, whereas a considerably higher proportion is used to make synthetic oil (Figure 10.8).

Peak extraction of oil is about 10 per cent lower than in the fixed demand Base Case, and prolonged from 1985 to 1990 (Figure 10.10). Synthetic oil is produced earlier and on a larger scale, thereby enabling a reduction in imports, especially around the middle of the programme period. Domestic oil consumption is higher over the first twenty years, at the expense of exports of both crude oil and oil products and (to a much lesser extent) of oil-fired electricity generation (Figure 10.11). Oil consumption is very much higher after the turn of the century: again, this is made possible mainly by reduced exports of oil products.

Since gas consumption is very much lower, extraction is much smoother over time, with the peak extraction rate about 40 per cent lower and deferred from 1985 to 1995 (Figure 10.12). There are no imports, and it is even possible to export up to 2b. therms per year from about 1992 to 2012. Synthetic gas is produced on a much more modest scale, although it still accounts for the bulk of consumption by 2025.

The lower total consumption of electricity is accommodated mainly by a reduction in nuclear energy, although the pattern of nuclear elec-

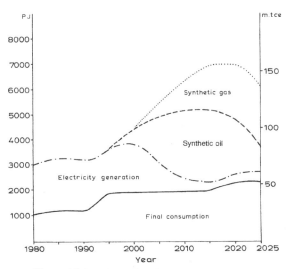

Figure 10.8 *Uses of coal (variable demand)*

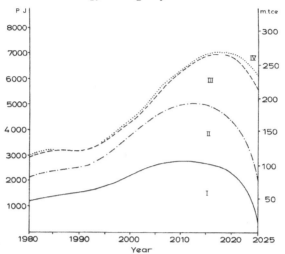

Figure 10.9   *Coal extraction by tranche (variable demand)*

tricity replacing coal and oil generated electricity is broadly the same (Figure 10.13).

Despite the increase in oil consumption, its shadow price follows a similar time pattern to that in the fixed demand model, in both cases reflecting the possibility of importing at exogenously determined world prices (Figure 10.14). Gas shadow prices are generally lower, reflecting the lower consumption. (Gas imports are generally unprofitable, hence the world price is less relevant.) Electricity consumption is lower in

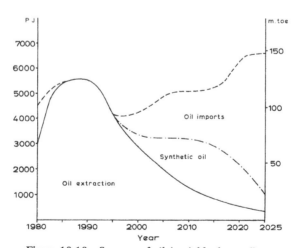

Figure 10.10   *Sources of oil (variable demand)*

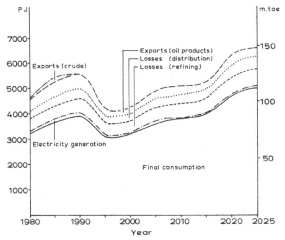

Figure 10.11   *Uses of oil (variable demand)*

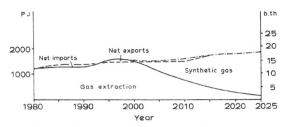

Figure 10.12   *Gas industry (variable demand)*

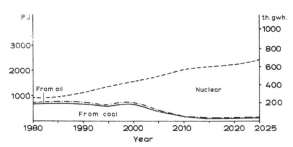

Figure 10.13   *Electricity generation (variable demand)*

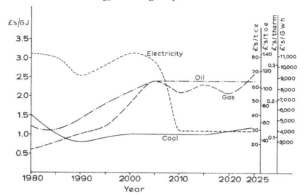

Figure 10.14   *Shadow prices of fuels (variable demand)*

2000 when nuclear capacity constraints are binding; hence the electricity shadow price does not rise dramatically. The shadow price of coal remains low (except in the first period).

In the fixed demand model, coal accounts for over half the primary energy by 2025, more than double the proportion accounted for by oil (although by 2025 these proportions have slipped back to 50 per cent and 29 per cent, respectively). With variable demand, coal rises to only 43 per cent of primary energy, just exceeding oil which still accounts for 40 per cent. The proportion of nuclear is slightly lower.

To appreciate the above information, we may evaluate the earlier fixed Base Case results against the present variable Base Case results. Assuming the latter to be 'correct', and after allowing for the differences in final consumption noted in the previous section, the major 'errors' of the fixed demand model are as follows: (1) Synthetic oil production is underestimated, whereas crude oil imports (after 1990), crude oil exports (before 1995) and oil product exports (throughout) are overestimated. (2) Gas extracted (before 2000), gas imports (around 1985) and synthetic gas production (after 2000) are all substantially overestimated. (3) The rate at which the electricity industry goes nuclear is slightly overestimated.

10.7   Alternative Scenarios

We have rerun the variable demand model under a variety of different assumptions and scenarios, just as with the fixed demand model. In this section we note for each case the main similarities and differences between the two models.

(1)   Elasticity of Demand
Demand elasticities are the subject of great controversy, and it would be possible to explore a vast number of alternative assumptions. For

reasons of time and space we limited ourselves to testing only two such alternatives: one in which all elasticities are increased by 50 per cent (both own-price and cross-price, in all periods), and the other in which all elasticities are reduced by 50 per cent (i.e. halved).

In the case of higher elasticities, final consumption of gas is about 20 per cent lower after the turn of the century; consumption of coal and oil are slightly lower, consumption of electricity slightly higher in later years. Production of synthetic gas is reduced, and the coal thus made available is used mainly for synthetic oil, which replaces oil imports. Total coal extraction is very slightly down (1 per cent over the programme period); tranche IV is required in only two periods after the first, and then on a very small scale.

With lower elasticities, final consumption of oil is about 18 per cent higher by the year 2025, while final consumption of coal is 21 per cent lower. The additional oil is provided mainly by increased imports and to a much lesser extent by faster extraction and increased production of synthetic oil. Both synthetic gas and gas exports are reduced slightly.

Perhaps changes in *relative* elasticities of demand for fuels would have a more significant effect, but the above results suggest that 50 per cent changes *across the board*, whether increases or decreases, do not substantially affect the value-maximising energy policy.

(2)   Terminal Values
The same terminal values were placed on coal, oil and gas reserves as described in Section 6.8. The effects on consumption were negligible, the largest change being a slight decrease in gas consumption in the final period. The production of synthetic oil is gradually increased after the turn of the century (by about 11m. tonnes in 2015 and nearly 16m. tonnes in 2025). This allows a corresponding reduction in oil imports, but also necessitates a corresponding increase in coal extraction. Apart from this, changes in energy policy are negligible. (It is worth noting that, whereas in the fixed demand model terminal values led to a significantly slower rate of depletion of oil reserves, the variable demand model has already led to a somewhat slower depletion rate before imposing terminal values.)

(3)   Oil Import Dependency Constraints
Recall that these constraints prevent imports of crude oil from exceeding 40 per cent of the total volume of crude oil passing through UK refineries. With fixed demand, the effects were to slow down extraction and increase synthetic oil production in order to reduce oil imports. This in turn necessitated an increase in coal extraction and the transfer of coal from synthetic gas to synthetic oil, which in turn led to an increase in the import of gas.

Exactly the same effects occur with variable demand, except that they are in some cases more dramatic and are accompanied by changes in final consumption. Oil imports, previously as high as 125m. tonnes by 2025, are completely eliminated! The gap is filled partly by evening out the depletion rate of oil reserves (with the 1985 peak rate down by 10m. tonnes), and partly by reducing final consumption of oil (about 10m. tonnes lower throughout), but mainly by a vast programme of synthetic oil production. To obtain the necessary coal, the extraction rate rises from 265 to 320m. tonnes in 2015, then, instead of falling, it continues to increase to 370m. tonnes by 2025 (using tranche V). In addition, the production of synthetic gas is limited to a fifteen-year period, and then at the severely reduced level of 5.4b. therms. Gas exports are therefore eliminated, and imports expand to meet demand, which is itself somewhat reduced in the last few periods.

The net cost of this constraint is £11 billion, substantially higher than in the case of fixed demand. The reason for the great difference is that with variable demand, the opportunities are taken to expand oil consumption from imports, thereby substantially increasing the degree of oil import dependency. To achieve a 40 per cent oil import dependency thus requires a much greater adjustment than in the case of fixed demand.

(4)   Balance of Payments Constraint
Recall from Section 7.4 that this constraint required that the average annual deficit on the balance of payments for energy products should not exceed £1,300m. The main effects in the fixed demand model were (1) a severe reduction in the rate of domestic oil extraction and an increase in oil imports and synthetic oil production; (2) a dramatic increase in the production of synthetic gas in order to eliminate imports five years earlier than they otherwise would be and to export gas later; and (3) a substantial increase in coal production to an annual peak of about 4.5m. tonnes by 2025. The net cost of this policy constraint was £9.12b. present value.

In the variable demand model there is little change in the oil industry, apart from a 30 per cent reduction in oil imports in the last decade. About two-thirds of this is met by an increase in synthetic oil and one-third by a reduction in consumption. The production of synthetic gas is dramatically increased in order to allow gas exports, as in the fixed demand model, but once again there is a contribution from reduced consumption. Coal production increases, but not to quite the same level as in the fixed demand model. The reduction in total net benefit is £4b. present value. Thus, when consumption can be adjusted as well as production methods, the cost of imposing this balance of payments constraint is reduced by half.

(5)   Coal Imports
When coal imports are allowed, they do not begin until 2010, but then rise steadily to 328m. tonnes in the last period. Domestic extraction actually increases slightly up to the year 2020 (by about 7 per cent), but this is more than offset by the 40 per cent reduction in the final period. The additional coal is used to produce synthetic oil, which replaces oil imports to an even greater degree than before. Production patterns for other fuels are unchanged, as are final consumption patterns of all fuels. The net value of allowing coal imports is about £269m. present value.

The envisaged import of coal is very substantial, but by no means as drastic as in the case of fixed demand, where imports were predicted to reach 530m. tonnes by 2025 (see Section 7.5), with important repercussions for oil exports, the production and import of gas and the choice of fuel for electricity generation. As in the fixed demand case, it is still true that the UK coal industry itself is largely unaffected by coal imports. (This conclusion does *not* hold, it should be emphasised, if costs of domestic extraction are not held down. If domestic costs rise at 1 per cent per annum, relative to world coal prices, domestic extraction never rises above 190m. tonnes, and falls to below 75m. tonnes by 2025.)

If the world price of coal is assumed to increase at 1 per cent per annum, it is not economical to import any coal during the whole of the programme period. Evidently synthetic oil made from coal imports has only a narrow cost advantage over imported oil, so the world price of coal is a quite crucial parameter in this model – but, again, crucial only for the production and import of oil. Even a parallel 1 per cent annual increase in domestic coal extraction costs does not provoke any coal imports, since replacement of domestic extraction is not the most relevant use for coal imports.

(6)   Non-nuclear Policy
Section 9.3 described the effects of a ban on further construction of nuclear plant. With fixed demand, the main effects were (1) to replace nuclear power by oil, gas and especially coal-fired plant, (2) to increase coal extraction by 50 per cent in the later periods, reaching nearly 400m. tonnes by 2025 and relying heavily on the unexplored tranche V, and (3) to replace both synthetic fuels by increased imports. The net cost of the policy was £35.5b. present value.

When a non-nuclear policy is applied in the variable demand model, coal-fired plant replaces nuclear capacity, with only a slight increase in oil generation in the end periods, and no use of gas. Electricity consumption is in any case somewhat lower than with fixed demand (620,000 GWh in 2025 compared to 765,000 GWh), and is now lowered further (to 546,000 GWh) in response to the higher cost of generation.

Coal extraction needs to be increased only slightly, using a negligible amount of tranche V, since final consumption of coal is reduced, synthetic oil is not produced, and production of synthetic gas is reduced (Figure 10.15). However, oil imports are vastly expanded after 2015 in order to replace synthetic oil and provide increased fuel for electricity generation (Figure 10.16). Mainly, however, they are used to meet a sharp increase in final consumption of oil after 2015, which reflects a switch away from electricity because of the latter's much higher (shadow) price (Figure 10.17). Synthetic gas is gradually replaced by gas imports (Figure 10.18).

The net cost of the non-nuclear policy is £20b. This is about two-thirds of the cost in the case of fixed demand, but none the less still much higher than when strict (IIED) conservation is in effect (cf. Section 9.5).

212

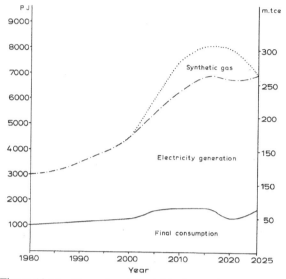

Figure 10.15   *Uses of coal (variable demand, non-nuclear)*

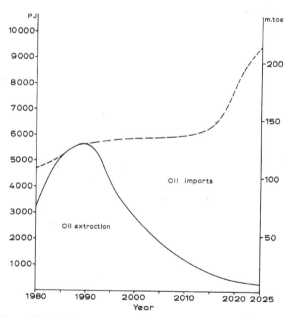

Figure 10.16   *Sources of oil (variable demand, non-nuclear)*

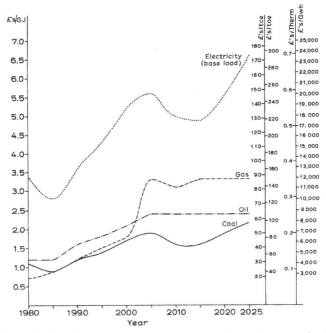

Figure 10.17   *Shadow prices of fuels (variable demand, non-nuclear)*

(7)   Conclusions

It is impossible to summarise the results of this section in a single paragraph, but three points are worth making. First it *does* make a difference whether demand is variable or fixed, because in numerous cases the imposition of a constraint, or the adjustment of market conditions, led to changes in final consumption as part of the process of adjustment, and to ignore these would be misleading. Second, however, the changes in consumption patterns were, on the whole, relatively small compared to the changes in production patterns, and often there were no changes at all in final consumption – though this could of course be different if

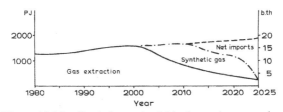

Figure 10.18   *Gas industry (variable demand, non-nuclear)*

price elasticities of demand were higher. Third, the differences in the effects of policy restrictions or variations in parameters were probably less significant than the differences between the fixed and variable demand Base Cases. In other words, the 'errors' in predicting demand and choosing a strategy in the first place are probably more significant than the 'errors' in predicting and choosing *changes* in demand and strategy in response to variations in conditions and objectives.

10.8   Rising World Prices after 2000

Section 6.7 explored the effects of assuming world prices of oil and gas rising at, respectively, 2 per cent and 1 per cent per annum after the year 2000, instead of remaining constant. With demand fixed, the main effects were to slow down the rate of extraction of domestic oil, to replace most oil imports by synthetic oil, to increase coal production substantially after 2010, and to increase imports of gas in order to reduce the amount of coal used to manufacture synthetic gas. The energy bill was £372b. higher.

With variable demand, all sectors respond in some way to the higher fuel prices after 2000. In the Domestic Sector electricity tends to be substituted for gas. The Industrial Sector uses less coal and less fuel oil. The Transport Sector economises on motor spirit. The Commercial Sector uses much less gas and oil, but slightly more electricity. In aggregate, final consumption of gas is down by about a quarter, oil and coal are down by about a tenth, and electricity up by about a tenth. Consumption of energy as a whole is down by 7 per cent.

The time pattern of domestic oil extraction is unchanged, but synthetic oil is substituted for imports as before. Production of synthetic gas is lower to reflect the lower consumption, and gas imports are not required. Coal production is substantially increased after 2010, although the increased demand for electricity is met by nuclear energy. Thus the effects of rising prices are basically the same as when demand is fixed, but rather less drastic (no change in oil extraction and no gas imports), since some of the pressure is absorbed by reductions and substitutions in final consumption.

It might be argued that it is more plausible to assume rising oil and gas prices after 2000 than constant prices: in other words, this might have been a more plausible Base Case. It is therefore worth exploring briefly the effects of the various sensitivity analyses and policies under this assumption, to see whether the effects are the same as in the variable Base Case.

(1)   Elasticity of Demand
The effects of 50 per cent changes in elasticities of demand are more or less as before. With higher elasticities, final consumption of gas and oil is down, while that of coal and electricity is up, especially in later periods. There is greater production of synthetic oil to replace oil imports, but otherwise higher elasticities do not make a great difference.

With lower elasticities of demand, oil and gas consumption is higher, met mainly by higher oil imports and higher synthetic gas production.

(2)   Terminal Values
The only significant change here is that coal extraction is reduced by 95m. tonnes in the final period. Almost all of this (89m. tonnes) is accounted for by a reduction in synthetic oil production (replaced by oil imports); there is also a slight (6m. tonnes) reduction in synthetic gas production (leading to correspondingly lower final consumption).

(3)   Oil Import Constraints
The 40 per cent oil import constraint has virtually no effect, except to reduce oil consumption slightly in later years, with a corresponding reduction in synthetic oil. The other modifications associated with this policy constraint have already been induced by the rising world oil and gas prices after 2000. The cost is only £124m.

A zero per cent oil import dependency constraint completely eliminates oil imports, leading to lower oil consumption and exports and higher production of synthetic oil. This necessitates a lower production of synthetic gas and an increase in gas imports. In effect, gas imports are substituted for oil imports. The net outcome is almost identical to the case of constant world prices, since the severity of the oil import constraint reduces foreign trade to a negligible level. The cost is quite substantial (£7.6b.).

(4)   Balance of Payments
Imposing the £1,300m. energy balance of payments constraint reduces oil and gas consumption slightly, has no effect on the oil extraction pattern, and replaces oil imports by synthetic oil to a greater extent: all these effects are as before. The main effects of rising world prices are (1) slight differences in the time patterns of imports and synthetic oil (the latter being higher up to 2020 but lower in the final period); (2) a reduction in synthetic gas production (instead of a massive increase), with gas exports discontinued except in 2005; and (3) no significant increase in coal extraction. As with the oil import dependency constraint, several of the effects of the balance of payments constraint have already been induced by the rising oil and gas prices. The cost of the constraint is £29b.

(5)   Coal Imports
With constant world prices of oil and gas after 2000, the main effects of allowing coal imports (at constant price) were (1) to speed up domestic coal extraction, (2) to import coal on an increasing scale, but only from 2010 to 2025, and (3) to produce synthetic oil to replace oil imports. Final consumption was unchanged, there were no crude oil exports, and the production of gas and electricity was unaffected.

With rising world prices of oil and gas, it is more sensible to consider the case where world coal prices rise (at 1 per cent per annum), since this is the reason for the rise in oil and gas prices. Nevertheless, the effects of imports are basically the same. Domestic coal extraction, which was held down to 162m. tonnes in 2005 before soaring to 433m. tonnes in 2025), is now speeded up, reaching 206m. tonnes in 2005, and 375m. tonnes in 2020, before falling to 225m. tonnes in 2025. There are no coal imports until 2015, but then they rise sharply to 393m. tonnes by the end of the programme period. They are mainly used to make synthetic oil available five years earlier, and on a much larger scale by 2025 (using 431m. tonnes compared to 278m. tonnes of coal). Production of synthetic gas is increased (taking 82m. tonnes instead of 65m. tonnes of coal by 2025), which allows gas consumption to rise from 13.6b. to 16.6b. therms. Final consumption of coal also rises slightly, from 78m. to 88m. tonnes in 2025.

The net benefit of these coal imports seems rather small, at £626m. present value. It should be borne in mind, however, that this is the present value (at 5 per cent discount rate) of certain benefits which for the most part are not received until about thirty-five years later. The value of the benefits around the year 2015 will be about £3,453 million, which is equivalent to a benefit of about £335m. in each of the subsequent fifteen years (or about £28 per annum per average family).

It is interesting to note that when domestic coal extraction costs also rise at 1 per cent per annum, the effect of allowing coal imports is slightly less drastic. Domestic production reaches a much lower peak in 2020, which allows tranche IV coal to be replaced by cheaper coal in the cost period. Coal imports are slightly higher in 2015 and 2020 but lower in 2025. Less synthetic oil is produced in the final period, and oil imports are higher and continue longer.

Thus, when oil and gas prices rise after the year 2000, coal imports *do* displace domestic production, and the pattern of imports is affected by domestic extraction costs (in contrast to the cases of fixed demand and variable demand with constant prices).

(6) Non-nuclear Policy
The nature of the policy is essentially the same as with constant oil and gas prices after 2000, except that it is no longer economical to make the sharp switch from electricity to oil consumption in the final decade, with the result that coal extraction is necessarily higher (to produce electricity in the absence of nuclear energy) and oil imports are substantially lower. The cost of the non-nuclear policy is £27b.

(7) Conclusions
Once again, it is impossible to summarise these results. In some cases rising oil and gas prices after 2000 make a difference, while in other cases they do not. Policy constraints geared to reducing imports, especially of oil, are less necessary since rising prices already provide incentives in this direction. On the other hand, a policy such as allowing coal imports now displaces domestic extraction, depending upon the movement of coal extraction costs. Thus, the levels of world oil and gas prices after 2000 are clearly significant, but their precise effects depend upon

policies with respect to other fuels, notably nuclear energy and coal imports.

10.9 Lagged Demand

It is generally agreed that consumers (whether domestic or industrial) do not respond immediately to changes in the prices of fuels. They may be 'locked in' to equipment which uses one particular type of fuel, or they may doubt whether the price change will be permanent. It is conventional, therefore, to distinguish between short-run and long-run elasticities of demand, where the former reflect the immediate response and the latter the response after sufficient time has elapsed for adjustment of stocks of appliances. Empirical evidence suggests that this distinction is important and that long-run elasticities are of the order of twice short-run elasticities (Pindyck, 1979).

All versions of the Birmingham Energy Model described so far assume that energy demands depend upon prices in the same period. No distinction is made between long- and short-run elasticities. (The elasticities used are intended to correspond to long-run elasticities.) It is, however, possible to specify and incorporate demand functions which depend upon prices in two or more periods, thereby allowing a distinction to be drawn between short-run and long-run responses. In this section we report briefly upon the results of one such attempt.

To explore the effects of such a distinction, the BEM was modified by specifying the demands for fuel in period t as linear functions of prices in periods $t-1, t$ and $t+1$. The coefficients in each period were set equal to those in the current period (as described earlier in this chapter) weighted by a Koyck-type lead–lag coefficient. The ratio of the sum of these coefficients to the coefficient in the current period can be interpreted as the ratio of long-run to short-run elasticity. Consequently, to reflect the empirical evidence found by Pindyck, the sum of the three lead–lag coefficient for periods $t-1, t$ and $t+1$ was set equal to twice the lead–lag coefficient in the current period t. (Since the latter was set equal to unity, the sum of coefficients for periods $t-1$ and $t+1$ was also set equal to unity. The final degree of freedom was used to maintain symmetry in the objective function coefficient matrix, which embodied the discount factor.) For further details see Carey and Littlechild (1980).

The model results are very little different from the base case results reported above. Final consumption of oil is about a tenth higher in the final period, that of coal about a tenth lower. Oil is extracted slightly faster, with the higher oil consumption in middle to later years met by higher oil imports. In fact, imports replace synthetic oil slightly. Gas is no longer exported in the middle periods, and gas consumption increases slightly then. Coal production is unchanged, except for being slightly lower in the final period.

Similar results were obtained in other runs. In so far as one can judge from just a few runs of the model, the results suggest that the distinction between short- and long-run elasticities may not be so important for long-term planning models as it is for year-to-year operational purposes.

References

Beale, E. M. L. (1968), *Linear Programming in Practice*, Pitman, London.

Carey, M. (1977), 'Integrability and mathematical programming models: a survey and a parametric approach', *Econometrica*, vol. 45, no. 8.

Carey, M. and Littlechild, S. C. (1980), 'Benefit functions with intemporal cross-elasticities of demand', mimeo, January.

Charnes, A. and Cooper, W. W. (1961), *Management Models and Industrial Applications of Linear Programming*, Vol. 1, Wiley, New York.

Common, M. S. (1981), 'Implied elasticities in some UK energy projections', *Energy Economics*, vol. 3, no. 3.

Dantzig, G. B. (1963), *Linear Programming and Extensions*, Princeton, New Jersey.

Department of Energy (1977), *Report of the Working Group on Energy Elasticities*, Energy Paper No. 17, HMSO, London.

Department of Energy (1978), *Energy Forecasting Methodology*, Energy Paper No. 29, HMSO, London.

Hicks, J. (1956), *A Revision of Demand Theory*, Clarendon Press, Oxford.

Hotelling, H. (1938), 'The general welfare in relation to problems of taxation and of railway utility rates', *Econometrica*, vol. 6.

Hurwicz, L. and Uzawa, M. (1971), 'On the integrability of demand functions', in J. S. Chipman *et al*. (eds), *Preferences, Utility and Demand*, Wiley, New York.

Kouris, G. (1981), 'Elasticities – science or fiction?', *Energy Economics*, vol. 3, no. 2, April.

Lancaster, K. (1973), *Mathematical Economics*, Macmillan, London.

Pearce, D. W. (1980), 'Energy conservation and official UK energy forecasts', *Energy Policy*, September, pp. 245–8.

Pindyck, R. S. (1979), *The Structure of World Energy Demand*, MIT Press, Cambridge, Mass.

Taylor, Lester D. (1977), 'The demand for energy: a survey of price and income elasticities', in W. D. Nordhaus (ed.), *International Studies of the Demand for Energy*, Ch. 1, North Holland, Amsterdam, New York, Oxford.

Uri, N. D. (1979), 'Energy substitution in the UK, 1948–64', *Energy Economics*, vol. 1, no. 4.

Willig, R. D. (1976), 'Consumer's surplus without apology', *American Economic Review*, vol. 66, no. 4.

11
Summary, Updating and Conclusions

11.1 Summary of Results

In this final chapter we shall first summarise what has been learnt from the construction and operation of the Birmingham Energy Model, then show how the model may be updated to provide a revised appraisal of the energy situation current at the time of going to press. Finally, we offer some brief reflections on the possible future application of the model.

Our aim was to construct an integrated model of the UK energy sector which could be used for the analysis of long term energy policy. The Birmingham Energy Model which we developed is essentially a means of generating an energy strategy, that is, a schedule of production, investment and trade for each fuel in the UK energy sector on a five-year basis over the next fifty years. Each strategy is calculated to optimise a specified objective subject to a set of technological, economic, political and social constraints. The so-called 'cost model' minimises the present value of all costs incurred, whereas the 'demand model' maximises the net benefits of energy output (i.e. benefits of consumption less costs of supply). The Base Case assumptions on technology, cost and demand were essentially those embodied in the 1978 Green Paper on energy policy, but sensitivity analyses were conducted on a wide range of alternative assumptions. A variety of policy constraints were then imposed, reflecting the urgings of various special interest groups. (It would have been equally possible to explore the effects of alternative policy objectives had sufficiently plausible ones been proposed.)

The main results obtained were as follows.

(1) The strategy for minimising the costs of meeting Department of Energy forecasts made in 1978 involves

   (a) fast extraction of domestic oil reserves, followed by increasing dependence on oil imports and synthetic oil production;
   (b) gradual replacement of domestic natural gas, first by imports then later by synthetic gas;
   (c) a gradual but decisive switch from coal to nuclear energy as the major source of electricity;
   (d) a steady expansion in domestic coal production as the rising demand for synthetic fuels more than offsets the declining demand for electricity production (Sections 5.2–5.5).

(2) This minimum-cost strategy is very similar to the 'reference scenario' described in the 1978 Green Paper, the main differences being that the latter envisaged a slightly slower rate of oil extraction and more rapid rate of gas extraction (Section 5.7).

(3) If the Green Paper target of 170m. tonnes of coal production capacity by 2000 could be slightly increased, the savings in energy costs in the 1990s would be of the order of £66 per additional tonne of capacity (net of additional operating and investment costs at the assumed reference level). Similarly, it would be worth paying over twice the standard cost of a nuclear station to instal nuclear capacity in excess of the 40 GW limit in 2000 envisaged by the Green Paper (Section 5.10). Both these estimates do, however, depend crucially upon the levels of demand projected in the 1978 Green Paper (which are now generally acknowledged to be too high).

(4) The minimum-cost energy strategy is quite robust with respect to the levels of UK oil and gas reserves but more sensitive with respect to the projected rate of increase of world prices of these fuels. The total energy bill, on the other hand, is more sensitive to UK reserves than to world prices. The effects of changes in these assumptions are generally not felt until around the turn of the century (Section 6.6).

(5) If world oil and gas prices are assumed to rise after 2000 the effects on the energy bill are negligible, but the minimum cost strategy requires substantial and immediate conservation of oil (compared to the 'base case' and 'reference' scenarios), with extraction held at about 106m. tonnes during the 1980s and 1990s, and a great increase in coal extraction from 2010 onwards (Section 6.7).

(6) An 8 per cent (as opposed to 5 per cent) discount rate slows down the replacement of imports by synthetic fuels, and very slightly reduces the shift from coal-fired to nuclear plants, but the overall effects are not large. In contrast, a zero discount rate leads to a drastic change in strategy: complete postponement of oil and gas extraction for twenty years, meeting consumption entirely by imports for that period, and a trebling in domestic coal production between 2010 and 2025 in order to produce synthetic oil on a large scale. However, this 'zero discount rate' case seems of little practical interest (Section 6.9).

(7) If, in order to limit dependence on Middle East supplies, oil imports are constrained not to exceed 40 per cent of oil refined, the minimum-cost strategy is to slow down domestic oil extraction and greatly increase synthetic oil production, thereby reducing oil imports after the turn of the century; in addition, it is necessary to increase coal extraction, severely reduce production of synthetic gas and vastly expand gas imports. The energy bill is increased by about £2b. (1 per cent). However, 50 per cent import dependency could be achieved for half the price of 40 per cent dependency (Section 7.3).

(8) If the energy balance of payments deficit is constrained to a maximum of £1,300m., the minimum-cost strategy is to reduce oil extraction (saving it for later years), export synthetic gas, and considerably increase coal production; such a policy would cost £9b. (present value) but there are doubts as to the feasibility of the required gas exports and coal production (Section 7.4).

(9) If coal imports are allowed, they would take place only on a negligible scale if the world coal price is assumed to rise at 1 per cent per annum. However, if world oil and gas prices were also to rise after 2000 at 2 per cent and 1 per cent per annum, respectively, then coal imports would rise steadily after the turn of the century to over 450m. tonnes by 2025. These imports would be used to produce synthetic oil and gas, thereby replacing oil and gas imports, and eventually allowing oil to be exported again. Domestic coal extraction would be largely unaffected, even if operating costs rose at 1 per cent per annum. In effect, coal imports would create new jobs rather than destroy existing ones. It is questionable, however, whether coal imports would be feasible on such a scale, and whether Britain would have such a comparative advantage in synthetic oil production as to make oil exporting profitable (Section 7.5).

(10) If the future demand for energy in the UK follows the pattern described by soft energy advocates such as Leach and the IIED, rather than that projected by the Department of Energy in 1978, there will be very considerable savings in the costs of meeting UK energy requirements (a 44 per cent reduction in the national energy bill – worth about £415 per annum per household). Energy imports will not be a drain on the balance of payments and the UK will be much more secure against disruption of foreign oil supplies. On the other hand, there may be difficulties in adjusting coal production to fluctuating demand (unless further stabilising constraints are imposed) and the cost of achieving the specified level of energy conservation is as yet unknown (Section 9.7).

(11) The costs and consequences of a non-nuclear policy depend crucially upon the assumed levels and growth of demand for energy. Assuming Department of Energy 1978 projections, a non-nuclear policy will slightly increase oil import dependency, substantially worsen the energy balance of payments, render the UK dangerously dependent on domestic coal, and increase the energy bill by 17 per cent. If, instead, the IIED low energy projections are assumed, a non-nuclear policy substantially increases oil import dependency, converts the energy balance of payments surplus to a deficit, increases coal output but not to an unmanageable level, and increases the energy bill by only 5 per cent (Section 9.7).

(12) If our own assumptions about price elasticities of demand are coupled with the Department of Energy's 1978 assumptions about growth in national income, and if energy prices are assumed to reflect marginal costs of production, the predicted aggregate demand for energy as a whole over the next fifty years tallies

almost exactly with the Department's projection. However, there are differences in the composition of this demand. Compared to the Department's projection, our calculations suggest that demand will be greater in the Transport Sector, lower in the Commercial Sector and much lower in the Domestic Sector; also, the demand for coal, electricity and gas will be lower, whereas the demand for oil will be much higher. Most strikingly, the Department's projections assume that by 2025 oil will meet a lower proportion of final demand than coal, whereas the BEM suggests that oil will still account for over twice as much final demand as coal (Section 10.5).

(13) To take account of this price-sensitivity of final demand (in what we call the 'variable demand' case), the minimum cost strategy should be modified to exhibit greater production of synthetic oil, partly to reduce imports and partly to meet the increased final demand; there should also be lower extraction and imports of natural gas and lower production of synthetic gas (Section 10.6). This 'maximum net-benefit' strategy just described is not sensitive to across-the-board changes in price elasticities of demand (Section 10.7(i)).

(14) With price-sensitive demand, the effects of imposing the various policy constraints do not differ very significantly from the fixed demand case, except that it is much more costly to reduce oil import dependency, and somewhat less costly to reduce the energy balance of payments deficit. The changes in consumption induced by these constraints are generally quite small compared to the changes in production patterns already examined (Section 10.7).

(15) With price-sensitive demand, rising oil and gas prices after 2000 make a difference to the effects of some policies but not others. For example, policy constraints geared to reducing oil and gas imports are less necessary since rising prices have already induced changes in this direction. On the other hand, coal imports do displace some domestic extraction (Section 10.8).

(16) The incorporation of time lags in the demand side of the model, thereby effectively distinguishing between short-run and long-run responses to changes in prices, does not significantly affect the optimal energy strategies. It could be relevant for year-to-year forecasting, but seems unlikely to be important for long-term planning purposes (Section 10.9).

11.2 Updating the Model

The above results are based upon data and beliefs taken mainly from published and official sources circa 1978. Specifically, the Base Case demand projections, and the turn-of-the-century targets for nuclear power station construction and coal production, are taken from the Department of Energy's 1978 Green Paper. However, it was subsequently felt by the Department of Energy (and more strongly by most of its critics) that these 1978 demand projections and nuclear and coal targets were seriously on the high side. During 1979 these assumptions were publicly modified. In this section we report briefly upon the results of rerunning the Birmingham Energy Model to reflect this change of view.

The Base Case assumptions described in Chapter 4 were revised in four respects.

1. Demand Projections
These are now based on the revised projections issued by the Department of Energy (1979), which at the time of writing are the latest published official projections. They differ from the 1978 projections in assuming very substantially lower initial output and growth in the Iron and Steel Sectors (with its 2025 energy demand only 46 per cent as high), and lower growth in the Domestic Sector (2025 demand 85 per cent as high). Energy demand is marginally lower in the Industrial Sector, identical in the Transport Sector, and marginally higher in the Commercial and Other Sector (the latter reflecting the higher assumed growth rate in the Services Sector). The overall demand for energy grows at an annual rate of 1 per cent (rather than 1.2 per cent), and reaches 238mtoe in 2025 (rather than 253mtoe – about 6 per cent lower). As regards individual fuels, the main difference is that the demand for electricity grows more slowly, reaching only three-quarters of its former level in 2025. (The revised level of total demand in 2025 is very similar to the total demand of 235mtoe in the variable Base Case discussed in Chapter 10, but the composition is quite different, both by sector and by fuel. In the revised fixed-demand model, the Iron and Steel Sector accounts for a much lower proportion of final demand, and oil accounts for only 31 per cent rather than 45 per cent of final demand in 2025.)

2. Nuclear Programme
The 1978 Green Paper assumed that a maximum of 34 GW of additional nuclear capacity could be constructed by the year 2000, making a total of 41 GW available then. Such a rapid construction programme now appears to be unrealistic. In the revised model, the maximum nuclear construction programme by the turn of the century is reduced to 13 GW (i.e. 10 new power stations with an average capacity of 1.3 GW each), making a total of 20 MW available in 2000. While the present government is not explicitly committed to this programme of construction, a statement by the Secretary of State for Energy (in the House of Commons, 18 December 1979) indicates that such a programme is thought to be feasible.

3. Coal Production
The 1978 Green Paper incorporated the National Coal Board target of 170m. tonnes of coal by the year 2000. In the 1979 Department of Energy projections, coal output at the turn of the century was forecast to be in the range 120–150m. tonnes. The top end of this range was

assumed to be the maximum output possible, and the 150m. tonne limit is accordingly incorporated in our revised model.

4. *World Prices*

World prices of oil and gas are assumed to rise at 3 per cent per annum until the turn of the century, and thereafter at 2 and 1 per cent, respectively (as in the sensitivity analysis described in Chapter 6). World prices of coal are not specified because coal imports are assumed to be precluded.

The minimum cost energy strategy implied by these revised assumptions is broadly the same as before, with the following principal differences:

(1) Coal is extracted at a lower rate up to the turn of the century, but at a higher rate thereafter. The lower availability of nuclear stations before 2000 means that more coal is required to generate electricity, though this is partly offset by the lower demand for electricity; there is also a fall in final demand for coal, so that the net effect is lower coal extraction up to 2000. Furthermore, additional capacity in 2000 would be worth less than half what it was under the original Base Case assumptions. After the year 2000, however, it is economic to increase coal extraction in order to produce synthetic oil and gas on a larger scale. This reflects the greater availability of cheaper coal tranches and the higher world prices of oil and gas.

(2) Depletion rates of oil and gas remain unaffected, so the increased production of synthetic fuels allows a reduction in oil and gas imports, and a slight increase in the use of oil for electricity generation before 2000.

(3) The nuclear programme is held back by the lower limit on construction, even though there is a substantially lower demand for electricity. The (shadow) value of additional nuclear capacity in 2000 is about 20 per cent higher. In the year 2000 only 18 per cent of electricity generating capacity is nuclear, but in the next five years nuclear production and generating capacity doubles, and by 2025 over three-quarters of electricity generating capacity is nuclear. (The feasibility and desirability of such a development needs further examination.)

At £201b. the total energy bill is about 6 per cent below the Base Case level; this matches the 6 per cent reduction in final demand.

In the variable demand model, the exogenously specified levels of demand have also been revised according to the Department of Energy 1979 projections. As before, this principally affects demand levels in the Iron and Steel Sector. GDP growth rate and GDP elasticities of demand for fuels whose demands are endogenously determined are identical to those in the variable Base Case (i.e. GDP growth rate of 2 per cent per year and GDP elasticity of demand of 0.5 for all fuels except aviation fuel and diesel oil in transport whose elasticities are 1.0).

The 'maximum-net-benefit' energy strategy implies a slower increase in total final demand for energy, rising to 191mtoe in 2025, which is about 20 per cent lower than the Department of Energy 1979 projection. Oil meets nearly half this demand by 2025, rather than one-third. To achieve this the UK oil depletion rate is slowed (peaking at 124 mtoe in 1990 instead of 135mtoe in 1985), and there is a significant (40 per cent) increase in synthetic oil production after the turn of the century, which in turn necessitates an increase in coal extraction (compared to the revised minimum-cost strategy just outlined). The final demand for gas is only half as high, and production of synthetic gas is reduced accordingly. Electricity production is less than three-quarters as high, but as before nuclear production increases rapidly after 2000, virtually displacing electricity from coal and oil by 2025.

To summarise, the energy strategy implied by the revised 1979 assumptions is broadly similar to the 1978 strategy, except that (a) total energy demand is significantly reduced; (b) production of coal and nuclear power are lower – and therefore more plausible – up to the turn of the century; but (c) after 2000, the switch to nuclear power and synthetic oil, and the increase in coal production, are even more dramatic, and therefore to be viewed with some reservation.

11.3   Concluding Reflections

Even the revised 1979 assumptions described in the previous section have been gradually outdated by subsequent changes in the economy and in government policy. The recession has deepened, and energy demand in 1981 was down about 5 per cent against 1980, which in turn was down 7.8 per cent against 1979 (*Financial Times*, December 3, 1981). The dangers of nuclear power are still much debated, and a group of scientists and economists has challenged the CEGB's assumptions 'that new plants will be built on schedule; that their performance will match expectations; and that nuclear fuel costs will remain low while coal costs grow' (*The Times*, February 3, 1982). Finally some observers have argued that even 150m. tonnes of coal production by the year 2000 is unrealistically high (Robinson and Marshall, 1981). In moving the second reading of the Coal Industry Bill, the Under-Secretary of State for Energy acknowledged that 'neither the world, nor the coal industry's own performance, had matched the expectations of 1974 . . . Since 1979, oil prices had not risen as steeply as was feared, while the NCB had not achieved hoped-for cost savings. Output per man-shift in 1980–81 was still below its 1972–73 level . . . It was therefore right – and inevitable – that the industry and the Government should reappraise the industry's plans' (*The Times*, February 3, 1982).

An energy strategy, even a long-term one, cannot be expected to last for more than a short while: it needs constant revision in the light of changing circumstances. The general thrust may well remain the same but the details will generally change, and those which are of immediate relevance for policy are particularly important. What is therefore required is a convenient mechanism for regularly updating the strategy.

At the time the present research began, the Department of Energy was analysing policy by means of a collection of separate (and somewhat disparate) fuel industry models linked by a demand forecasting-cum-allocation model. These models have subsequently been revised, but the same philosophy seems to be held.

Our own view was that the construction of a single integrated model of the whole UK energy sector was a practical proposition, and that such a model would be considerably more flexible and convenient to use. This turned out to be the case. The Birmingham Energy Model involved financial support from the SSRC totalling approximately £50,000 over seven years, the bulk of which financed nine man-years' of research associate time; in addition, the two principal investigators were engaged part-time on the research. As for operating the model, even under our rather awkward arrangements each run took only about a day; to add constraints took a few hours, and to vary the parameters of the model took a few minutes. (Under favourable circumstances these construction and operating times could be considerably bettered: four experienced investigators could probably design and implement a comparable model in a couple of years, and access to powerful computer facilities could provide direct interactive capabilities.)

It will be clear from the work described in this book how a model such as the BEM could be used by the Department of Energy as an aid in designing and updating UK energy policy. It could also be used by other government departments and by fuel industries and firms as a means of appraising policies implemented or proposed by the Department of Energy. For example, we have seen how it can be used to calculate whether a particular strategy is the least-cost means of meeting pro-jected energy demands, what would be the cost of imposing specified constraints (e.g. in response to environmental or industrial lobbies), what would be the consequences of allowing coal imports or curtailing oil imports, how the strategy would vary as demand projections were revised, and so on.

The BEM also constitutes a check on the plausibility of other models used in energy policy-making. In this context, it is currently being used to help validate the British component of a European energy model developed by the EEC for use in setting policies concerning European import dependency and the utilisation of new technologies.

In most developed countries there are now several large scale models which regularly appriase government macroeconomic policy and predict that country's likely economic performance. In the USA, formal models are beginning to be used for regular appriasal of energy policy too. Our hope is that the Birmingham Energy Model will have played a pioneer-ing role in the systematic appraisal of long-term energy strategies for the UK.

References

Department of Energy (1979), 'Energy projections 1979', a paper by the Department of Energy, London.

Robinson, C. and Marshall, E. (1981) *What Future for British Coal?* Hobart Paper No. 89, Institute of Economic Affairs, London.

Notes on the Authors

S. C. LITTLECHILD   Professor of Commerce, and Head of the Department of Industrial Economics and Business Studies, University of Birmingham, since 1975. Visiting Professor at New York, Stanford and other US universities in 1979/80. Has published about 40 articles on theory and applications of mathematical programming, game theory, public utility pricing and investment policies, telecommunications economics, Austrian economics and nationalised industries. Co-author and Editor of *Operational Research for Managers* (1976); author of *Fallacy of the Mixed Economy* (1978) and *Elements of Telecommunications Economics* (1979). Has acted as a consultant to HM Treasury, the Electricity Council, American Telephone and Telegraph Co., and the World Bank.

K. G. VAIDYA   Lecturer in Economics at the Management Centre, University of Aston, since 1972. He has published articles in Energy Modelling and Economic Development and has worked as consultant to various international organisations.

I. H. SLICER   Has been Principal Lecturer (Research) in the Department of Government and Economics, at the City of Birmingham Polytechnic, since 1970. Before that he had 20 years experience as an industrial chemist and technical manager. He obtained his M.Sc. and Ph.D. from Warwick University, writing dissertations on the price of milk in the UK and on Unilever. He has also carried out research on the evaluation of recreational benefits. Current research interests include inland waterways and energy.

J. ROUSE   Is currently Principal Lecturer in the Department of Government and Economics, at the City of Birmingham Polytechnic, where he has been since 1970. He obtained his Masters degree from Leicester University in 1970. During 1975/76 he was a visiting scholar at the Public Sector Economics Unit at Leicester University. Published a report on Local Authority Highway Investment Appraisal for Department of Environment. Current research interests include economic appraisal of inland waterways and energy policy. (Dr. Slicer and Mr. Rouse have published a number of papers in the Department of Government and Economics, City of Birmingham Polytechnic, on inland waterways for recreational purposes.)

M. CAREY   Assistant Professor in the School of Urban & Public Affairs, Carnegie-Mellon University, since 1979. Formerly statistician at the Department of Trade and Industry (1970–72) where he worked on their energy models, and Research Fellow, Universities of Aston and Birmingham (1974–77). Has published several articles on mathematical programming.

P. G. SOLDATOS   Obtained his M.Soc.Sc. in national economic planning and Ph.D. from the University of Birmingham. Worked as

Research Fellow on the Birmingham Energy Project for a couple of years, mainly on the computer programming side, then took a job with West Midlands Gas Board for a year before returning to work for a private company in Greece. Published several papers on solar and nuclear energy.

M. A. ANARI Obtained his Ph.D. at the University of Birmingham, where his thesis incorporated a linear programming model of the energy sector. Subsequently appointed as Research Fellow working on the Birmingham Energy Model. He was formerly employed in the Iranian National Oil Co. and hopes to return to a university post in Iran.

D. BASU Lecturer in Econometrics, Oxford Institute of Agricultural Economics, since 1980. Formerly Research Associate at the University of Birmingham (1976–77) and Research Officer at the Department of Applied Economics, University of Cambridge (1979–80). Author of *Future Energy Policies for the UK* (1981) and several articles on quantitative aspects of planning. Current research interests in stochastic optimal control and impacts of trade negotiations on domestic economies.

Index